Uncovering the Secrets of a Southern Family

A Memoir

by

Wayne E. Busbice with Patricia Busbice

*To Connie, a good friend —
Best of luck, Wayne Busbice*

authorHOUSE®

AuthorHouse™
1663 Liberty Drive, Suite 200
Bloomington, IN 47403
www.authorhouse.com
Phone: 1-800-839-8640

Printed in the United States of America
Bloomington, Indiana
This book is printed on acid-free paper.

ISBN: 978-1-4343-3349-0 (e)
ISBN: 978-1-4343-2366-8 (sc)

Library of Congress Control Number: 2007931711

DEDICATION

To my children and grandchildren, to give them a true history of their ancestors: who they were, where they came from and how they lived, and to help them better understand and appreciate their heritage. Also, in honor of my ancestors, whose genes, values and circumstances made me who I am today.

CONTENTS

FOREWORD

Anyone who looks back on his life and those who touched it usually thinks of a teacher first, after family. By teacher, I mean anyone who made a major impact and taught important values by example. For me, Wayne Busbice heads that list. To say Wayne made a big impact on me at a critical time in my life would be a vast understatement. If our relationship were based on paybacks, I'd still be in debt after all these years.

As a boy in a poor farming family in the heart of the Great Depression, Wayne grew up picking cotton in Louisiana. But his parents instilled in him the importance of education as a means to a better life and a good future. The joy of playing and singing country music with brothers and cousins proved to be a welcome pastime and a break from his studies and farm work. As his musical skills progressed, Wayne began performing publicly.

Although he became an officer in the Air National Guard and maintained a career as teacher, counselor, and later principal, Wayne never lost his love for country music and performing. In 1956 he made his first commercial recordings. By this time, the rock 'n' roll movement was taking the country by storm. To stay abreast of the times, Wayne wrote and recorded a few titles merging country lyrics with a more contemporary beat, a style often referred to as rockabilly. Some of Wayne's records have gone on to become highly prized collectors' items among rockabilly aficionados, especially in Europe.

Dr. Busbice was the principal of Gaithersburg Junior High in Maryland when I entered there in the fall of 1973. He was the first non-medical doctor many of us students ever knew. Dr. Busbice and I were only casually acquainted until he found out about my playing bluegrass and country fiddle. The orchestra teacher, Ellsworth Briggs, had noticed me, and advised Dr. Busbice that I played fiddle a lot better before and after class than I played classical violin during class. Thanks to their initiative, that year we performed as a trio -- Dr. Busbice on guitar and vocals, Mr. Briggs on bass, and myself on fiddle -- at the school variety show and other functions. The audience was enthusiastic, and word started to spread among students and parents. We found ourselves performing several times a year for community events in addition to school functions.

During eighth and ninth grade I was first on the student council, and then class president, so I worked very closely with Dr. Busbice. Our mutual love for traditional music made it easy for me to respect, relate to, and learn from him.

Wayne Busbice became an educator on many different fronts beyond his initial degree in agriculture. It is amazing how he found the time to perform his duties as a school administrator, stay active in military service, remain a strong presence in the community, perform on stage, and be a devoted husband and father. Somehow, Wayne seemed to do everything well, never faltering or showing stress. The pressures of managing an overcrowded school must have been overwhelming at times, but Wayne was ever the professional. He never lost his temper or lost control of a situation. Even problem students respected him, because he gave everyone, even those who may have tested his patience, a fair deal. All the while he tried to pass along what he has learned to others, and to instill in us students the desire to excel.

Dr. Busbice continued to give me tremendous encouragement after I went on to high school and for several years thereafter. I sought Wayne's counsel personally and professionally on many things. His advice was always logical and on the right track. Most of his advice I took, and that which I didn't take, I wish I had.

Wayne's younger brother Bernarr, professionally known as Buzz Busby, had made a name for himself as an extraordinary bluegrass vocalist and mandolin virtuoso. Dr. Busbice and his brother Buzz decided to do an album together in 1977. They recruited me to play fiddle on the project and it became the very first recording session I ever participated in.

I went on to pursue a career as a professional musician for eighteen years, playing fiddle with the Johnson Mountain Boys, then Kitty Wells and Johnny Wright. I also worked as a disc jockey in Washington, D.C. In 1995, I achieved a lifetime goal when I moved to Nashville, Tennessee. Within two weeks of arriving in the country music capital, I was hired by the Grand Ole Opry as a regular announcer on WSM, one of the most famous radio stations in the world. There were five people lined up for the job but I, the new kid in town, was the lucky one. Had it not been for the early stage experience Wayne arranged and the connections I made with his help, my life may have taken a very different path.

Upon retiring from the school system, Wayne established a recording studio in his home, with his own record label and music publishing company. The studio and the label served not only as a vehicle for Wayne and Buzz to make recordings, but also as an opportunity for other musicians to make records that might not have been accepted by a major independent label.

Family continues to be the most important part of Wayne's life. His appreciation of family ties underlies his desire to know more about his ancestry. After much research, Wayne has traced his heritage, uncovering information he never dreamed of. In a life that continues to be well-lived daily, he has witnessed a great deal that he has graciously shared in these pages. His journey has been an amazing success story, with peaks and valleys, triumphs and tragedy.

Wayne's respect for others, his humility, and above all, his integrity are obvious to those who know the man. He always seems to place others before himself. It's been said that you can't go through life and always take -- you have to give back. Wayne Busbice has given back a great deal. He is truly a special man. But in testimony to his character, I don't think he's ever realized it. To him, regardless of the role he was in, he was just doing his job.

To make a contribution in a person's life is one thing, but making a difference is another. Countless are the lives Wayne Busbice has touched, contributed to, and made a difference in. His name is a good name – and one that those who have known him will never forget.

Eddie Stubbs
WSM Grand Ole Opry Announcer
Nashville, Tennessee
September 17, 2006

PREFACE

I began my deep study of people on the front porch of my father's farmhouse.

After the day's work was done in the cotton fields my father would sit out on the porch swing with his two daughters and seven sons surrounding him. Neighbors and uncles wandered over, barefoot and in their overalls, to share the day's events and roll a cigarette from a Prince Albert can. On that porch we heard many stories about people we knew: their foibles, their mishaps, their tragedies, and their rustic ways. Most of the stories made us laugh, often till our bellies ached.

This gave me an insight into human nature and the spectrum of behavior of all kinds of people. Many of these stories became folklore in the family and are still being told today, seventy years later.

I serve as a sort of album of family memories. I am the one, of all my brothers, sisters, and cousins, who seems to be the repository of all these stories; they still live within me. I can go back in a moment to the 1930s, to that front porch near Eros, Louisiana.

From these sessions I learned to analyze character – and to accept people as they are. Learning what makes people tick became a motivating factor in my life. As a boy I developed an intense interest in people. I became more and more conscious of this as a young teacher. I now recognize that helping others answers a deep need of my own. My career paths, and indeed my whole life, are testimony to this concept.

I was a Southern boy living in poverty in the economic depression of the 1930s, but with a rich, full family life. I also lived amid mysteries. As I grew, more and more questions occurred to me about my family's history and circumstances. Why did I have three grandfathers, when my friends had only two? Why did the grownups whisper when they talked about my Grandpa Cap Rusheon? Why did we live in such an out of the way community in the backwoods? How come my parents were so capable, and yet so poor?

In my youth, I searched for answers to uncover my identity. My parents kept giving me mysterious responses – and sometimes, no responses. That spurred me on to try to solve the mysteries.

My parents instilled in my mind early on that education would be the way out of my humble beginnings. I embraced that belief all through my life's journey. When my father passed away I was only 14 years old and I made a commitment to myself to obtain as much education as my motivation and talent would allow.

Throughout my military, education, music and political careers, my interest in my family's heritage continued. When I look back on the many facets of my life, I recognize key people who had a significant influence on me. From my humble beginnings I never dreamed I would go such great distances from my backwoods cotton farm, encounter so many inspiring people, and have so many opportunities to shake hands with history.

The storytelling that began on my father's front porch   continues today. Only now, I'm the storyteller. My wife and others have encouraged me to write down some of these life stories. But I have to say, my search for my identity has been ever present. It is the motivation for writing this memoir.

Wayne E. Busbice
September 5, 2005

ACKNOWLEDGEMENTS

Over lunch one day in October 1972, I told my family background to a young woman I was just getting to know, and she immediately suggested I write a book. Patricia, now my wife, convinced me over the next thirty years that my stories are worth telling. She was kind enough to write them with me. For this endeavor, she gave generously of her time, encouragement, wise counsel, computer skills, professional-quality editing and research.

My most heartfelt thanks to Kit Ingalls, a skilled professional writer, who offered excellent advice, wise editing and valuable recommendations on organization to make my stories flow. Kit taught me how to ensure clarity, when to expand and when to curtail the writing, and how to enhance my stories. Her belief in this project carried me through many setbacks. If this memoir is a reflection of my experiences, she breathed the life into it.

I also want to express gratitude to others for their contributions:

My friend Steve King, the author of several books, for assisting with the technical aspects in preparing the manuscript;

My cousin Roger Busbice, family historian, and my cousin Donald Busbice, who shared valuable information;

My Busby online genealogy community who shared data and research leads.

Wayne Busbice
September 2006

~1~

Prosperity

One day in 1914, Oates Oliver Busbice boarded a train that would change his life. As the railroad cars clattered through the northern Louisiana hills, the young farmer met a nineteen-year-old schoolteacher, Talitha Fay Connella. When he left the train at West Monroe, Oates knew that he had to see Fay again. He did, and the two began courting, became sweethearts and planned to marry.

Their marriage was twice postponed -- first, by the death of Fay's father and second, by Oates's induction into the United States Army and service with the Allied Expeditionary Force in France.

After the war ended, O.O. Busbice received his discharge from the Army on April 26, 1919, his character described as excellent. Five months later -- five long years after their courtship began -- Oates married his sweetheart.

Monroe Morning World
Monroe, Louisiana
A wedding of interest to their many friends is that of Oates Oliver Busbice of Eros, La., and Miss Talitha Fay Connella, of Buckner, La., which was celebrated Wednesday at 3:30 p.m. at the home of Mr. and Mrs. J.D. McGee. Pink and white roses formed the decorations of the house. Miss Mattie McGee presided at the piano, accompanying Miss Heloise Connella, who sang "I Love You Truly". Miss McGee played Mendelssohn's Wedding March for the entrance of the bride and groom. Rev. S.C. Rushing performed the impressive ring ceremony. The bride wore a dainty costume of white organdy over white satin, and carried an arm bouquet of bride's roses. After the ceremony, a two-course luncheon was served to the guests, who included only members of the families and intimate friends. Mr. and Mrs. Busbice will be at home after November 1 in Shawnee, Okla.

My father Oates (pronounced Otis) was born Oliver Allen Busby, Jr. in Laurens County, Georgia, on May 21, 1893. He was the fifth son and sixth child of Oliver Allen Busby and Mary Frances Byrd Busby. Their children would eventually number thirteen.

When the family came to Louisiana in 1899, Daddy's name was changed from Oliver Busby to Oates Busbice. Subsequently, he chose to

1

reclaim the Oliver and drop the Allen. He became Oates Oliver Busbice, known affectionately to his friends as "Double O."

Oates grew up on a farm in Frantom, five miles southeast of Eros. Every child in the family had a responsibility to keep the farm going and to help put food on the table. Double O spent his youth plowing with mules, chopping and picking cotton, and working in the cornfields. He hunted, fished, rode horseback to church every Sunday, and went to the small country schools in Frantom and Jumping Gully.

When Oates finished eighth grade, his education ended. High school did not exist in the rural areas. For two years, Daddy's oldest sister, Eva Mae Belle, was his teacher in a one-room school.

Eros was the school, church and social center for several small communities in the surrounding area, of which Frantom was one. In a radius of about ten miles were settlements called Hog Hair, Jumping Gully, Indian Village, Salem, Guyton, Flat Creek, Head Settlement, Vernon, and Fuller Town. Right down the road was the hamlet of Bug Tussle. Some of these small communities were located in Jackson Parish and some in Ouachita Parish, but almost all citizens sent their children to the Eros school and received their mail via rural mail carriers from Eros.

The Tremont Lumber Company founded Eros. Mrs. Pearl Collins, a well-educated resident who was interested in astronomy, suggested that the town be named after the asteroid Eros, discovered in 1898. Of course, the asteroid was named after the ancient Greek god of love. During the early twentieth century Eros, Louisiana, was a sawmill boomtown.

Inhabitants of the small communities surrounding Eros often came together for socializing at box suppers, which were used to raise money for a variety of causes. On one of these occasions, Oates had arranged to meet a girl from Indian Village who he was dating, one of the Griggs girls. When he arrived with his brother Elton, friends told them that an angry, jealous, drunk boyfriend of the Griggs girl was there, talking big about how he was going to cut Daddy to pieces. The friends warned Oates that he should be very careful because the jealous boyfriend was mean when he was drunk.

Uncle Elton and Daddy thanked their friends for the warning and continued to walk toward the entrance. As they were entering the building Uncle Elton slipped Daddy his small .22 caliber pistol and said, "Take this just in case."

Daddy outbid the jealous boyfriend for the box lunch his date had brought for the auction. Sure enough, when they sat down to eat it together as was the custom in those days, the angry boyfriend, with his knife open, started staggering toward Daddy shouting he was going to cut him to pieces. Someone standing next to Uncle Elton said, "You had better go help your brother; that crazy guy has a knife." Uncle Elton replied, "That's okay, Oates can handle it." "What do you mean?" the friend asked. "He's got the difference in his pocket," said Elton with a sly grin. When the angry boyfriend got within ten feet, Daddy pulled out the pistol and everybody ducked behind their seats or hit the floor as the would-be assailant fled toward the exit where the deputy sheriff caught him. Fortunately, the deputy had been alerted, saw the whole episode and did not charge Daddy with anything. In those days, carrying a gun was no big deal.

My father, Oates, as a doughboy in France, World War I

Oates grew up learning how to farm from his father and older siblings, but, once he met Fay, he decided that he would like to go out on his own and carve out a career as a roughneck in the oil fields of Oklahoma. There he hoped to save enough money to wed the girl of his dreams. Daddy was still in Oklahoma when he received greetings from Uncle Sam to join in the fight to stop Germany's aggression in Europe.

Oates Oliver Busbice was inducted into the service of his country on September 5, 1917, in Seminola, Oklahoma. On his way to Camp Shelby, Mississippi, he stopped in West Monroe, to say a tearful goodbye to Fay. He promised he would help win the war and return to marry her after the war was over.

Momma was born Talitha Fay Connella on November 11, 1894 on her father's 400-acre plantation on the Ouachita River, in what is now the city of West Monroe, Louisiana. Fay, as the family called her, was the eighth child in a family of eight girls and two boys.

Fay excelled in school and received encouragement at home, where her parents and older sisters placed great emphasis on education and independence. This was unusual, even avant-garde, at a time when women could not vote and had few occupations open to them. Most women made their economic contribution in the home assisting their husbands with farming and caring for the children. Women were responsible for doing all the domestic chores involved in running the home, and their education beyond eighth grade was generally considered unnecessary.

At the age of fifteen, Fay lost her mother to cancer, after a long illness. The following year, 1911, Fay graduated from Ouachita Parish High School. Under a program that allowed students in the top ten percent of their class to take a teacher's exam, Fay began teaching in a one-room schoolhouse in Evelyn, some ten miles west of her home.

In 1917 and 1918, while Oates was in the Army, Fay attended Tyler Commercial College in Tyler, Texas, studying telegraphy and bookkeeping. She received a diploma as Master of Accounts, setting a school record for finishing the course early.

After basic training, Daddy was shipped to Camp Kilmer in New Jersey, where he boarded a troop ship to France. He sailed from the United States on June 20, 1918, to France via England. He was seasick all the way to France, and said he'd never been so sick in his life. He experienced the same problem leaving France for the United States.

Oates was selected to join an elite group to become a messenger on the front lines of the war in Europe. He was engaged in the battles of Villers-en-Haye Sector, St. Mihiel, Puvenelle Sector and Meuse Argonne. Daddy's role was crucial because, during World War I, officers, commanders, and noncoms did not have telephones, radios, and other electronic devices to use on the front lines to communicate during battle. They were dependent upon messengers to get through the lines and deliver handwritten messages in order to control the troops and keep all personnel informed about battle strategy.

4

My mother, Talitha Fay Connella, circa 1918

During one of Daddy's missions, he was caught in no man's land and was shell-shocked and knocked unconscious. While he was blacked out, the Germans released poison gas over the battlefield where he lay. Oates was rescued when the battle was over and placed in a field hospital. The doctor told him that the exploding artillery shell that knocked him out actually saved his life. Daddy did not receive any visible wounds during his tour of duty on the front lines but his lungs were affected by the poison gas and he drew disability pay for about ten years.

The war ended with an armistice signed on November 11, 1918, Fay's twenty-fourth birthday, but months passed before Oates could return home. The agony of his wait is reflected in this letter to Fay, written on February 27, 1919:

Dearest Fay,
I have been thinking of you all day so I couldn't go to bed without telling you about it. I haven't heard from you or any one else from the

5

U. S. A. in six months. I get so disgusted at times and think I will never write any more, then again, I think maybe you write and something is wrong with the mail so that I don't get my mail. Anyway, I find myself continually writing. What are you doing nowadays. Are you still holding your position at the same place? Dear, you don't have any idea how bad I want to see you. I would give worlds to even hear from you. I still perform my last duty before retiring at night by kissing your picture. I hope to see you soon. I think now I will be home within the next two months. I have been transferred to the 85th Division for transportation home and immediate discharge. I am stationed now at Le Mans France. This is the hardest battle I have had to fight, having to wait. My dear I will have to close - my candle is beginning to come to an end.

Yours, Oates

337 Infantry Company D, A. E. F.

After Oates mustered out of the Army and married Fay, the two returned to Shawnee, Oklahoma, where their first child, Oates Oliver Busbice, Jr., was born.

When his father passed away two years later, Oates, Fay and their young son returned to the farm near Eros to care for my grandmother and her farm. Daddy worked the land for about a year, and then bought a drugstore in Chatham in partnership with Dr. Gill, the town physician.

By 1920 Eros had grown to be the largest town in the parish, with a thousand residents. It boasted a post office, three hotels, a newspaper, a company commissary, three doctors, a drug store, three churches, a jail, a bank, its own telephone exchange and Jackson Parish's first high school with six hundred pupils. However, in 1920, a cyclone touched down in Eros and destroyed and devastated the town and the sawmill.

The people of Eros did not give up. They consolidated all of the one-room schools in the surrounding area and children were bused to Eros. They rebuilt the sawmill and operated it.

Disaster struck the town again in 1926; this time a fire burned the sawmill down to the ground. Since most of the timber in the area had been harvested, the mill company decided not to rebuild and moved its operation to Olla, Louisiana, about sixty miles south of Eros. A few hundred citizens of Eros decided to stay and keep the sleepy southern town operational.

Most of the citizens who remained in the town after the fire commuted to Chatham to work at the smaller sawmill in operation there, or carpooled to West Monroe to work at the Brown paper mill. Many of the lumber and pulpwood workers who remained either cut logs and hauled them to the mill in Chatham or cut pulpwood and delivered their product to the paper mill.

Oates and Fay had moved to Chatham after he purchased the drugstore. Fay taught at Chatham High School and their family grew, with the birth of their second son, Connella, and then of daughter Helen Fay. In March 1928, Momma gave birth to twin boys, Temple and Charles LeMoyne.

I was born on March 28, 1929, just one year and two weeks after the birth of my twin brothers. Since my mother had three children within one year, two of my aunts, who were without children, begged my mother to give me to them. Of course, my mother and father would not hear of such a thing. So I grew up as the third in the phrase, "the twins and Wayne," often spoken as one word of four syllables.

The stock market crashed seven months after I was born, marking the beginning of the Great Depression, but I hasten to tell people that my birth was not the cause of this terrible disaster. In my opinion the credit goes to President Herbert Hoover and his failed policies – policies that left my family, and millions of others, just one bad day away from hardship.

~2~

Working Hard and Making Do

Shortly after my first birthday, Daddy's drugstore burned. He had no insurance on the property and the economy was already devastated by the onset of the Depression. Daddy had to move back to the family farm in rural Frantom.

Daddy would spend the weekdays on the family farm with his brother Emery, and the weekends with us in Chatham, a seven mile trek through Flat Creek swamp, which was filled with snakes and deep bog holes. He spent five or six days of the week in grueling farm labor from sunup to sundown, then took this walk to rejoin us every weekend.

For the next year, the family stayed in Chatham. My mother continued teaching until enactment of a law providing that only one spouse in each household could hold a job. The intent of the law was to try to ensure an income in every household. Unemployment had soared due to the Depression.

When I was two years old, and Momma could no longer work, we all moved to the 360-acre family farm, which straddled the Jackson-Ouachita Parish line. My brother Billy was born when I was two. I have no memory of our lives before Billy was born.

My first remembrance of the farm is that we had no electricity, no running water, and no indoor plumbing. As some people would say, it had four rooms and a path, referring to the "two-holer" outhouse out back. We used chamber pots at night so we didn't have to go outside to use the outhouse.

There was no telephone, radio or TV. Our only source of news was the *Monroe Morning World* that was delivered by the rural mail carrier Monday through Saturday. There were many days when the mail carrier was the only motor vehicle that passed our house.

Daddy would get up before daybreak, care for the stock, and work an hour or two in the field before sunup, when Momma brought him his breakfast. He would come home for the noon meal then return to the field and work until darkness made it impossible to continue.

The farmhouse was humble, made of wood left in its natural state and covered with homemade pine shingles. We read by kerosene lamps and cut our own firewood to burn in the fireplace and in the wood stove on which Momma and the girls cooked. Using a three foot long cylindrical

8

bucket at the end of a rope which was wrapped around a pulley, we drew water from a bored well sixty feet deep with wood curbing about a foot square. Everybody got a bath in a number three galvanized washtub on Saturday night, whether we needed it or not, using hot water from the kettle to take the chill off of the fresh water drawn from the well. Two kids would use one tubful of water; then it would be dumped and filled again for the next set. During the week, we took pan baths to wash our faces, hands and feet.

My mother had her hands full with the twins, Temple and LeMoyne. Since I was born so soon after, Helen became my prime babysitter and caretaker. She was only five years old when I was put in her charge.

When I was about two and Helen was seven, Momma asked her to use the water shelf (a shelf that supported the water bucket and family dipper) to change my diaper. The water shelf was located at the end of the front porch, about eight feet from the ground. Helen took the diaper off, washed me with a cloth and then turned to reach for a clean diaper. While she looked away, I began fidgeting, rolled over, and fell eight feet to the ground. Helen thought I was dead when she saw me lying still. Refusing to give in to her feeling of panic, she jumped off of the porch, picked me up and patted my back. I began to breathe again and didn't even cry. There were no broken bones, scratches, or bruises so she kept it a secret from Momma, but confessed some time later. (Brain damage? --- I wonder.)

One day when I was four, Daddy took my mother, Billy, Helen and me to our Aunt Belle's house in Eros. Belle lived five miles from our farm, and she was a teacher at the Okaloosa School. Aunt Belle put my mother to bed at about ten o'clock in the morning. She assigned Helen to look after Billy and me and told us to stay on the porch or in the yard, but not in the house. Soon cousin Lucille came out and told Helen, "We need some milk. Take the boys down to Mr. Bennett's and get some. Don't hurry, just take your time and be home for lunch." The doctor arrived at the house as we were leaving.

Mr. Bennett lived about a block away and he kept several cows. We dawdled on the way, played on the porch of the church, threw a few stones, arrived at the Bennett house, and bought a bottle of raw milk from Mrs. Bennett. Mrs. Bennett kept us occupied with a long conversation about our farm and our animals and our games.

I was anxious to get back to my special toy car, which I had left on the porch at Aunt Belle's. As soon as we returned, Cousin Lucille said, with a big smile, "Come in here, boys, I want to show you something." Momma was propped up on pillows and she was glad to see us.

Lucille showed us a baby boy lying on a blanket in a cardboard box. "Your little brother came while you were gone." We were excited, but never thought to ask where babies came from. I never noticed when my mother was pregnant. She was always a little heavy. To me, she was just Momma.

Back at the farm, I was the one who got to run into the house and tell everybody, "We've got a little brother, we've got a little brother!' My parents named him Bernarr Graham Busbice.

Marilyn, my youngest sister, was born in 1935 when I was in the first grade. I remember waking up in the middle of the night and being told to keep quiet because Momma was giving me a new baby sister. She was born in the farmhouse without benefit of a doctor, only a neighbor lady serving as a midwife. She was really cute, very friendly and kind. All of her siblings spoiled her and made her the mascot for our "team." As she grew older, my father would tease her and say that she was so pretty, she was sure to marry young. This would cause her to blush and turn beet-red.

Each new baby got a lot of attention from everyone else in the family. My parents doted on their children and the rest of us followed their lead.

My father and Uncle Emery were the only two of the seven brothers who remained on the family farm. Between them, they had a total of fourteen children – Daddy and Momma had nine and Aunt Ivie and Uncle Emery had five. We were raised together as an integrated family, although our houses were a mile apart. We played, worked, socialized and went to church together. We shared fieldwork on the farm and when work was done, we had enough kids to make up two complete string ball teams for a pickup game. The two sets of siblings on the family farm grew up feeling as if we were brothers and sisters. Momma and Daddy brought us up to regard our aunt and uncle as two more parents.

Four little boys:
Wayne, Temple, LeMoyne and Billy, 1932

My family followed the common Southern practice of calling the children by their first and second names -- Helen Fay, Marilyn Kay, Connella Allison, Temple Allen and so on. However, I went against this tradition. My name at birth was Wayne Evan Busbice, but my mother wished everyone to pronounce my middle name "ee-von", French for Evan, so she changed the spelling to Evon. To me, it sounded feminine. When I started first grade, it didn't sound too good to be called "Yvonne", a girl's name. To avoid teasing from my classmates and brothers, I used only Wayne.

In our family of seven boys and two girls, the boys were expected to do work on the farm when they reached the age of six. The girls were never required to do field labor, but were expected to help Momma in the house. When I turned five years old, my job was to carry water to the field for my older brothers, my father, my bachelor uncle Allison Connella, and two hired hands. The hired hands received a dollar a day and room and board. They shared a room with my two oldest brothers.

I was extremely bowlegged as a baby and my parents feared that I could never learn to walk. They consulted the country doctor who said straightening my legs would require breaking and resetting them. Fortunately, the doctor conferred with a specialist who suggested that time would probably solve it; but if after three or four years the problem still existed, he would consider an operation. Luckily, my legs grew straight enough for me to walk, albeit rather clumsily for several years.

When I became water boy at age five, my right big toe would sometimes get caught in the inside seam of my left pants leg causing me to trip and spill the water before I could deliver it. This was very embarrassing to me, but I outgrew the defect by the time I was ten.

Living five miles from the nearest small town made transportation a real problem. My earliest memories of this inconvenience include going to Oak Grove Baptist Church six miles from home in a wagon pulled by a team of mules and falling asleep on a pallet on the way back. Daddy would drive the wagon over five miles to the general store in Eros or Chatham to buy groceries, plowshares, and other items needed on the farm. On occasion Daddy let me accompany him and watch the mules in the wagon yard while he shopped inside the store. My duty was to run inside and tell him if the mules were getting too restless. Billy or the twins usually came with us.

When times were prosperous Daddy and Momma each owned an automobile, but they were unable to afford the cars after the Depression hit. Then, in 1934, Daddy obtained a job in Monroe, twenty-five miles from home, during the winter. He worked as a timekeeper for the Works Project Administration (WPA), established by President Roosevelt's New Deal Program, which was draining Desiard Bayou to make room for expansion of the city limits. At first Daddy would hitchhike to Monroe on Sunday evenings and return home on Friday nights. After a few months, he and Momma cashed their World War I bonds and bought a used Ford coupe that made the commute easier for him.

This coupe did not have enough seating for our family but Daddy could be very creative. Late one afternoon he positioned all the children on and in the coupe with the two oldest brothers on the running board, Billy and me in the open trunk, Helen sitting between my parents, the baby, Bernarr, on Momma's lap, and Temple and LeMoyne each hugging a headlight and sitting on the front fenders. We visited Uncle Emery and his family who lived about a mile away and there were no other vehicles on that stretch of lonely country road so safety was not a factor with Daddy driving ten miles an hour. We stayed until after dark. On the return trip, LeMoyne, who knew only of candles and kerosene lamps, yelled back at Daddy not to drive too fast or he would blow the headlights out.

12

A few months later Daddy purchased a 1934 Ford sedan and this was much more comfortable for the family to ride in together. Still, it did not transport the entire family at one time. When Daddy later acquired a school bus to fulfill his contract to drive the Eros children to school, we finally had a vehicle that would hold our large family of eleven with room to spare.

About this time, the WPA had transferred Daddy closer to our home to coordinate the Texas tick fever eradication program. The government built several dipping vats filled with chemicals that would kill the ticks. One of the vats was placed on the west end of our farm. Farmers in our community were required to drive their small herds to our farm. Each animal was dipped, or immersed, for a number of times until the ticks were all gone.

In our rural area the three major topics of discussion were weather, religion and politics – politics being the most animated. Huey Long's political antics and campaign humor provided some of Frantom's best entertainment when I was growing up. The men in our area used to gather in neighborhood groups, sitting around the fireplace in the winter or the front porch in the summer, and repeat "Huey stories" over and over.

It would be years before I heard the word charisma, but I learned what it meant by listening to stories about Huey Long. He could excite people just by appearing before them.

Huey liked to create myths about himself. He grew up in Winn Parish, adjoining Jackson Parish, where I grew up. Winn was one of the poorest parishes in Louisiana. The farmland soil was very thin and it was very difficult to make any serious money in farming, but his grandfather speculated on land and this gave the family status; they were recognized as one of the most financially well-to-do families in the parish. Nevertheless, Huey fostered this myth of being abjectly poor and he did it with great skill. He would adopt the manner of yokel or country bumpkin when meeting those from outlying farms and backwoods.

Daddy and Uncle Emery told stories about hearing Huey speak on the front porch of the mercantile store in Chatham in the late 1920s, when Huey was running for governor. On one occasion, when a crowd of about 300 people had gathered to hear him, Huey in a momentary lapse forgot his country bumpkin myth. He used sophisticated language that many of the farmers in the area didn't quite comprehend – along the lines of, "When I am elected governor I will have the fiduciary responsibility to provide for the health and education of our families, especially our children, to give them the opportunity to grow up in an educated environment."

13

Huey caught himself being articulate and quickly switched to more simple language. "That just means this: when your children go to school, they will have free books, free pencils, free paper and all the materials they need to get a good education. Not only that, I'll see that they have a good nutritious lunch, free of charge for those who can't afford it."

Hearing the simpler version, Ole Man George from Hog Hair, who was standing at the very back of the crowd, yelled out, "HOORAY FOR HUEY! – HOORAY FOR HUEY!" Mr. George had a voice like a bullhorn. He startled the crowd and all eyes turned to look at him. One member of the audience said, "I take it you're really strong for Huey." Ole George said, "Yes, HOORAY FOR HUEY and I'm gonna' vote for him if I live to get to the polls!" The crowd chuckled. Huey just ate that up and went on with his speech. Everybody knew that the reason Ole George was so excited about Huey's plan was that he had twelve children, and free lunch for them meant a lot in 1928.

Huey Long grew up in the center of the bible-quoting redneck country and, of course, he was a Southern Baptist. When he ran for governor, he took his campaign into Cajun country, which generated one of Frantom's favorite "Huey stories." When Huey first arrived in French-speaking southern Louisiana, a local supporter reminded him, "Remember one thing, Huey -- down here, we have a lot of Catholic voters." Huey inserted the following anecdote in every speech he gave that day: "Now I know there's a lot of good Catholic folks here today. I just want to tell you folks this: when I was a boy I would get up every Sunday at 6 a.m. to hitch our horse to the buggy and take my good Catholic grandparents to Mass. After I took them home, I'd hitch the horse up again and take my Baptist grandparents to church for the 11 o'clock service." The anecdote played well with the voters, especially in Baton Rouge. That night, his aide said, "Huey, you've been holding out on us. I didn't know you had Catholic grandparents." Huey eyed him and replied, "Don't be a damn fool. We didn't even have a horse."

From the conversations I overheard, I surmised that folks were not under illusions about Huey Long. They knew he was a scoundrel, that he was corrupt. But they admired the way he was able to tax the big oil, gas, and railroad industries to raise funds to construct roads, bridges and public buildings. Of course all of these projects bore Huey's name inscribed prominently on them so the voters couldn't help but see it and marvel at how he got things done.

After men in Frantom tired of stories about "ole Huey," their conversation would usually shift to President Roosevelt (pronounced "ROOZ-eey-velt") and his secretary of agriculture, Henry A. Wallace.

They admired President Roosevelt for his New Deal program but blamed Henry A. Wallace for getting the government involved in their farming decisions. In fact, I have never met a farmer who didn't resent the intrusion of government regulations in his farming business.

I remember Old Man Watt telling my father one day, when we were visiting his blacksmith shop, "I wish the gubbermint would mind its business and let me mind my own. Why, there was a gubbermint man on my farm just yestiddy telling me how many hogs I could market and how much cotton I could plant. I had a strong urge to go in my house and get my gun and run him off, but I was able to control my temper and appear civil while he was here. I don't think he knows how lucky he was to be able to walk away in one piece."

Under the provisions of the Agricultural Adjustment Act (AAA), a farmer was told how many acres of cotton he could plant or how many hogs he could raise. The AAA program compensated the farmers for adjusting their programs by paying them parity for the reduced revenue. This was referred to as the annual "P" check. At my early age, I didn't understand all of the ramifications of this kind of talk and I thought they were referring to how much money they made based on how many *peas* they had sold.

Bernarr became very ill with colitis the summer he was two. He was hospitalized in Monroe, and my mother stayed there with him. Daddy arranged for Temple, LeMoyne and me to spend a few weeks in Shreveport with Uncle T.O. and Aunt Edith, and Uncle L.B. and Aunt Mamie. Uncle T.O. and Uncle L.B. were both high school principals.

It was there that I saw my first movie, which starred Shirley Temple – who was then my age, five. The process puzzled me. I tried to figure out how those people could dance and move around on a screen. I had a lot of questions for the grownups after the movie.

Whit White, Aunt Mamie's brother, owned a typewriter and we played with it a lot. Whit suggested we use it to write a letter to Momma. Temple, who was six, sat down at the machine, while LeMoyne and I hovered around telling him what to say to Momma.

Many years later, I would find this letter in Momma's keepsakes.

Shreveport, Louisiana
July 19, 1935

Dear Mama,

I hope you and Benard are getting along fine. We are having a good time here at Mrs. White's. We stopped in Ruston and ate supper. We also stopped Uncle LB and spent the night. Then Whit came after us and brought us to Shreveport. We went to town lastnight to see Barkadale

*field, Municipal airport and to seen picture show. Whit also said he would
take us to the street carnival.*

*We want to ride the ferreas wheele, horses, cars and the Worldes Fair
Thiller. Funny lady came here today and Mrs. White bought us abook
called jolly ghost stories. The funny lady wrote it.*

With Love,

Wayne, Temple, and% LeMoyne

My formal education began when I was five years old. When my
twin brothers Temple and LeMoyne started to school, I wanted to learn
to do schoolwork, too. So Helen taught me to read, spell and work with
numbers, as well as to write. This gave me a leg up when I entered the first
grade. I really enjoyed those tutoring sessions. It was obvious that Helen
loved teaching and some of that enthusiasm rubbed off on me.

Momma thought it would be good to have three children graduate
at the same time. Since I was only one year younger than the twins, she
asked permission from the school principal to allow her to home school
me for the first grade so I could begin the second grade with Temple
and LeMoyne. In support of her request, she pointed out that she was
a capable, trained teacher and I was already reading, spelling and doing
math right along with the twins. Permission was readily granted and I felt
very special to be able to receive this attention from my mother and my
big sister, Helen.

Early the following spring, Momma told me that I would not
be joining the twins in the second grade, after all. The teachers at the
Okaloosa School said it would be better for me to follow along with my
own age group and some of them feared that there might be some unhealthy
competition among the three of us. I was a little heartbroken, but soon got
over it. Momma smoothed it over by explaining that I would be ahead of
the other students in my class and Helen continued to work with me. She
let me read stories to her and complimented me on my progress and that
made me feel good.

My cousin Bobby's sister Vivienne was tutoring him, too, and he and
I were progressing at about the same rate. My sister Helen and my cousin
Vivienne were truly sisters in feeling and sharing. Both girls were beautiful
and academically gifted.

Vivienne was the only girl in her family, with four brothers.
Throughout her youth, which spanned the Great Depression, she helped
Aunt Ivie with all the chores required to cook, clean, iron and sew for a
family of seven. But these responsibilities, as difficult as they were, pale
in comparison to the one she took on when she was only seven years old.

Bobby was born on September 6, 1929, when Vivienne was seven. Aunt Ivie had a very difficult time with Bobby's birth and suffered from severe, lingering problems afterward. Aunt Ivie hemorrhaged and she needed a D and C. There were no social programs at that time to provide help. Times were very hard and the family had no money for a doctor. They asked Ivie's father but he either refused or was unable to lend them the money. For a year, Aunt Ivie was bedridden and not expected to live.

The Busbices, like most farmers in our community, prided themselves on being independent and taking care of their own. But there were no grandparents, aunts or cousins nearby who could take time from their own families to care full time for the new baby. The solution was to rest with Vivienne, who was taken out of second grade to become Bobby's full-time caregiver.

Years later, when he was an adult, Bobby wrote the following poem, dedicated to Vivienne:

MOTHERHOOD AT SEVEN
By Bobby Busbice

She was only seven when the baby was born,
And she wasn't much bigger than an ear of corn,
Her mother was ailing the whole first year,
And how anyone survived is not very clear,
Kids were farmed out here and there,
As the family tried to cope with this utter despair,
The next step was pitiful and I don't mean maybe,
The seven year old was taken out of school to tend to the new baby,
Now take a look at the second graders in your school,
Could they assume such a responsibility as a general rule?
Few have enough maturity to come in out of the rain
But to take care of a baby...well it was just insane
But she managed somehow day by day
To keep that baby alive and the hearse away.
It was out on the back gallery so they say,
She gave this baby a bath in the old fashioned way,
First she stripped off its clothes and laid it on the floor,
She took a wash pan, some lye soap, and what's more,
She scrubbed that baby with an old sugar sack,
As she cleaned it up from its heels to its back,
Now that bath was thorough, I'm telling you,
She took off the old dirt along with the new,
I happen to be the described herein,
Who never saw the inside of a real playpen,

But who owes his life to a dear seven year old,
Who had to grow up awfully fast so I've been told.
I'm awfully glad she did or I wouldn't be here
To dedicate this poem to someone so dear.
Sister, I can never repay you for the agony you went through,
But please accept these humble words as a tribute to you.
You have come a long way and this is long overdue,
So I'll end this poem with a loving – THANK YOU.

I was six months older than Bobby. We were together from elementary school all the way through college. I was as close or closer to Bobby than I was to any of my brothers, and he was my best friend, too. We liked the same things, and enjoyed each other's company. He could see the humor in just about any situation and could tell funny stories almost as well as his father, Emery.

Bobby and I wore a path walking the mile between our houses. We frequently spent the night together in his bed or mine. We talked about the books that our sisters had asked us to read, and read to each other to show how well we could do it. At his house, Aunt Ivie would exclaim and encourage us with lots of praise. She also took time away from her housework to play checkers and dominoes with us. I always felt that Aunt Ivie really cared about me, partly because Bobby and I were so close.

When I started school, the teacher, Miss Ellen Peevy, treated me differently from the other first grade students since I was scholastically ahead of them. She made me her assistant and stationed me at a table in the back of the room. While she did her regular teaching, I worked one-on-one as a peer tutor with the pupils who were having difficulty keeping up with the class. She gave me a set of look-say cards and I would practice with the students until they mastered the exercise. I also helped them with their ABCs, numbers, spelling and reading. I spent most of my first grade in back of the classroom tutoring others. Being ahead of the other students in the first grade gave me a lot of confidence that kept me in good stead the rest of my school experience.

The Three R's came more easily to me than my classmates, and I couldn't understand why some of them had difficulty learning. I thought it was because they were lazy, not trying or didn't care. After a career in education, I now know that there are many valid reasons why students learn at different rates.

I had started asking questions about my grandparents when I was five. But when I went to school, we had Grandparents Day, when we were invited to stand up in class and tell about our family. I wanted to contribute, but I couldn't stand up, because I didn't know any grandparents. This bothered me.

Later that day, I was weeding with Momma in her flower garden, while she was gathering flowers to take to church. I asked my mother what happened to my grandparents.

Me: "I know you named [my older brother] Connella after your father. Do I have a Grandpa Connella?"

Momma: "Yes, but he died before you were born. All your grandparents have passed away."

Me: "What about Daddy's father? Do I have a Grandpa Busbice?"

Momma, with hesitation, diffidence: "Oh, he passed away in Georgia before the family moved to Louisiana."

Me: "Well, who is Grandpa Rusheon that everybody talks about? And why does he have a different name?"

Momma: "Mr. Rusheon married your grandmother, and that makes him a step-grandfather to you."

Me: "That means I have three grandfathers?"

Momma: "Yes, Mr. Rusheon knew your grandmother back in Georgia. She married Mr. Rusheon when she came to Louisiana."

Now I could go back to school and brag that I had three grandfathers, one more than my classmates. But the concept of a third grandfather bothered me. And I reflected on my mother's reluctance when telling me this – so different from her usual frankness. I knew there was more to the grandfather story.

I had heard the word Georgia before, when I was playing in the fields where the men were working, and I came upon a huge grass-hopper. I asked Otis Jackson, our hired man, "What do you call this big grasshopper?" He said, "That's a Georgia grasshopper." I asked him what that meant, and he told me Georgia was a state, and probably there were a lot of them there. He told me my daddy came from Georgia.

I learned to read books, but never learned to read music. When I was very young, in the early 1930s, I sat by the fireplace in the wintertime and listened to Daddy teaching my two older brothers, Otis and Connella, how to read notes and sing parts by shape-notes in a Stamp Baxter's Quartet Songbook. ("Shape-notes" is an old system from colonial times for learning notes based on different shapes. It is sung *a cappella*.)

Daddy learned music from his father and the summer singing schools held at local churches. In the early twentieth century, churches conducted singing schools during the summers. Today, churches have replaced these with vacation bible schools. My father and his contemporaries learned to read music and sing parts when they were growing up. As I grew older,

I enjoyed the moving gospel songs that we sang at Oak Grove Baptist Church and Frantom Chapel Methodist Church.

Momma made a major contribution to our family's music heritage. Recognizing that her children all enjoyed music, she traded a setting hen and fifteen chicks for a windup Victrola and some 78rpm records. This was in the depth of the Depression and money was scarce, so bartering was very prevalent. The records were mostly by country artists of that era including the father of country music, Jimmie Rodgers, the Monroe Brothers, Bob Wills and the Texas Playboys, Roy Acuff, Bob and Joe Shelton, the Carter Family, Gene Autry, Fiddlin' Arthur Smith and some other early cowboys.

I was six years old and my life's course was set. Tutoring kids in the back of the classroom was the start of my teaching career. Listening to the popular country songs on our windup Victrola led me to a passion for music. And I was finally old enough to work in the fields with my brothers.

~3~

Pickin' Cotton and Guitars

When I turned six years old, I had to begin doing regular farm work in the field. My chores included picking cotton, chopping cotton, thinning corn, carrying out bushes that were cut by an older brother, cutting down cornstalks, and knocking down dead cotton stalks with a big stick. I did all this work by hand, along with my brothers, to make it easier for the plow to break and till the soil.

As I grew older my responsibilities increased in scope. Each of the siblings had additional chores to perform after the workday in the fields was finished. My chores usually included milking one or two of the family cows, morning and afternoon. I was eager to learn how to plow like the big guys. Plowing seemed to be a rite of passage for boys on the farm. The day after I was first permitted to plow, I couldn't wait to tell my friends at school all about it.

Each of our fields was given a name, such as Bunn Bottom, Luther New Ground, or Virgil Cut to identify the location where we were to work each day. Neighbors' names were given to our fields because their property abutted ours or they had helped clear the land.

In our farm community, we worked with mules. They were preferable to horses as work animals because they were more docile, easier to train, and had more stamina than horses. However, we did have a riding horse for a short period of time.

I can remember the first time I was assigned to plow in the Boozy Cut. I was plowing with Old Blue, a large mule, and when it came lunchtime, I had to undo his traces and take him home to water and feed him before I could join the family at the dinner table. When I went to undo Old Blue's traces from the singletree, I walked up from behind the mule and the next thing I knew I was sitting on the ground, dazed. It all happened so swiftly that I didn't realize at first that he had kicked me right in the pit of my stomach and knocked the wind out of me. From then on, I always approached mules from the front so they knew what I was doing when I began working with their gear. Texan Sam Rayburn, Speaker of the House of Representatives, used to say "There is no education in the second kick of a mule." I had a visceral understanding of his good advice.

To train a mule when he became big enough to work, we would hook him up to a ten-foot log. Temple would get on one side of the mule's head holding a lead, and I would get on the other. Daddy would take the plow lines and walk behind the mule, talking to him and teaching him to respond to "get up" to move forward; "gee" and "haw" to move right or left. On the appropriate command, we pulled the leads to teach the mule what was wanted. This continued until the mule followed verbal directions and we could remove the leads. The mule also had to learn different gaits for different chores. When plowing a young crop, he had to walk slower to prevent covering up the cotton or corn with dirt. As the plants grew taller, he could go faster.

We had what was known as a three-mule farm. Most of the family farms in the area were two mule farms. The number of mules defined a farmer's status and indicated how much land he could cultivate to grow cotton. Mechanization – tractors, cultivators, cotton pickers and the like – did not come into use in the Louisiana hill country until after World War II. Family owned and operated farms began to decline as a result of mechanization.

Uncle Allison, Momma's bachelor brother, came to live with us and to farm his own crops on shares for several years in the early 1930s. Uncle Allison was strong and healthy and very intelligent about some things, but he had suffered moderate brain damage at birth and was somewhat devoid of social graces. He could complete farm tasks fairly well when given directions, but was unable to plan and carry out tasks without specific guidance.

Daddy assigned him to feed corn and hay to the mules each night after the day's work was done. The first night after supper, Uncle Allison went out to the barn to do his duty and returned very shortly thereafter. Daddy realized that Allison hadn't had time to do the job correctly so he asked, "Allison, did you finish feeding the mules"?

"Yes," replied Allison.

Then Daddy asked, "Did you shuck all that corn in that short period of time?"

"No" said Allison, "I just threw it all in the trough, shucks and all and let them deal with it."

"That won't do because the mules will just throw it all on the ground and waste it," said Daddy.

Allison replied, with confidence, "They may throw it on the ground tonight, but they'll pick it up tomorrow night!" And sure enough they did, and that changed our method of feeding the mules from that day forward.

I didn't have a real understanding of the dimensions of our farm, although I knew it was about a mile and a quarter from one end to the other. And I recognized that there was a place where the farm was very narrow. One day, I asked my daddy how our land was laid out. He said, "Hand me that loaf of bread and I'll show you." He took two rectangular pieces of bread, made an L out of them, and connected them with a small overlap inside the elbow of the L. He said the north piece of bread was 200 acres, and the south piece was 160 acres.

We lived in gently rolling hills. About two thirds of the farm was arable, and the rest was in timber. The main timber crop was fast-growing slash pine, or short leaf pine, used for pulpwood. There were two large pastures fringed by woods in our section. And we had a three-acre hog lot where we kept two or three brood sows. Scothorn Branch ran through the southwest section, where Uncle Emery lived, but there was no creek in our section, so we dug a sky pond (fed only by rain and runoff) in the pasture near our barn. The Soil Conservation Service dug a pond in our other pasture for cattle, as a part of its program to assist farmers.

For years, there had been a monstrous piece of machinery with a huge blade like a road grader rusting by the woodpile at the far edge of our property. It was of a size that would take four horses or mules to pull it, when the blade was engaged. I was told it was a terracing machine, bought by Grandpa Rusheon and Uncle Seaborn.

When Grandpa first started farming in Louisiana, farmers used the water ditch method for flood control. People didn't pay much attention to erosion. They plowed on the contour, but land was so cheap and plentiful that if a natural runoff ditch occurred they just cleared another few fields. Grandpa brought his terracing skills with him from Georgia, where it was the most effective method to prevent erosion. For a time, Grandpa and Seaborn, his oldest son, created a farming revolution in our community with their terracing method.

Grandpa was willing to lend his terracing machine but it was too big and clumsy for other farmers to use, and too expensive to buy. Instead, Grandpa Allen Rusheon taught his neighbors to construct terraces with a huge turning plow, using the services of a surveyor to plot the contours. By the time I was born, the machine had been retired to the woodpile.

For sport, we boys caught fish in Scothorn Branch, put them in a bucket and then transferred them to the pond, where we could catch them again. Donald and I were the two avid fishermen in our families. Occasionally we caught one big enough to eat. We created a problem once when we caught a catfish in the branch and put it into the pond. It ate all the fish eggs. We soon discovered we didn't have any more fish. We had to wait until the dry season in the fall when the pond receded to knee-deep and we could use a feed sack to seine out the catfish. Then we restocked the pond with perch and bream.

In our section of the farm, there were three storage barns, one near the house and two near the location of the old house that Daddy's brother Elton had built in the 1920s. The large barn was across the road and used primarily for feedstuff for the animals. The far barns were used for harvested cotton or for storing produce and equipment. There was a fourth barn near our yard for cattle, with milking stalls and a feed compartment.

We usually had three cows. Two were always kept in lactation. We had a neat way of calling the cows for milking. They were fed from old metal washtubs. If they were not at the cow barn at milking time, we'd bang on the tub so they could hear it, and they'd come running.

Suppertime was Daddy's time to be chairman of the board. He would begin with a report of his day's work, which might include his political contacts, how many acres he had plowed, or how much cotton he had planted with the hired hands. As children, we were never allowed to plant cotton because, if it was not done right, there would be no crop.

After Daddy finished, each of us explained what we had accomplished that day or what problems we encountered. We all looked forward to sharing the story of our day. I couldn't wait until it was my turn to tell about how I sank a basket at school, how I beat everybody at marbles during recess, or how many bushes I had cut and removed from the field. Daddy had a way of making each of us feel good about whatever we had done. Also at the dinner table, Daddy assigned our tasks for the next day's farm work.

Our workweek was generally six days. Some of the farmers would take Saturday afternoon off to go hunting or fishing or just relax to get away from the hot sun and hard work, but Daddy had a different philosophy regarding the workweek. It wasn't until the beginning of World War II that our father allowed us to take off a half day on Saturday afternoon.

My oldest brother, Otis Jr. (who spelled his name differently from Daddy), was usually in charge of our farm work crew. Generally our work detail included Temple, LeMoyne, Billy and me. Because the four of us were close in age, we were grouped together for all our farming assignments. Junior would have us work real hard for a few hours and then take a break.

During the break, we could rest under the trees and play around, talk about school or hunting and fishing. Junior would read a magazine or some book he was able to smuggle out of the house without my parents' knowledge. He was an avid reader, always eager to get back to whatever he was reading at the time. He would read anything he could sneak out under his shirt. We took these breaks a couple of times during the workday.

We usually accomplished more work than my father expected, so Junior was never disciplined for letting us have some rest.

Farmers with large acreage would clear land of trees and brush when they wished to expand their production. I remember Daddy employing Amos Lee, one of our next-door neighbors, to help him clear one new ground. As a young man, Amos had migrated to our neighborhood from Alabama by horseback, with all of his worldly goods packed on. He was known as the man with the best looking horse around.

Daddy and Amos Lee spent most of the winter cutting down underbrush, piling it up and burning it in huge bonfires. They cut down the large trees and sawed them into logs about twenty feet long. Word went out that there was to be a "log rolling" at the Oates Busbice farm and all able-bodied men were invited to give a hand, free of charge of course.

The farmers rolled the smaller logs in a suitable pile and used mules to move the larger logs. The wives and children were invited as well. Women were asked to bring a covered dish to help feed everyone. A "log-rolling dinner" meant a huge feast. This was akin to the barn-raising days of the pioneers. It was hard work but a great social event as well.

After the logs were removed, Daddy allowed the stumps to rot in the new field for several months, then doused them with kerosene and burned them to reduce their size and strength. We wrapped chains around the stumps, inserted a strong pole between the stump and chains, and then attached a doubletree at the long end. Attaching two singletrees to the doubletree allowed two mules to be hooked up to the rig so they could pull together in a circular motion and twist the stump out of the ground. A doubletree was an attachment with hooks that was usually connected to a plow. In this case we used it to pull stumps using mule power.

Singletrees, two feet long, were attached to a doubletree, three feet long. Each was made out of hickory wood, which was the hardest wood on a Louisiana farm. Daddy took us out to the woods to saw down a hickory tree with a two-man crosscut saw – manual, of course. We cut the trunk into segments of two and three feet in length. Using a drawing knife with a two-foot long blade, we removed the bark and molded and honed the timber to the proper size so the hooks could be attached at each end. The mules' traces were then attached to the hooks, which gave them a better leverage to pull with.

In Jackson Parish, transporting children to school had been privatized. In 1936, my father won the contract to deliver the children on our route. That meant that he needed a school bus.

Daddy bought the shell of a brand new 1936 Ford truck. It had a driver's seat and a windshield, but no cab and no bed in back. Our neighbor Amos Lee was what we called a shade-tree carpenter, meaning he was self-taught, worked out in the open, not in a shop, and had no certification. Daddy bought lumber, tin, and cloth, and the talented Amos then constructed a school bus body attached to the truck between July 4, when the crops were laid by, and the start of school right after Labor Day.

This vehicle had a double row of benches down the center, backs to each other, and a long bench on each side. It could hold 40 children. We had to crawl by dozens of knees to get to our seats.

Since Daddy owned his own bus, during the summer he would take the middle seats out and load up the bus with crops to sell to people in the neighboring small towns. Cotton was our cash crop, but we grew tomatoes, watermelons, and cantaloupes as minor cash crops.

Daddy usually took at least two of the kids with him to assist. It was a wonderful treat for each of us when we were allowed to go. We would sleep on a pallet in the bus at night, eat in restaurants, and enjoy seeing the different places. We took these trips after the crops had been "laid by," meaning that they no longer needed to be cultivated.

Daddy took Helen, Vivienne, and our cousin Hollace from Boeuf River on one of his watermelon-pear trips in the school bus. Daddy had driven down to Baton Rouge to bring back a whole load of pears to take to market with our homegrown watermelons. One of his marketing techniques was to say to buyers, "You can see, these pears are all fruit -- hardly any core at all." He then would cut off the slim top of the pear to show them. Of course from that angle the pear looked like it was all meat with very little core. The technique was effective and Daddy did very well with it.

After parking in the shade of big trees in each little town, Daddy would join some politicians in the courthouse square to discuss local politics. On this trip, Daddy demonstrated his pear technique to Hollace and asked Hollace to handle the pear sales while he was away from the bus. The first customer came up, and Hollace got confused. Saying, "These pears have hardly any core at all," Hollace cut across the big bottom of the pear by mistake, exposing the largest part of the core. Embarrassed, he closed it up quickly and threw it back into the basket, but his suspicious customer left without buying. Helen and Vivienne and Hollace came back from the trip roaring with laughter about Hollace's pear technique.

The first vacation we ever took was during Christmas school vacation in 1937. Daddy decided to go visit Aunt Pauline and Uncle Allen and Aunt Mae Belle and Uncle Penn in Port Neches and Port Arthur, Texas. We took out the middle seat of the bus and installed a mattress and some quilts, since we would be driving all night. Daddy turned over the driving to Otis Jr. and Connella, who were 18 and 16. I was so excited I couldn't sleep, so I moved up front to listen to Junior and Connella talk about girls, sports and school. They got so involved in laughing and chatting they failed to watch the road. Before they knew it, the paving ran out, and we drove into a construction area.

I know exactly where it happened – between Lake Charles, Louisiana and Orange, Texas – because I was bouncing up and down with excitement about crossing the state line. Connella slammed on the brakes, and the bus fishtailed, which woke up Daddy and everyone else. I was terrified, but Daddy took it all in stride and just quietly told them to be more careful.

This was my first trip out of Louisiana, and it was awesome just to be in the state of Texas, where I saw my first real cowboy -- Aunt Pauline's neighbor -- complete with hat and spurs. But my ideal cowboy lisped. He was attracted to my sister Helen, and several of us went for a walk with them. But he spoiled the macho effect when he said, "Hold up a thecond. I theem to have thome mud on my thpur."

Returning to school, I was elated to be able to brag about my Texas vacation to my classmates.

In the late 1930s, the state mandated that any new school bus must have a steel body. Our old wood-body bus was grandfathered in, but when Daddy wanted a new bus, the steel body was mandatory. Nobody in our area could do the job, so he had to drive the new truck frame all the way to New Orleans -- 250 miles -- to have a steel body installed, since nobody in our area could do the job.

Allen Head and his wife, good friends from Hog Hair, went with Daddy. The three of them were totally exposed driving along, as the truck frame had only an engine and windshield – no doors, no roof, no cab. In New Orleans, a wheel broke off a truck coming toward them, rolled into their front bumper, bounced up thirty feet over the windshield and came down right next to Daddy, grazing but not injuring him. Only after he returned home did we all learn that Daddy had survived the freak accident by a matter of inches.

Our house was on a local parish road. Repairs to these dirt roads were the responsibility of the local farmers. In spring and fall of each year, all the farmers would get together and bring shovels, posthole diggers, rakes, and axes to put in their required number of workdays on the roads. They would fill in potholes and deep ruts; they would cut down small pine trees and place them crosswise on hilly grades to give cars and trucks enough traction to climb the hills in the wintertime. These dirt roads were referred to as washboard roads because of the humps made by the pine poles.

In 1938, the state built a new gravel highway about a half a mile further south of our dwelling and closed our farm-to-market dirt road. This meant that Daddy had to build a new house to give us access to the new road. Fortunately, my grandfather had built several tenant houses on the farm for sharecroppers and farm laborers in the early twentieth century and some still had good lumber in them. We tore down our current dwelling and some of the old tenant houses and Daddy purchased what new lumber was needed to build a larger home on the state road.

The new state road ran right through the middle of the farm, whereas the house we had been living in was at the very northeast edge of the farm. My father hired two or three local farmers who were "jackleg" carpenters to help the family members construct the new dwelling. My daddy and all the brothers helped with the building details.

One of the most interesting things to me about building the new house was making shingles for the roof. We found a large cypress tree about five miles away and purchased it from a man who was known as "Baby Doll" Ford. I was lucky enough to help make the shingles and learn how to use a fro, which is a dull instrument that looks like a small scythe. That's where I learned the origin of the saying, "This tool is dull as a fro." It is placed on top of the wood block. When hit with a wooden mallet, it makes the wood split off from the block and the shingles fall away magically. My job was also to help stack the shingles and load them on the bus to be hauled to the building site. And to my surprise, that one huge tree provided all the shingles necessary to cover the entire roof.

The new house was completed in 1939. It was much larger than the one we had been living in and gave each of us a little more privacy. Still, there was no running water or electricity or indoor plumbing.

During the construction our whole family moved to a rented house half-mile away. It was really too small for comfort, but it had a good, though drafty, barn. My two oldest brothers and I were privileged to have a "semi-private room" in this structure. I slept on a cot and Junior and Connella shared a double bed. Daddy installed a wood heater to keep us warm on cold winter nights. It was like having our own apartment. We had a washstand, and a kettle we could put on the heater to get hot water to wash with. We had a cupboard for snacks, lots of books and coal-oil lamps to read them by. Sometimes I got to read Junior's detective and wild west magazines.

I felt very special because I was singled out to live with the two older boys, whom I admired. I felt like a big guy. I loved to listen to their conversations as they talked about girlfriends and plans they had made with their friends. But my classmates in third grade teased the devil out of me when they found out I was living in a barn. So in later life when people asked me, "Why don't you close that door? Were you brought up in a barn?" I could say, "Yes, I was."

My daddy was a hard worker and generally held down two or three jobs in addition to farming. In the late thirties, when the U.S. government began distributing surplus food to people on welfare, Daddy obtained the contract to transport commodities from regional warehouses to local distribution centers. The bus was ideal for this project since it was fully enclosed and weatherproof. On occasion, Daddy would let a few of his sons accompany him.

I remember one trip vividly, when I was about ten. Daddy told me and two or three of my brothers we should bring a sandwich and some snacks, since his schedule did not allow for us to stop at a restaurant. We went thirty-five miles to Ruston to pick up a load, and delivered the commodities to Columbia, sixty-five miles away.

Daddy kept to a steady thirty-five miles per hour all the way. When we arrived at the distribution warehouse across the street from the Columbia courthouse, people were already lined up to receive their food. They had come by wagon, buggy, old car, and horseback. I noticed the individuals in the waiting crowd seemed downcast and anxious; they were dressed in ragged clothes and were unkempt and bedraggled. As I stood on the pavement, people shuffled past me into the warehouse, carrying old feed sacks, flour sacks, and dilapidated suitcases.

An old man came up riding an old horse. He was wearing faded overalls and a holey fleece-lined jacket. His horse walked very slowly and cautiously, as if feeling its way. I asked the stranger standing beside me if there was something wrong with the old man's horse. He explained that the horse was blind, but it was the owner's only means of transportation, so he had trained him to walk that way to avoid bumping into things. The man standing next to me said the old man lived alone in a small house just outside town, and seemed to be able to take care of himself.

When the old man dismounted, it was obvious he was unsteady on his feet. The work staff filled his bags, and helped him tie them onto the horse. I felt very sorry for him. Even today when I hear stories about people in dire straits, I remember that old gentleman and his blind horse.

Each year, after the first frost, it was time to harvest the corn. That included pulling each ear off the stalk by hand and throwing it in the wagon as the mules pulled slowly along. When the wagon was filled, we unloaded it in the corncrib to be used during the winter to feed our farm animals. On occasion, we would take corn to Mr. Spillers's corn mill and have it ground into meal for Momma to make cornbread.

We also harvested sugar cane to make syrup. Stripping cane and hauling it on the wagon to the mill was a very hot and difficult job. Usually, we ended up cut and bruised from the sharp leaves. The work was exhausting. Decades earlier, this job had been relegated to slaves -- it had carried a very high mortality rate because of the leaves, the sharp cane-cutter tool, the weight of the stalks, and the heat.

We owned the only syrup mill in the community and my uncle Emery was the best syrup maker in the area. Therefore, most farmers nearby brought their sugar cane to our mill to make syrup. They usually paid for this service with an agreed-upon number of gallons of syrup in exchange for the process. It was my job at the syrup mill to feed the stalks into the cane grinder as the mule, attached to a long pole, walked in circles to turn the grinder to squeeze out the juice into a barrel. People would come by and use a cup to dip into the cool cane juice barrel and get a free drink. We could hear them exclaim that this was a real treat. The syrup mill operated in the late fall and just about everyone in the community dropped by to get a cup of cane juice. It was a great time for neighbors to socialize and swap a little gossip.

Potatoes and black-eyed peas were our staple foods. We grew plenty of them and preserved them in the same manner that farmers had going back to pioneer days. The growing season was long enough to produce two crops of Irish potatoes, one in the spring and one in the fall, which gave us plenty during warm seasons. During the winters, we stored the Irish potatoes in the cool portion of the smokehouse or barn and sprinkled them lightly with lime to keep them from going bad. We grew large crops of sweet potatoes, dug pits about six inches deep to get below the frost line, and covered them with pine straw and leaves in order to preserve them through the winters.

Daddy usually planted his cotton late in the spring because he wanted it to be ready for cultivation when we were out of school in mid-May. Therefore, we boys had an opportunity to make a little money in late August. The farmers who planted in the early spring would have their cotton open and ready to be picked at least two weeks before ours was ready. We then hired out to neighbors – often to Amos Lee, whose only son was disabled and unable to work outside -- to help them gather the cotton. We used our earnings to buy new clothes for school, to save for the county fair late in September or to spend frivolously. I have picked cotton for as little as fifty cents a hundred pounds. If the cotton was thick, I could make almost a dollar by working hard all day long.

If we had time left during the summer, we would hire out to other neighbors or to people in town to furnish winter firewood. Together with friends, we performed a lot of odd jobs for neighbors to be sociable, to earn extra money, and to buy a few things for ourselves that we couldn't expect our parents to give us for Christmas.

In September, we boys were not allowed to attend school after the first day of enrollment until all the cotton had been picked. Still, our parents expected us to keep in the top ten percent of our classes regardless of how many days we missed in order to get the cotton picked and taken to Chatham or West Monroe to be ginned. Of course we complained, but things always seemed to work out.

Our family was so large that I wore mostly hand-me-downs. Rarely did I get new clothes made or purchased just for me. Until we were in the sixth grade, we boys would go everywhere, except church, barefoot, from Easter to Thanksgiving -- even to school. Daddy always made sure we got a new pair of shoes after the cotton was sold in the fall. Since girls matured earlier and were more conscious of their appearance, they began wearing shoes when they were in the fourth grade. But we boys would say, "Heck, we don't wanna' wear shoes until we have to."

My father, who had many community duties off the farm, had to wear shoes. A man couldn't go barefoot one day and wear shoes the next; his feet would get too tender. Feet had to be conditioned to be tough on the farm. Usually farmers, like my Uncle Emery, went barefoot all their lives.

One time, Emery walked a mile and a half in his coveralls, barefoot, to discuss farming with our neighbor, Mr. Luther Kilpatrick, who was a state representative at the time. While they were chatting on Mr. Luther's front porch, a state senator dropped by, all spiffed up in his white linen suit and Panama hat. While Mr. Luther and the senator were discussing politics, Uncle Emery felt a little left out, so he methodically rolled a cigarette, pulled out a big wooden match, and nonchalantly but noisily struck it on the bottom of his callused foot. The senator's eyes got, as Uncle Emery said in the retelling, "big as saucers." After the senator left, Uncle Emery and Mr. Luther had a good laugh and Mr. Luther told the story all over the neighborhood.

Wayne as a schoolboy

Daddy cut the boys' hair on weekends, using shears and hand clippers, but because there were seven of us boys it was difficult. He got tired of doing that at least one weekend a month. As we grew older, Daddy made an arrangement with the only barber within fifteen miles, Mr. Hayden, who had a barbershop in Eros. Uncle Emery had made the same arrangement with the barber for his sons, so that equaled eleven Busbices for the barber to cut. We were told to go to the barbershop to have our hair cut and put on the tab. One day I went to get a haircut and I thanked Mr. Hayden and told him to put it on the tab. Soon after that Uncle Emery came in to get his haircut, and when he started to pay, Mr. Hayden asked, "Do you want to pay for your son who came in here last week?" Uncle Emery said, "None of my boys have been in here recently, it must have been one of Oates' boys." We worked together, played together, and were even thought to be brothers. We liked that status and got a good laugh when people would get us mixed up.

We were basically one family and "favored" (Louisiana lingo for looked like) each other. Lots of times I'd walk down the street and Daddy's buddies would point their finger at me and say, "Busby!"

Not, "Hello." Just, "Busby!" And, "I don't know if you are Emery's boy or Oates's. Whose boy are you?" I would explain, and they would say, "Well, I knowed you was a Busby, I just didn't know which one!"

In those days in Louisiana, it seemed extremely important who your daddy was. Usually the first question asked of me when being introduced was, "What's your daddy's name?" or "Who's your daddy?" The second question was usually, "What church do you go to?" The answers to those questions gave you status and identity in the mind of the questioner.

The Busby name came up with some regularity. Once after I had seen someone on the street who came right out and said "Busby!" instead of Busbice, or instead of saying hello, I asked my mother why they called me Busby instead of my real name. She just grinned and replied, "Busbice is kind of hard to say and that's probably why they chose to say Busby." Further questions got me nowhere.

One spring, Daddy, two hired hands, Temple, LeMoyne, Billy and I were working in the field preparing to plant cotton. Momma sent Bernarr out to the field with a copy of that day's newspaper. Daddy looked at it, tied up his mule, and excused himself. He didn't return to the field that day.

That evening Daddy brought home a subdued Junior. There had been an item in the paper about Junior's arrest in Monroe for drunkenness. I overheard our neighbor Hardy Fuller ask Daddy if he had met Police Chief Busby, and whether we were related to him. Daddy replied, "Yes, we are." Our ears perked up at this further mention of the name that was so much like ours. But there was no more discussion and we didn't dare to ask.

I remember vividly one of the fishing trips that Daddy took the boys on. We dug up worms, gathered up the fishing gear, placed our sleeping quilts in the bus along with all of our personal gear, and set out for Cheniere Creek about 20 miles away. Going fishing at night meant fishing for catfish by setting out hooks along the creek bank, called a trotline. We set out a number of hooks and checked them periodically until about midnight.

It was one of those moonless nights that swallow you up in darkness. We had to walk a log to get across the 40-foot-wide creek to check the hooks on the side across from where we were camping. My brother Temple was in charge of making the run with me to remove the fish from the lines and place them in the bucket.

We were using a carbide light, and on our way back to the log the light went out. Temple was also in charge of the carbide light, which was our only source of illumination on the very dark creek bank. We had to put more carbide in the lamp and add water, but much to our dismay, we discovered we didn't have a match. We yelled to Daddy for assistance. After assessing

33

the situation, he said, "Don't panic. I'll empty my Prince Albert tobacco can, put some matches in it and throw it across the creek. The matches will stay dry, even if it lands in the water."

Because the creek was so wide, we were not sure Daddy's pitch would be successful. We looked at each other and silently remembered that Daddy didn't throw too accurately on the rare occasions when he played ball with us. We waited anxiously, holding our breath as Daddy hurled the can of matches to our side of the creek. Before he made the pitch, he told us, "Listen to where it lands so you can locate it in the dark."

Temple and I weren't too confident but as luck would have it, Daddy threw a perfect strike and the tobacco can landed a few feet from us. We felt around with our hands in the dark and found it, took out the matches and Temple got us going again. We located the log that was our safe and dry passage to the others and gave a big sigh of relief.

Sometimes we would go fishing, or go swimming in the nude in Scothorn Branch on our farm, or in Flat Creek. About two miles from our farm, Flat Creek ran between two hills, and was bordered by trees on either side. It was as deep as fifteen feet where it curved around the bend; legend had it that the creek had been dynamited at that point, to make it deeper. This could have happened when road building was occurring nearby, or when farmers were blowing up tree stumps to clear the land. Because of the depth and the strong whirlpool current at the bend, and also the fact that someone drowned there during a co-ed skinny dipping party years before, our parents forbade swimming in Flat Creek. When our older brothers were around, my brother Junior or my oldest cousin, Lannie Mack, we chose not to go there or risk being thrown in the deepest part. And we younger kids couldn't swim yet.

As we became older and bolder, Donald, Bobby, Billy and I sneaked over to Flat Creek, determined to learn to swim. We discovered that empty syrup cans with their lids on were buoyant, and could serve as water wings. With one syrup can under each arm, you could stay afloat and maneuver in deep water by kicking. As we got better at it, we held the cans at arms' length and could almost swim. Finally, we were able to dispense with the cans and dog paddle confidently.

But we were very careful when we went over there to the cool water of Flat Creek, and we spent the afternoons swimming, water-fighting and sometimes fishing. Swimming in the creek was a guy thing; the girls did not participate.

Our family didn't have a radio until the early 1940s. When the United States entered World War II, my father, a WWI veteran with two sons in the military, decided it was important to keep up with the war news. Our first radio ran on A&B batteries because we had no electricity. We discovered that the radio brought in the Grand Ole Opry on Saturday nights, and this expanded our music exposure primarily along country and western lines and offered many more artists than we had on records. The Opry was an instant hit at the Busbice residence. My siblings and I adopted various artists as our favorites and tried to emulate them while we were working in the fields and doing our chores around the house and barns.

Growing up with eight brothers and sisters, I had to learn negotiation, diplomacy, and coping with the small society that was our family.

I was a year and two weeks younger than the twins, Temple and LeMoyne. Temple was thirty minutes older than LeMoyne and the more aggressive socially. LeMoyne was calm, quiet and had the reputation of having a greater work ethic. Individually, either one of them would have been a hard act to follow. Being the only twins in the extended family gave them automatic recognition and status. Consequently, I felt that I had to work harder to keep up with them, so I tried to do everything they did to earn some recognition on my own. I believe this was an important factor in making me strive to achieve throughout my life.

I admired Temple for his leadership qualities. His avid interest in reading inspired me to follow his lead. On cold, rainy, windy days when we couldn't go outside, Daddy would crawl up in his bed and invite the four middle children to climb in with him while he read Big Little Books. These were stories about popular characters like Dick Tracy, Kit Carson, and Gene Autry, which were designed to bridge the gap between children's stories and adult books. After an hour or so, Daddy would ask Temple to take over briefly while he rested his voice.

LeMoyne and I enjoyed hunting, boxing and playing music together. He was larger and stronger than I was, but he was careful not to do me any harm. We used 16-ounce gloves and he taught me a lot about the art of self-defense that gave me the skills I needed to be competitive with my classmates at school.

Billy was two years younger than me. We shared an interest in sports and liked to argue about which major league baseball team was the best. He was always pulling for the St. Louis Browns and I favored the Cardinals. These were the closest major league teams to Eros. We got our sports results from the newspaper until 1942, when Daddy finally bought a radio.

I was six years younger than Connella, whom I tried to emulate. He was always upbeat, friendly and involved with people. He was active in sports and he was good at them. I admired him for that and I could see how his involvement in sports, combined with his good looks and friendly demeanor, made him very popular. In our family, we viewed Connella as bigger than life. My father gave him the nickname of "Mr. Personality."

Bernarr was four years my junior so we didn't pal around much in the early years. If he wanted to do something, he made sure he could do it faster and better than anyone else. Although he was the youngest boy, in the cotton field he wouldn't give up until he had picked as much as his older brothers. His drive to excel extended to school. He graduated as valedictorian of his high school class. By the time he was eleven, Bernarr was totally focused on music. He loved Bill Monroe's music with a passion. I had learned the rudiments of playing a mandolin I borrowed from Alan Crowell, and I had the privilege of teaching Bernarr the basic concepts of noting and rhythm styles on both the guitar and the mandolin.

Marilyn was pretty, friendly, kind and dutiful. She helped my mother with the household chores. And as the adults used to say in those days, "Marilyn never gave her momma a minute's trouble." She was a real treasure in our family.

Our family worked half of the 360 acres and Uncle Emery's sons, Donald, Lannie Mack, Lancelot and Bobby, worked close by on the other half of the farm. Sometimes we boys got together. We would work on their chores for a while and then we would all go back over to our field and work there. This way we could socialize, sing duets and quartets, teach each other new songs we had heard on the Grand Ole Opry, plan a fishing trip or hunting trip, and enjoy ourselves. It took the drudgery out of the hard work.

Temple and I used to team up and sing duets – he sang lead and I sang harmony. When we were in our early teens, our neighbor Travis Kilpatrick needed help harvesting his cotton and he offered to give us his guitar and fiddle if we would pick his cotton for a week. Temple, LeMoyne, Billy and I readily agreed to work, and at the end of the week we received the musical instruments. (We acquired our Model T in 1944 the same way: neighbor Dennison Smith traded it for a week's cotton picking.)

LeMoyne, Temple, Billy and Wayne with fiddle and guitar

Allen Crowell was the best homegrown musician in our community. He played the fiddle, guitar, and mandolin equally well. He preferred the fiddle because it was the lead instrument used in those days to excite the square dancers at the local gatherings. People would say, "I hear that fiddle ring out and I gotta' get up and dance!"

Allen never learned to read music. He had a natural talent for learning to play a song or fiddle tune by listening to it only once. When I was about fourteen, Allen was in his mid-thirties, and he lived a half-mile from our farm. Straight from a hard day's work without bathing or changing clothes, I would frequently go over to visit him and jam on his front porch. I sang and played guitar, while Allen played fiddle. By this time I had learned the guitar chords but needed practice to know just when to make the changes.

37

While Allen fiddled, he would call out the chord changes to me so I could keep proper time.

My cousin Bobby, who had a beautiful tenor, would join Allen and me on the porch sometimes so we could sing harmony. Of course we had no telephones and Bobby's house was a mile and a half away from Allen's. We worked out a plan that after supper, Bobby would sit on his porch and listen. The sound carried over the fields and he could always hear us. In the twilight, Bobby would hurry on down the gravel road to add his voice to the harmony.

Walking by Your Side
   By Wayne Busbice
   Pub. Old Home Place Music

If you want to meet Him tomorrow
If you want to feel satisfied
Just ask the Lord to guide you
And He'll be walking by your side.

Chorus:
When you reach the river of Jordan
When you have to cross that great divide
Jesus will be right beside you
Oh, he'll be walking by your side.

You can't find the way without Him
You must give up your foolish pride
Just take your Savior by the hand
Then He'll be walking by your side.

I learned a lot jamming with Alan Crowell and I kept my mother informed of my progress. Momma asked me to invite Allen to our house to practice so she could observe how good I had become. Allen accepted the invitation and I was surprised when he arrived all cleaned up, freshly shaven and wearing his "Sunday-go-to-meetin' clothes." As I invited him to come up on our front porch and have a seat, I asked, "Why are you all dressed up, do you have somewhere else to go after practice?"

He replied, "I would never insult Miss Fay by coming to her house in my dirty work clothes, because I have great respect for her." I tried to explain that she would not mind if he came over in his work clothes just to practice – besides, I went to his house in my work clothes. Allen explained that was different. "This is Miss Fay," he said, and he had too much respect for her to do that.

~4~

Momma

To the neighbors, she was "Miss Fay", teacher, church leader, and mother of nine – a strong, intelligent, hardworking woman who drew respect from all who knew her. To me, she was Momma.

It was a point of honor for the Busbice men that the Busbice women would do no fieldwork, and would be treated with respect and dignity as all "Southern belles" should be. But that didn't mean they led a life of leisure.

With no electricity, Momma was responsible for preparing all the meals from scratch: breakfast, dinner –the noon meal -- and supper each day, with meat at each meal.

Before daybreak, Momma got up and made hot biscuits on the wood-burning stove. I liked to stand by and feed wood into the stove as she worked to watch the efficient way she squeezed off a lump of dough with her hands to get each biscuit the right size. Then she'd make coffee in a percolator pot, fried eggs, bacon, oatmeal, and cocoa for the children, and put homemade butter and our own sugar cane syrup on the table. It was important to feed the adults and hired hands first, so they could get to the field by sunup. Next, we children would eat in shifts. Soon we left for our before-school chores; mine was to milk the cows while others fed the hogs and chickens, and geared up the mules for plowing.

Finally, after all the workers and children left for field and school, Momma could sit down and enjoy her meal. That old saying, "A man's work is from sun to sun, but a woman's work is never done," was true in her case.

Helen was Momma's only helper and she washed dishes and made beds. For many years, she was overburdened as the oldest girl in our family of nine children --my sister Marilyn was born when she was eleven. Helen and my mother were very close. While they worked in the kitchen, Helen confided about her friends and boyfriends to get Momma's advice. I was always curious at home, and I tried to listen in. But I always kept what I heard to myself.

Mondays and Fridays were washdays on the farm. Momma had a large cast iron wash pot to heat the water to boil our extremely dirty clothes in lye soap to get the dirt out. She used several washtubs and a scrub board to clean and rinse the clothes that were not quite so soiled. After washing, the clothes were hung outside on the line to dry.

My mother was an avid reader. In spite of the little time available to her during the day because of all her duties, she tried to read at least one book a week. She was able to read mostly after all the children went to bed. She read bestsellers, popular novels, and history by the light of a coal-oil lamp. Usually she had to use two lamps at a time to see well, and she placed them in reflector devices to focus all the available light on the page. From her father, she had inherited a good library, which included a series of books about Lincoln, an encyclopedia, a dictionary, and Shakespeare's writings, among others.

After she read a good book, Momma would gather the younger children in front the fireplace. We couldn't wait to hear her tell us the whole story, with explanations where we needed them. Watching her pleasure from reading gave all of us an appetite for books. She did the same thing with movies.

It was really unusual for Momma to be able to go to a movie. I'll never forget how exciting it was to hear her tell about "Gone with the Wind". It took her at least three evenings after supper to tell the story. She made each character come alive as she described them and what they did, and why.

There weren't many people in our neighborhood who were readers, but Momma encouraged all of us children, especially me, to read for pleasure. I especially liked to read in the cold winter months, when I buried my face in a good western novel in front of the fireplace. Momma made sure I received at least one novel for Christmas, and kept me well supplied with stories of the West. My favorite author was B.M. Bowers, who wrote a series about Chip of the Flying U. Chip was an adventuresome boy who got into scrapes that were over his head, but with courage and diplomacy he always managed to come through unscathed. This was my favorite theme in reading. I identified with Chip, who was struggling to be a man and be accepted by the older, rowdy boys, while still following the rules of society.

Uncle Allison saw me reading the westerns, and fed my imagination with his story of seeing Frank James, the notorious brother of Jesse, as a young boy. Uncle Allison had seen Frank when the former outlaw was hired as a celebrity to fire the starting gun for the horse races in West Monroe.

Aunt Ivie was famous for her homemade tea cakes. She seemed to always have a batch ready when I was there, and I dearly loved them. I liked to visit Aunt Ivie and sit in her kitchen while she worked.

40

She said, "Did you know this was your grandma's kitchen?" This was startling, for I knew the house as Emery's and Ivie's house, and had never known my grandparents used to live there. "Your grandmother loved her children and she was so good to them," she went on. "She was a good cook and a wonderful person, and I just adored her." But about Grandpa, all Ivie would say was that he was difficult. It was clear to me that she refused to talk about him because she had nothing good to say. This only raised more questions in my mind.

Momma belonged to a group of women who enjoyed quilting. One of their favorite quilting parties involved making a friendship quilt. Each lady would make a square for the top and put her name on it. At the quilting bee, all the women gathered in one house to decide how the squares fit together. They put up a frame to lay out the quilt so they could work on it. After many meetings at different homes, it was ready to stuff with cotton.

In order to get the cotton filler (batting) for the quilt we kids had to go out and pick "quilting cotton", after the main crop had been harvested. We had to glean the remainder after the two main pickings. We hated to do this because the bolls were gnarled and sharp, and some of them were not fully opened due to boll weevils. The cotton was scattered and it was hard to gather a sackful. It took a full morning of picking to get enough. The cotton was then taken to the gin to have the seeds removed, so it could be put in the quilt.

Quilting cotton was also called scrapping cotton, because it was the leftover scraps. Sometimes there'd be enough of this to make a mattress. Our neighbor Nancy Fuller and my mother usually teamed up to make a mattress. I would hear Momma discuss the best place to buy mattress ticking with Nancy. I thought this meant ticks. I thought it was strange that they wanted to buy mattress ticks.

Often there was visiting back and forth among the neighbor ladies – my Uncle Emery called them the Hot Stove Gossip League. And of course they also visited one another with hot food and cakes when someone was sick. My Aunt Belle and my Aunt Zona, Momma's sisters, visited regularly. I would listen to them talk about old times when they were young, and what their sisters were all doing. Every year, Momma invited her nieces Lucille and Elaine to spend a whole week with us. Momma also socialized with the ladies of the Women's Missionary Union of the Baptist Church.

During the depression years in the 1930s, nobody had money to buy many of the things needed for everyday living. But we were luckier than most because we were able to grow our own food. For the household food, we raised black-eyed peas, brown crowders, and purple hull peas in a joint pea patch with Uncle Emery's family. At pea-picking time, usually at the hottest time of the summer, when the peas were just ready for the dinner table but not yet ripe for canning, Helen and Vivienne arranged to meet in the pea patch several times a week to pick them for dinner.

Occasionally when I was not required to be working in the field, I'd go with them to listen to their gossip. Naturally much of their gossip was discussing their boyfriends. Because I was younger, and a boy, they developed a code language of their own to keep me in the dark so I wouldn't spill the beans to my brothers. Once in a while I would break the code and tell them I could understand them. They were always quick to deny what I had deciphered, though.

We spent many hours shelling peas for Momma to can in a pressure cooker. On occasion we would invite some of the neighbors over for a "pea shelling". At times we might have as many as ten people on the cool side of the porch socializing and shelling peas all week long. The neighbors who helped shared by taking several jars of canned peas home for their winter stores.

We could purchase salt, flour, sugar, and other staples at the general store, which also carried a lot of things other than groceries -- clothes, plowshares, tools, and cotton sacks.

Momma made nearly all our clothes from cloth purchased at the country store, or from feed sacks, flour sacks and cornmeal sacks, which came in colors and prints for this purpose. People joked that folks bought the brand of flour and meal that had the prettiest cloth rather than the best quality food.

Momma sewed shirts, pants, coveralls, jackets and dresses. She even made our underwear. She made one-piece BVDs, which served as pajamas. She exchanged patterns with other wives, in different sizes as their children grew.

I liked to lie on the cool pine floor and watch Momma pedal the sewing machine. I waited for the bobbin to run out, so I could change it for her. While I lay there, we talked about school, church, my friends, and family. I felt very close to her at these times, and I was always eager to help her.

Momma even made our cotton sacks to use for picking cotton. We had to drag them on the ground behind us, long enough to hold a lot of cotton, but not large enough to weigh us down. She measured each of us to make sure we had a sack long enough. For example, at age ten when I was picking 100 pounds a day, my sack would be about six feet long. As I grew and my volume increased, my sack would get longer. An adult might use an eight-foot sack. She also had to compute the volume in the sack for each picker, since dragging more than fifty pounds (for an adult) would tire you too quickly.

In order to earn money to buy Christmas presents, Momma raised chickens. To get good quality laying stock, she ordered biddies from the Sears Roebuck catalog. A biddy is a two- or three-day old hatchling. The mailman delivered them in a box lined with hay, with holes punched in the top.

Biddies have fuzz, not feathers, and they are very sensitive to the cold. So if the chickens were delivered during a cold spell, I slept out in the brooder house with them to maintain the fire during the night. When I was seven, Momma had me set up a wood heater inside the brooder house, and stuff blankets and old clothes in the walls for insulation. And I stayed there for two or three nights until the biddies could survive without extra heat. I always volunteered to work in the brooder house – none of my brothers was interested in raising chickens.

Todd Holloway was the senior deacon in our church, and also the egg peddler. And, he practiced medicine without a license. One day I went outside with Momma when Deacon Holloway drove up to buy eggs. I had big swollen glands in my neck, and Momma mentioned she was concerned that I might have mumps, and wondered what she should do about it. She asked his opinion, and Mr. Holloway agreed that it looked like mumps. "But," he said, "there's one sure way to know. Have him eat a sour pickle. If it hurts him to eat it, he's got mumps." I never did like sour pickles. And when I took a bite, it hurt, and I puckered. But as an adult, I got the mumps for real, and realized Mr. Holloway's diagnosis was lacking.

Momma raised broiler chickens for us to eat. For breeding, she had two huge red roosters. The older one was cock of the walk – he dominated everything in the barnyard by sheer assertiveness, even after the younger rooster grew to be as big as he was. The younger rooster had trouble mating with the hens -- the old rooster never allowed him to get close enough. My two oldest brothers, Connella, and Junior, had a theory that the young rooster could probably beat the strutting old rooster, if he would just fight.

The old rooster had a distinctive bright red wattle and comb. One day while our parents were out, I watched with great interest as Connella and Junior took the old rooster right into the living room and rubbed soot from the fireplace all over his wattle and comb. Then they set the old rooster out in the yard with his new appearance, a black wattle and comb, and waited.

When the young rooster spied him, he didn't recognize his nemesis. He thought this was a new interloper in his kingdom, so he sped over to

43

the old rooster and attacked. When the flying feathers cleared, the young rooster had won, and chased the old guy away.

Momma returned, and saw that her prize rooster had a different look "Boys, come in here!" she called. They had to wash the old rooster clean, but his domination in the chicken yard was over. He had to share his hens from then on.

From this, I learned about the psychology of roosters and teenage boys.

While I received my academic education in school, it was from my family and the farm that I received a wide, general education about the world we live in. Living on a 360-acre farm, I learned how to build your own house, how to select the best breed of hog for meat, how to sever barbed wire without wire cutters, how to repair farm machinery and almost anything else with haywire, how to wring a chicken's neck, and how to feed a family without money. Learning how to fall back on my own resources and use initiative was to benefit me all my life.

Tragedies of a Southern Family

I was in first grade the year that Mr. McBride, the principal, came to our classroom door and asked me to step outside. He said, "Wayne, I just wanted to tell you that your Aunt Laura passed away today." I looked up at him, puzzled. "I don't have an Aunt Laura." He replied, "Yes, you do. Laura is your mother's sister. I'm terribly sorry, I just wanted you to know."

When I got home, Momma simply said that Laura was her older sister, and had been living in a hospital in Alexandria. She didn't tell us that Pineville was an asylum for the insane. Aunt Belle, a widow with a rich boyfriend, drove Momma to the funeral in her new 1935 Chevrolet.

Momma's parents were Charles Allison Connella and Sarah Nobles Connella. Around 1870 Charles had inherited a large portion of his father's cotton plantation, which he farmed with black farmhands and sharecroppers. These people were primarily descendants of slave families that had belonged to the Connella plantation in the years before the Civil War. After emancipation, most former slaves had nowhere to go to make a living so they stayed on the plantation to sharecrop or work as day laborers.

Charles and Sarah were married in 1880, and soon they had two daughters, Belle and Alice. One morning when Alice was two, Sarah was outside doing yard work amid burning piles of leaves on the plantation lawn. Alice was playing, and she fell and tumbled into a flaming pile. Sarah rushed to pull her out, but she was burned so badly that she could not live. Her mother held her and tried to comfort her until she died just before midnight.

Sarah put the charred dress and the baby's doll and toys in a small trunk, and placed the trunk and her cradle in the corner of a room. Daily, she visited the little shrine, held the doll, kissed the dress, and mourned her daughter. Three of Sarah's children died in infancy, but Alice would be the one she would mourn for the rest of her life. She never stopped blaming herself for the accident.

Sarah died of cancer in 1910, leaving her husband and seven children: Belle, Laura, Jettie, Zona, Charles Allison, and Heloise, and Fay.

Grandpa Charles Connella and Grandma Sarah Noble Connella, around 1905

Charles stopped doing his own farming and began to rent out some of his arable land and subdivide other portions of his holdings. In addition to the plantation, he owned other big farms in Union Parish to the north.

Grandpa Charles Connella was very protective of his daughters, especially after they came to marrying age. When Belle, at twenty-six, wanted to marry Edmund Williamson, a fifty-two-year-old widower and owner of a plantation twenty-five miles away on Boeuf River, Grandpa reluctantly gave his permission with the requirement that they come back to visit the family at least once a month. Mr. Williamson agreed to do this. He kept his word and was welcomed and accepted by the family.

When another daughter, Jettie, fell in love with Jim Faust, Grandpa refused to allow them to marry because Jim had a reputation of having an uncontrollable temper and being cruel to his animals. He was once seen beating a calf with his fist.

Jettie pressed Grandpa constantly and begged him to allow her to marry Jim. Finally Grandpa agreed but said there would be conditions. And the conditions were that they must live in a house he would build for them on the plantation about a hundred yards from his, and that Jim must be good to Jettie. Jim owned a few acres about ten miles away and made his living as a carpenter and part time farmer.

It wasn't long until the new couple began having marital problems. Within a few years, a son and daughter were born to Jim and Jettie. When Jim became abusive to Jettie she would take the children and go back to her parents' home and ask Grandpa for help. There were no social programs or shelters for battered women in the early 1900s. This was the responsibility of the family and extended family.

After spending a few days at home with her parents, Jettie would take the children back to her residence and try to patch things up with her husband. On one occasion, Jim beat her badly, and Jettie came home again and asked her father for protection. Grandpa said he would protect her and the children but she had to make up her mind that the move back into the Connella family home would be permanent. Jettie agreed, because she and the children couldn't tolerate the mistreatment anymore. Grandpa stated that with this proviso, he would provide support and protection for her and the children.

A few hours later, Jim Faust appeared at the Connella residence and demanded to see his wife and two children, James Jr., and Elaine. He returned many times with the same demand. Grandpa informed Jim that Jettie had asked for his protection and he was going to take care of her and the children. Jettie did not want to see him because she was afraid he would strike her again and she had asked through her father that Jim not be allowed to see her or the children. Jettie had hoped that a cooling off period would give Jim time to calm down. It had just the opposite effect: Jim became more angry and unreasonable. He reasoned that his wife and children morally and legally belonged with him.

Grandpa was large and strong, six feet two inches tall and weighing about 220 pounds, and not afraid of a physical confrontation. But Jim was small in stature. Jim cogitated on the situation awhile. He went to downtown Monroe, had a few drinks, and returned to the Connella residence armed with a handgun.

MONROE NEWS-STAR – Monday, August 16, 1915
TRAGEDY IN WEST MONROE
C.A. Connella Shot and Killed by His son-in-law, Jim Faust
Slayer is Arrested
Family Troubles is Given as the Cause of Killing of Well Known Citizen of Ouachita Parish
–Slayer Says "He had to do it," But Expresses Regret for Killing
Charles A. Connella, well known citizen of Ouachita parish, was killed at his home in the upper portion of west Monroe shortly before 9 o'clock Saturday night by his son-in-law, J.M. Faust. Family troubles are given as the cause. Five bullets from a 32 caliber pistol struck Mr. Connella in his body and arms. Faust, after doing the shooting disappeared from the scene and was not located until about noon Sunday when his brother telephoned Sheriff Parker he was at his home, 6 mi. west of Monroe, and was ready

to surrender. Mr. Parker went out soon afterwards and took Faust into custody, placing him in the parish jail at 3 o'clock Sunday afternoon.

"I had it to do," was all the statement that Faust would make when he reached the jail, adding that he regretted the killing very much.

According to the best information obtainable Faust and his wife had trouble Saturday morning when he is alleged to have abused her. She took their young son and went to the home of her father. Faust declared he intended to take possession of his child. Saturday night about 8:30 o'clock he went to Mr. Connella's home where he demanded the child. In spite of the warnings of his daughter not to go outside Mr. Connella left the other members of the family, stating he intended to go out and talk to Mr. Faust and try to settle the differences he had with his wife. He was unarmed. Only a few words had passed between the men when Faust pulled his pistol and began shooting Mr. Connella who begged Faust not to kill him. In spite of the pleadings of his father-in-law, Faust continued to shoot until he had emptied the pistol. Mr. Connella, though fatally wounded, walked up the steps at the front of his house and sat down in a large porch chair where he died a few moments later long before physicians arrived. Sheriff Jack Parker was located and went to the scene of the killing immediately, but could not locate Faust Saturday night.

Faust worked as a carpenter and was well known among the local members of the craft. Among the stories regarding the shooting is one current in west Monroe that he went around Saturday and paid every little bill he owed in town. Another report said he had on several times previous to Saturday had trouble in his home life. It is said that Faust had never been on good terms with his father-in-law since his marriage...

Coincidentally, my father, Oates, was at the Connella home courting Fay when the shooting occurred. When eight-year-old Edmund II arrived at midnight with his mother, Belle, he sat in Oates' lap and got so upset that he wet his pants and Daddy's clothes.

The Connella family was traumatized by the killing. Jettie was overwhelmed with guilt, believing she was responsible for her father's death, and this state of mind almost sent her over the edge. Laura was also teetering on the brink. She had recently lost her fiancé to scarlet fever and had barely survived the illness, herself. The ordeal left her physically and mentally weak.

Fay and Zona were both teaching school nearby and helping look after Heloise and Allison, who were minors and living at home. Heloise was still in high school. The family group at home now included five sisters and one brother.

The family agreed upon a plan to care for everyone as a cohesive family unit until things were sorted out. Fay and Zona took over running the household and supervising the two minor siblings while trying to keep Jettie, her son and daughter, and Laura on an even keel. Belle, the oldest, assumed the position of matriarch. All the young women relied on Belle's husband to make all the funeral arrangements and manage the property and financial matters until things could be worked out.

Fay used her share of the inheritance to further her education. She took a summer program at Louisiana State Normal College, and obtained a teaching certificate.

They could not resume their normal lives until Jim was brought to justice. It took six months for the court to set a trial, and to select and seat a jury of twelve men to try Jim Faust for manslaughter. There were several family meetings to plan strategies to deal with the very uncomfortable situation. The family council made it clear to Jettie that she and the children would be cared for if she would stick with the family, and the prosecutor requested that she not visit or contact her husband during this uncertain time.

Partly because of her aggravated mental state, the family begged Jettie not to make an appearance in the court. Family legend has it that Jim sent word to Jettie that he would kill her and the children if she did not come to court and show support for him. Of course, this information never made its way to the jury. She believed him, and felt that by obeying him she was saving the lives of her children as well as her own. The family had pleaded with her to stand by the family. Jettie must have felt she was in a no-win position and this weighed extremely heavily on her already fragile mind.

The *Monroe News Star* carried a short story in January 1916.

COURT CROWDED FOR FAUST TRIAL

The trial of Jim Faust charged with manslaughter for killing C.A. Connella in west Monroe continued to attract attention today in the district court. To complete the case as soon as possible a night session was held last night. The defendant went on the stand and described the killing and the events leading up to the tragedy. His testimony allowed that he feared Mr. Connella. The defense is placing his chief reliance in the evidence showing that Mr. Connella had an overbearing disposition and that his reputation in the community along this line was bad.

State of Louisiana vs. Jim Faust – case # 13152 was held in the Sixth District Court, Parish of Ouachita. No record of the deliberations survives, only a summary of the results. In those days, the district court did not have court reporters. Following is the summary, the only record in the court files:

Further evidence adduced and closed. Case argued. The jury after having heard the argument of counsel and the charge of the court retired to consult upon a verdict. The jury came into court and returned the following verdict: We, the jury find the accused Not Guilty.

This verdict sent a shock wave through the community and especially the Connella family, who responded with disbelief. The family and friends just could not believe that the jury could find him not guilty considering the evidence presented. Jim Faust had shot their father who was unarmed, five times, emptying his revolver, then fled. Charles Connella had not threatened him in any way but was adamant that he could not let him see his wife and children. According to relatives piecing together the story years later, the twelve men of the jury evidently reasoned that the wife and children were the property of Jim Faust and Charles Connella was interfering in his business. Also, the jury was probably swayed by Jettie's appearance in court with the children, and the defense attorney stated in his summation that she would take Jim back and live with him.

The verdict visited untold pain and suffering on the entire family, especially Jettie and Laura. The fallout from the court's decision and Jim's subsequent behavior caused great difficulty for the family. While Jettie was making preparations to take the children and return to live with Jim, her family made it clear that she could not be considered a member of the family as long as she remained with Jim Faust. In their anger and sorrow, the family chose to sever all connection.

Almost immediately after the trial, Jettie had a nervous breakdown and was committed to the mental hospital in Pineville, Louisiana.

Jim Faust, seeking revenge on the Connella family for his perceived wrongs, refused to pay Jettie's share of the taxes owed on the Connella property. Standing on principle, the other siblings refused to pay her share either because of Jim's misdeeds. Jim speculated that Jettie's siblings would be forced to pay her share of the taxes to prevent the plantation from being sold at auction by the sheriff. He reasoned that if there were a forced sale of the property, Jettie would get her rightful share of inheritance. Either way, Jim realized he would be ahead of the game financially and get revenge at the same time.

Members of the community were sympathetic to the plight of the Connella family and worked out a plan with the sheriff to allow Fay, Zona, Belle, Laura and Heloise to be the highest bidders. During the bidding, Jim had a "ringer" planted in the crowd to run up the price of the property so Jettie would get a larger sum for her share of inheritance. After a couple of bids, the sheriff walked over to the "ringer" and stared directly into his eyes, and he stopped bidding.

The result became a matter of public record:

MRS. JETTIE FAUST ET AL VERSUS MRS. BELLE WILLIAMSON ET AL

STATE OF LOUISIANA, PARISH OF OUACHITA
SIXTH DISTRICT COURT, NO. 9037

Be it known, that by virtue of and in obedience to an order of sale, dated the 27th day of April, A. D., 1916, issued on the judgment rendered in the above entitled and numbered suit, from the honorable Sixth Judicial District Court, in and for the Parish of Ouachita, and directed to the Sheriff of said parish, I, T. A Grant, Sheriff thereof, did on 27th day of May A. D., 1916, take into my possession the following described property belonging to the heirs of C. A. Connella, to wit: ... in a distinct and audible voice, I offered the said property for sale when Miss Fay Connella and Miss Zona Connella having bid the sum of $2,500.00 and their bid being the last and highest, and having several times cried their bid and solicited others, and no one bidding more, they became the purchasers for the sum above stated, and the said property was adjudicated to the said Miss Fay Connella and Miss Zona Connella ...

There were several other family properties sold that day and in the following months, but this was enough to settle Jettie's interest in the inheritance and rid the family of Jim's legal involvement with them. It took nearly all of 1916 to resolve the legal entanglements involved in dividing up the Connella estate and making proper arrangements for everyone, especially the two minor children, Allison and Heloise.

Jettie was released and recommitted to the asylum several times before she passed away in 1926 of encephalitis. Fay and Zona visited her on rare occasions, but she was not responsive.

At time of Jettie's death, her daughter Elaine was fourteen and her son Jim, sixteen. Both lived with their father, but the aunts – my mother and Belle-- took Elaine under their wing and often invited her to visit. In my childhood, Elaine often stayed with us. She was always lively and fun, and full of stories. But we were all warned by our parents never to mention her father in conversation.

When she grew up, Elaine Faust married Ed Hislop and lived in West Monroe. As her father aged, he was invited to live with the young couple. Soon after Jim Faust moved in, Ed and his father-in-law got into a heated argument, and Ed fled the house. Elaine returned from a shopping trip to find her husband gone. Ed finally telephoned from a nearby gas station and explained that he had argued with her father.

Elaine asked, "Why didn't you just stay here and work it out with him?" Ed replied, "He's killed one man, and I don't want to be next."

This was the first Elaine had heard about her father having killed someone. Nearly hysterical, she pressured Ed for details, but he told her only the bare facts: Jim Faust had killed her grandfather.

Aunt Belle, still the matriarch, was the person to tell the story. Ed drove Elaine to Eros for a conversation with Aunt Belle, who told her everything. Afterwards, Belle said, "I'm not making any judgments. You will have to decide that for yourself."

Jim Faust lived with his daughter Elaine for the remainder of his life. His grave is in the Connella plot of the Hasley cemetery, right next to my Grandpa Connella, the man he killed.

Laura was two years older than my mother. In her debilitated condition, the murder of her father was the incident that pushed her over the edge into unreality, and she, too, required hospitalization. Zona presented the petition to the court in her role of head of household, being the oldest of the five remaining siblings at home.

The petition stated that Laura had to be watched constantly to protect her from herself. She was caught wading out into the river trying to drown herself. According to the document, her symptoms included:

...forgetfulness, excitable, depressed, hears voices, believes she is being persecuted by the state, individuals and by Catholics. Believes she is being shadowed by detectives. Her symptoms are progressive, especially during the trial of Jim Faust. Adjudged insane by two physicians and was committed by Judge Ben Dawkins.

Laura lived in the Louisiana State Asylum for the rest of her life. She was very intelligent and responded well to treatment, and eventually became the librarian for the Pineville, Louisiana, mental hospital. She died in the asylum from cancer of the temple in 1936.

Although Laura died when I was six, and Jettie and Grandpa and Grandma died before I was born, I did not begin to learn the details until I was in my teens. While my parents were no strangers to tragedy, they kept these stories from us growing up, and our childhoods were warm and happy. The times we saw our extended families were generally set aside for celebration.

~6~

Family Days

Following a tradition started by my Rusheon grandparents, we always celebrated the Fourth of July with a family reunion and fish fry. By July the crops had been laid by, so farmers could take a rest. Most of my father's brothers and sisters returned for the celebration.

These events had started before I was born. When I was growing up, we all looked forward to the food, laughter, and the games with cousins.

My father's family gathered on the family farm where we lived. Some would stay at Uncle Emery's house, and some would stay with us. There was always a big noontime meal at Emery's house, which had been the Rusheon homeplace.

Generally it was too hot for a big crowd to gather and eat in the house. There was no air conditioning or electric fans because we had no electricity. Everyone used a handheld fan provided by local funeral homes and general stores.

Chairs were brought into the yard, and some people had to sit on stumps. The "first table" was for adults only. Children always ate last. There was always fried chicken, peas, butter beans, sweet potatoes, mashed potatoes, gravy, squash, tomatoes, and biscuits, all washed down with iced tea. The men sat in their own group while women did all the cooking and serving.

Traditionally, two treats were served for dessert -- watermelon and homemade ice cream. The homemade ice cream maker was filled with cracked ice, sprinkled with salt, and the ice cream bucket was filled with homemade goodies and inserted to make ready for thirty minutes of hand cranking. I always enjoyed helping with the hard work because I knew what the final result would be and I couldn't wait. Homemade ice cream was a real treat on the farm. There were no ice cream stores nearby, so to get ice cream, we had to make it. After we finished eating the watermelon, we saved the rinds so Momma could make watermelon rind preserves the next day.

There is a photo of my daddy's generation under the big oak trees: Mae Belle, Violet, Pauline, L.B., T.O., Seaborn, Elton, and occasionally Uncle Joe and, of course, my father and my uncle Emery. Some were named Rusheon, and some were named Busbice. Aunt Violet's children, Teddy and Frances Bixler, were the only Rusheon children I knew as a child. Not in the photo, but off somewhere having a rollicking time, were at least twenty-eight of us kids.

We had fireworks, went swimming, and played softball, volleyball, and red rover. To make a softball, or red rover ball, we got a peach seed or a walnut and wrapped it with string saved from feed and fertilizer sacks over a long period of time. The softball or "stringball" had to be repaired frequently during the game.

All the adults bragged about their children and how they were doing in school. Many of us were straight-A students, and it was not unusual for a Busbice or a Rusheon to be at the top of the class. Since L.B., T.O. Mae Belle, and Pauline were teachers, they questioned me about my schoolwork. I would joke that recess was my favorite class, but I did very well in all my subjects. Basketball was my obsession. The aunts and uncles always encouraged me to go to college.

Daddy's youngest sister, Violet, was born beautiful. As time went on, Violet became the legendary yardstick by which the family measured feminine beauty. All of Violet's seven brothers wanted their daughters to look just like Violet. Always, a debate would develop at these reunions: "Don't you think Vivienne looks the most like Violet?" "No, Helen looks more like Violet." "I think Lois looks more like Violet…" And every girl in my generation grew up hoping that she would be selected to be the most like Violet. To this day, at family reunions we still discuss which young girls are "pretty as Violet".

Violet was undeniably good looking, but it was the homeliness of her older sisters, Pauline and Mae Belle, that really made her stand out. When both Pauline and Mae Belle married men who could not have children, people in the family whispered that it might be a good thing not to pass along their looks to a baby.

Although sometimes we children were invited to hear some of the funny stories the adults remembered, in general it was understood that children did not mingle with the adults or listen in on their discussions. The abrupt halt in conversation when I entered the room made me wonder if secrets were being kept. So I listened intently whenever I was allowed to join my aunts and uncles and hear their colorful stories.

The talk I heard at these reunions was always about their father, Allen B. Rusheon, and his dictatorial and demanding ways. Most of my aunts and uncles were adept at describing their lives with Allen Rusheon, whom they all feared as children. Apparently the daughters got off lightly, but Allen's sons told stories about his harsh punishments and beatings.

My Grandpa Allen would decide he was going to teach a son to sing, or teach a son to read, and by golly, the young boy had better learn fast.

Because of their farm chores and obligations, the children only got to go to school on rainy days, but that was no excuse for falling behind. In the summers, he demanded that all his children go to singing school.

Emery told a story about coming home from an errand, and from far down the road he could see young Oates running out to the gate. Every few minutes Oates flew from the house to the gate, and back. When he got closer, he could see Oates was in tears. "Well," Emery said, "that was the day the old man was teaching Oates to read." Each time Oates missed a word he got whacked by his father.

An aunt by marriage would ask, "How did you manage to live like that?" And the answer would come, "Our mother was an angel. She kept everyone calm and she was very understanding."

In my childhood my daddy and all his brothers and sisters knew Allen Rusheon was really their father and not their stepfather, but Daddy and his siblings kept this fact secret from us.

Thanksgiving was another important day in our lives. The typical Thanksgiving Day on the farm included a visit from Momma's sister Aunt Belle and her daughter Lucille. They usually brought along some goodies for the dinner: sliced bananas topped with mayonnaise and ground-up peanuts, and an assortment of pies and cakes. Bananas, when fixed in this way, were a real delicacy. We did not feel deprived because turkey was not the centerpiece of our Thanksgiving. We had plenty of chicken, ham, squirrel, beef, and pork.

On Thanksgiving morning, my mother would pick up a fat yard chicken (today we would call it free range chicken) and, with one quick snap of the wrist, sever the chicken's head from its body. It was a violent act that I mastered when I was about ten years old and then it became my duty to kill the chickens.

If the weather was cold enough to keep meat from spoiling, we would also kill a hog for Thanksgiving. If not, we would go hunting. Either way it was a day of gunshots—the sharp sound of a rifle for the hog or the blast of the shotgun for squirrel. (There were a lot of quail on our farm, but no one in our family enjoyed killing those beautiful little birds.) I remember the anticipation of returning home from the woods with cold hands and face and looking forward to warming up by the fireplace and sitting down to a sumptuous meal.

I remember one Thanksgiving in particular. My brothers Billy, LeMoyne, and I took our hunting dogs and went into the deep woods near Smith bayou and the Kelly field. I was using the rifle and LeMoyne had the twelve-gauge single barrel shotgun that my father nicknamed "Long Tom" because he said it would "reach way out yonder and get the squirrels," but it had a kick – recoil -- like a mule. Billy loved dogs, and he always enjoyed being in charge of them and training them to become better squirrel and opossum hunters.

On this day the dogs treed a squirrel we could just barely see; it was about 100 feet up, in the top of a huge oak tree. LeMoyne tried the shotgun but it could not reach that far. All that was showing was one little ear and an eye on the little squirrel's head. I took careful aim with Daddy's .22 rifle, pulled the trigger, and to my surprise the squirrel came floating down. I was really proud of my marksmanship and when we got home I couldn't wait to tell everybody about it.

Until I left home for college, I had never eaten a chicken, steer or hog that I didn't know personally. Over the course of feeding and watering the hogs for months, we developed an attachment for these misunderstood and maligned animals. Contrary to popular myth, hogs are intelligent and clean. We gave them pet names, scratched their bellies and talked to them. But killing a hog was as natural a part of farm life as harvesting a garden. It didn't allow for very much emotion and sentimentality.

When the time came, my father would take his .22 rifle off the rack and walk down to the hog pen and select the ones to be slaughtered that day. One hog would start walking slowly toward Daddy, thinking he was about to be treated to an ear of corn or a scratch on the belly. My father would put the gun barrel between the hog's eyes, and pull the trigger. The hog would drop to his knees and then topple over. After the first one was killed, the others sensed danger and usually had to be driven to the killing spot. At least it was quick. At first I was squeamish but I soon became reconciled to this necessary process.

Once the hog was slaughtered, I would join my brothers and do my part. This involved helping lift the hog into a barrel of hot water in order to loosen the hair so it would come off easily when we took big butcher knives and scraped it off the carcass. We had to be very careful not to have the water too hot or the scalding water would set the hair and make it even more difficult to remove.

It's hard to explain, but one minute I was a little squeamish about the hog being killed and the next thing I knew I was helping scrape the hair off of its carcass and looking forward to eating fresh liver, pork chops or tenderloin. This whole butchering ritual made me think deeply about life and death for the first time.

Momma didn't use cooking oil in preparing food for meals as it was too expensive and not readily available. She and other farm wives used lard made during butchering time for their cooking. The fat was cut from the hog in small pieces, placed in a big iron pot and cooked until all the fat was liquefied. Then we drained the fat into buckets to be used for cooking throughout the year. The solid left after rendering lard was called cracklings and was eaten for snacks, like potato chips nowadays. We thought cracklings were a delicacy.

Squirrel hunting was fun. Unlike the poor hog, I told myself, the squirrel at least had a sporting chance. They were fast and had tall trees to hide in, but I was a pretty good shot and brought down most of them when I got them in my sights. I guess what I really enjoyed about squirrel hunting was watching the dogs' reactions—they moved instinctively and gracefully, weaving back and forth through the woods searching out their prey.

Every year at Christmastime we chopped down a very nice pine or holly tree -- there were lots of them on our farm -- and put it up a few days before the holiday. My sister Helen was usually in charge of decorating the tree. Most of our ornaments were homemade. We made paper chains colored with crayons for decoration.

Like all the farms in the area, since we couldn't have tree lights, we put birthday candles on the tree. But we lit them only on Christmas Eve because they were too dangerous to use all the time. We decorated the house with mistletoe and holly branches we gathered from the woods. Once about every four years it snowed and everyone was thrilled to have a white Christmas. Four inches of snow was the most I ever remember getting on the farm and it only stayed on the ground a day or two.

We had only an open fireplace and a couple of wood heaters to heat our home, and my mother cooked on a woodstove. The fireplace was decorated with stockings for all the younger children, and they were filled with fruit and nuts. Each child received one toy, such as a truck with battery-operated lights, a basketball, a baseball glove or bat, or a board game. My mother rose early and started baking a big, fat hen. First I killed it for her by wringing its neck, and then she plucked off the feathers, scorched off the hairs over a fire, and cleaned out the insides. If it was a big red rooster with big sharp spurs on its legs and too heavy to wring off its neck, one of my older brothers or my father would place it on the chopping block and cut its neck off with an ax. Then Momma cooked it with all the trimmings, including giblets and gravy.

My father went out to the smokehouse to retrieve the best ham which had been curing since late fall and set aside for Christmas. For weeks before Christmas, we made trips to the smokehouse, and even took visiting cousins and neighbors, just to view the Christmas ham with awe and anticipation.

After opening our presents we had fireworks. I particularly liked playing with the sparklers. Dinner was at noon, and we ate all day after that. After dinner we visited our cousins who were our nearest neighbors, a mile away at the other end of the farm. We didn't go to church unless Christmas fell on a Sunday.

All of these celebrations required a lot of work to prepare food for a large crowd. We did not have a refrigerator or freezer to preserve perishables. However, we had ice delivered once a week for our icebox to keep milk, butter, and eggs fresh and to provide ice for our favorite drink in the hot summer, iced tea.

~7~

Friends and Neighbors

Times were very hard in the 1930s and early 40s in our Frantom community, located in the southeast corner of the Eros area. There were no phones, electricity, or running water (except in the creeks), and transportation was limited.

Except for the poverty, I think the residents were fairly happy. They had an unbroken heritage of a rural life, gospel and country music, stories, customs and traditions that went back to the time of our early pioneers. The chief entertainment for men (women were always in the kitchen) was gathering in the barn on rainy days, sitting on bales of hay, and sharing tales of our colorful neighbors and ancestors.

Ninety percent of the families were cotton farmers and no one claimed financial success except Old Man Marion Bunn, who gained this status by lending money to poor farmers and foreclosing on their farms when they were unable to pay the note as it came due. He was eager to lend money but rather inflexible when it came time to settle up on a loan. Basically, he was the single source of financing a crop in those days because the bank was closed in Eros during the Depression.

Out of necessity, people socialized through personal visits, attending church, and functions sponsored by the schools. This lifestyle produced certain individuals who carved out their niche in life by exhibiting unique traits that made them stand out in the crowd.

There was very little mobility in the 1930s: communities became ingrown. Jack Fuller's family was an example of this. Although he was known as a hard worker, Jack was uneducated, as well as a poor manager and an inadequate family provider. Jack had married Edith, the oldest daughter of the Lawrence family, who lived nearby. Edith passed away after bearing one daughter, Annie May. Jack then courted and married Edith's sister Nancy, and they had two children. Edith and Nancy had another sister, Bertha, who married at sixteen. When asked why she married so young, Bertha replied, "I was afraid that Nancy would pass away, and I'd have to marry Jack."

Annie May Fuller, Jack's daughter, grew up to marry Jake Knox and they moved into our neighborhood. Annie May had only a second grade education. She and her husband had a large family they could barely support, even with the aid of government help. Several of the children were mentally handicapped. Annie May and her children enjoyed chewing gum, but they couldn't afford to buy it. Annie May figured out a plan. She got a hatchet, went to a large sweetgum tree in the woods, and chopped a large chunk out of the bark. As sweetgum sap gathered in that injured spot and hardened, it made good chewing gum. You never saw Annie May without a wad of gum in her mouth. When the sap stopped rising, Annie May went back into the woods with her hatchet.

Momma was the type who would never say anything negative about someone else. Mr. Will Burkett lived on a farm adjacent to ours on the east side. When I was eight years old, I asked Momma why we never visited the Burketts, and they never visited us. Momma just shrugged. This seemed odd to me. As a result, I observed closely whenever Mr. Burkett's name came up.

Later on in my genealogy research I came across Mr. Burkett's name in a court document about the trial of Jim Faust. Mr. Burkett had served as one of the jurors who failed to convict him for the killing of my Grandpa Connella.

Hog Hair was directly south and adjacent to the Frantom community, back in the sticks. Bob Brady was one of the few people around who owned a motor vehicle in the 1930s. About once a month, he would come by our farm on his way from Hog Hair to Eros or Chatham to do some shopping. He drove a black Model T Ford that he kept in good condition. Whenever he stopped in front of our house, we ran out to see the car, and marvel at our reflections in the shiny finish.

On one occasion, Bob stopped by Uncle Emery's house and asked if he would like to ride along and maybe do some shopping of his own. Uncle Emery joined him and they went on their way to Eros and Chatham. As they approached an area near Will Copeland's house, a big red dog darted across the road. Bob Brady continued at the same speed and made no attempt to slow down so Uncle Emery, being a dog lover, yelled, "Watch out for that dog!" Bob still made no effort to slowdown or use his brakes and stated very firmly, "That dog better look out for me because I'm on my way to Chatham!" Luckily, the dog moved out of the way and avoided a disaster.

Mr. Luther Kilpatrick's farm was adjacent to our farm and our families were very close friends. Mr. Luther was a fun-loving person and he liked to tell jokes on his friends just to embarrass them in a good-natured way. He was a local politician and was elected as a representative to the Louisiana legislature in 1936.

He was a strong supporter of Huey and Earl Long, and our political district was firmly behind the Longs. When Governor Earl Long and his wife were touring our area, they usually spent the night with Mr. and Mrs. Kilpatrick. It appeared Luther felt he was living in tall cotton (as we said) with that background, but when he ran for re-election in 1940, he lost. Therefore, he felt a little dethroned and he resumed farming with his grown son, Travis, and they raised garden crops and produced eggs to sell in Monroe. Luther didn't drive so Travis made the deliveries.

Once Travis had to be away from the farm on other business and he hired Denison Smith, a neighbor, to drive Luther to make the deliveries. Travis instructed him to be sure to deliver a crate of eggs to the St. Francis hotel.

When Luther reached the hotel, dressed in his sweaty work clothes and rundown brogans, he grabbed the eggs and was walking through the main lobby instead of going to the rear entrance, which was designated for deliveries. Luther became tired and winded because the egg crate was quite heavy. To rest for a moment, he set the eggs down on a beautiful table in the most elegant hotel lobby in Monroe, where the sophisticated urban patrons were socializing in their finery.

The hotel manager, observing this, came from behind the counter yelling at Luther, "DON'T SET THEM EGGS THERE!" Luther was embarrassed and insulted, and he reacted instantly by grabbing the manager by the collar, and stated loudly, "Now, you look-a-here, don't you talk to ME like that. You can't put the sons-a-bitches on ME. You may talk to your niggers and your workers that-a-way, but I DON'T TAKE-EM."

At this point the manager was the one who was embarrassed by the escalating scene so he apologized and quickly got the bellboy to take the eggs back to the kitchen and asked Luther to please use the delivery entrance in the future. Luther took pleasure in telling his friends how he got the best of the hotel manager and made him apologize.

During the Depression Luther Kilpatrick served two terms as a police juryman (same as county commissioner) in Ward One, which included the greater Eros community. The monthly salary for that elected position was twenty-five dollars, but it was considered a tidy supplementary income for that day and time.

Between Frantom and Hog Hair was an area known as Flat Creek and it was filled with bog holes and swampy topography. It was almost impossible to keep that portion of the road passable during the rainy season. The Hog Hair residents invited candidates for election to a box supper and gave them an opportunity to speak on behalf of their candidacy.

Ed Wingate was a ne'er-do-well petty politician and he was running against Mr. Luther Kilpatrick for a seat on the Police Jury. Ed had been very critical of Mr. Kilpatrick's efforts to keep up the roads, especially in the Flat Creek area connecting Hog Hair with the outside world. When Ed gave his speech, he laid it on pretty thick regarding Mr. Kilpatrick's lack of accomplishments in performing his duties. By the time Ed finished his speech, Mr. Luther Kilpatrick's face was beet red with anger.

When it was Luther's turn to speak, his speech went something like this: "Ladies and gentlemen, friends, and Ed Wingate: My opponent has accused me of digging turtle holes in Flat Creek swamp instead of fixin' the roads. If anybody expects me to build a paved road through Flat Creek swamp for twenty-five dollars a month, they should elect me governor of the state. I thank you." End of speech.

Ed Wingate lost the election. Luther Kilpatrick won re-election to the Police Jury, and four years later he was elected to the state House of Representatives.

Sometimes we worshipped at Frantom Chapel Methodist Church. The minister there was Jerry Fordham, who had a long tenure. He had a reputation for preaching long emotional sermons. Rev. Fordham would begin around eleven o'clock and was just getting warmed up an hour later. The longer Rev. Fordham preached, the louder and more emotional he got. Uncle Emery said he could preach sin and hell so hot you could feel the heat, and he wouldn't stop until there was not a dry eye in the house. Occasionally, people who were not moved to tears would pull out their handkerchiefs and fake it so the reverend would finish his sermon.

He was dearly loved and a legend in his own time. When Reverend Fordham was in his eighties and I was five or six, I remember seeing him preach one of his famous, moving sermons.

In early summer just prior to lay-by time for the crops, the men of the church went into the woods to gather trees and branches. They built a brush arbor by laying branches on a trellis frame made from saplings. People could gather under this leafy pavilion on a hot summer day for an "all day singing and dinner on the ground".

People came from all the churches for miles around to sing hymns led by Daddy, uncle Emery, Clarence Cockerill and other song leaders, and to listen to special quartets and vocal groups.

All the ladies brought covered dishes, coolers of cokes and ice tea, for a community feast. Each woman brought the cake or pie that was her specialty, hoping to get compliments. We children were instructed to go through the line and eat something nutritious before we attacked the dessert table. Momma reminded us to watch our manners. I relished the opportunity to load up on Mrs. MacBride's blackberry pie and Aunt Ivie's tea cakes.

After eating and socializing all afternoon, everybody returned to the church for more gospel singing. For weeks, anticipation would build as people wondered whether my Uncle Emery would be there to sing. When Emery got up and sang "O, They Tell Me of an Uncloudy Day" people clamored for encores. I loved the all-day singing so much that I was inspired to go around singing all the new gospel songs for weeks afterwards.

Church denominations in the larger community included Baptist, Methodist, and Apostolic. All were variations of fundamentalist beliefs, and the Apostolic church members, who we called Holy Rollers or 'Postolics, were the strictest among us.

The Baptist and Methodist denominations prohibited their members from dancing, drinking alcohol, smoking, attending movies, playing ball or fishing on Sundays. The Apostolic members were also prohibited from doing these things, plus the women couldn't cut or perm their hair or wear makeup. Also the Apostolics engaged in speaking in tongues, and rolling around in sawdust in front of the pulpit when seeking the Holy Ghost.

The nearest church for blacks was located in Chatham, about ten miles away from our farm. A small area of Eros contained a segregated housing section referred to as "nigger quarters". There were no black churches in the Eros community because there were only a few black citizens living there.

The Klan had been active in our area in the early years of the century. Occasionally when the older men got together I'd overhear them bragging about the "nigger whuppins" they'd been involved in as young men. From what I could determine, at the end of every crop year the officers of the KKK selected one male Negro as the victim, in order to "keep them in their place". By the time my father grew up, every young white man was expected to join, and he did. But the KKK's violent activities in our small community had subsided by that time. To my knowledge Daddy never participated in any violence, and knowing his nature, I can't believe he would have.

The South was not integrated in schools, churches, buses or any type of social gathering.

I was in college before I realized that everyone didn't take the Bible literally. I had been brought up thinking that to reject the Bible would "send your soul to hell".

The Catholic religion was something I only heard mentioned occasionally. I will never forget the first time I saw a nun. Momma took us to Monroe to do Christmas shopping when I was about twelve years old and we passed three ladies on the sidewalk all dressed in black, and after they passed by I was very curious about who they were.

Momma explained that they were Catholic nuns and they dressed that way all the time in public, and they never married. I was just a little less than shocked to learn about this, and I asked a lot of questions, and she explained all the basic facts to my siblings and me about Catholicism. There were no Catholic churches within twenty-five miles of our farm. Little did I suspect that I would meet and marry an ex-Catholic later on in my life's journey. And that a nun would become a good friend and my best groupie.

The two oldest senior citizens in my community were affectionately known as Old Man Watt Smith and Old Man Neal Cockerill. They took pride in their senior status and each boasted he was the oldest. This disagreement was well known in the community. They were both only in their sixties but that was considered really old in that time and place.

In his later years, Neal was on welfare and probably receiving an old age pension from the state. All he did was walk up and down the road and talk about the Bible or his experiences when he lived in west Texas.

Mr. Watt worked hard on his farm and was the only blacksmith we had. He made and repaired wagons, carts, plow stocks, plowshares, cotton planters, and an assortment of other farm equipment. He loved to boast about his work and would say, "I brought patching to this country." That he did, and he did this work for all of his neighbors free of charge. I loved to go over and crank his bellows to heat up the coal to make the chisels, plowshares and other metal objects white-hot so he could bend or shape them.

When asked to what he attributed his long life and health, Mr. Watt answered, "Hard work." One day I replied logically, "Mr. Neal doesn't work and he claims he is as old or older than you." Mr. Watt replied, "Ohh, weelll , Neal never *did* work, so that's a very feeble argy-ment on his part."

Both men liked to quote scripture, both were very religious, and both had ways of interpreting the Bible in their own inimitable style. Each would say he believed every word of the King James Version, but each would interpret it differently.

One issue Neal was stuck on was baptism. He contended that a person was not a saved, born-again Christian unless he was baptized by immersion. Every summer the church held a revival meeting and this particular summer the congregation was busily engaged in selecting a new minister. The plan was to have a prospective minister assist with the revival during the week of the "protracted meeting" in order for the members to evaluate him.

Neal let it be known he was going to be particularly assessing the candidate about his feelings on baptism. Frantom Chapel did not have a baptismal pool and they used the sprinkle method to conduct baptisms. Neal wanted that changed.

Neal attended every service, sat on the front row and listened intently during the revival. When the new members were baptized, the minister used the sprinkle method. The minister would take a bowlful of water, dip his fingers in it and flick water on the bowed heads of the converts as he recited, "I baptize you in the name of the Father, the Son, and the Holy Ghost."

When Neal was asked about his recommendation on the candidate to replace the regular minister, he said, "I'm against him. He talked all around the water, and when he baptized, he sprinkled 'em with water but he missed two or three of 'em. Therefore, those people were not really baptized and are not saved." He considered this a terrible injustice and as a result, he boycotted the services for a while.

Neal would have approved of my baptism. My parents belonged to Oak Grove Baptist Church in the nearby Okaloosa community and when I joined at the age of fourteen, I was baptized in Chapel Walters creek.

White Water Creek
   By Daniel Sipe
   Pub. Old Home Place Music

Take me down to White Water Creek
Where the memories run deep
On the banks where my mother used to pray
Though the water is so cold, there'll be a fire in my soul
When Jesus washes all my sins away.

Chorus:
Roll on, roll on,
Roll on White Water roll on,
On God's celestial shore, salvation evermore
Roll on White Water, roll on.

When I was a boy, oh how I enjoyed
All those Sunday dinners on the ground
That preacher would speak on the banks of White Water Creek
Seems like all of heaven would come down.

Mr. Watt Smith was born in the latter part of the nineteenth century and he carried all of the southern prejudices with him into the twentieth century. The only material he had to read was an old ancient history book, the Bible, and the *Monroe Evening Star* newspaper. He had no formal education but he had taught himself how to read at about the fourth or fifth grade level.

He was steadfast in his belief that Negroes, Indians, and Mexicans didn't have a soul. When asked about people with a mixed background he would state confidently that they were also without a soul. He always justified his beliefs by quoting the scriptures. Once I asked him what quantum of mixed blood would cause a person not to have a soul. His reply was an instant and authoritative, "One drop." He went on to justify his reasoning by referring to the Bible in Genesis Chapter Three in this way: "The Bible says that a serpent who was more sub-tile than any other beast of the field came to Eve and tempted her to eat the forbidden fruit of the tree." Then he asked me, "What beast of the field can talk? It's a nigger, of course," he continued, "and that's why we know that niggers are not on our spiritual level." He seemed pleased with his reasoning and interpretation of the bible. Luckily, hardly anyone believed his version.

Gene Yeager was another person from Eros who thought he had cornered the market on the absolutely correct way to interpret the Bible. He was a clerk at Mr. Pratt's general store and on one occasion I entered the store to buy a peanut patty for my lunch. He asked me if I really understood the real meaning of Eve convincing Adam to take a bite of the apple in the Garden of Eden. I told him I thought I did, but would he give me his version. He replied, "God was making it clear that if you take advice from a woman, you will go wrong every time."

In my family we referred to Mr. Smith, Mr. Cockerill and Mr. Yeager as the thirteenth, fourteenth and fifteenth apostles respectively, because each of them felt they were exceptionally well versed in the meaning of the Bible. Fortunately, they had very few followers.

Old Man Watt lived on a private dirt road about a mile back in the woods. He and his wife, Ma Babe, who weighed less than a hundred pounds, had nine children. Ma Babe's mother was appalled that her daughter was continuously pregnant. When she visited, she said, "Watt, every time I come over here Babe is pregnant. And she's a very small person. You should stop having children." Watt's reply was, "Oh well, that's what I married her for, and that's what she's gonna do, as long as she's married to me."

Watt and Ma Babe had six sons and three daughters. The daughters all produced children, but that wasn't good enough for Mr. Watt. He wanted a grandson to bear the family name. It gradually became apparent that all his sons were sterile and Watt would not have a grandson named Smith.

One son, Fred Smith, lived in Oklahoma with his wife, Lillian. Hoping to please the old man, they decided to trick Watt into believing they were going to have a child. They notified him that Lillian was pregnant. Old Man Watt was proud as punch; he told everyone he was going to have a grandchild, and he hoped it would be a son to carry on the name. The truth was, Fred and Lillian had signed up to adopt, and as soon as they got the baby, they brought him to visit. Mr. Watt was thrilled about that baby.

This deception lasted about three years. Perhaps Lillian confessed to one of her sisters-in-law, who leaked the truth. Mr. Watt was sadly disappointed; he lost hope of having a grandson of his blood. Although his friends and neighbors had compassion, they couldn't resist chuckling around the community about how Watt had been duped.

One of Watt's daughters had a son, who they often brought to visit. When it rained, the last half-mile of the Smith's private road was not passable by car; so the daughter and her husband had to park their car near our house and walk back to Watt's house. Of course my brothers and I hung around the car, which was a novelty, and we got to know the grandson, about ten at the time. He was a citified, prissy kind of boy who talked funny, and none of us could relate to him. Sometimes he let us sit inside the car and play the radio – a thrill for us, since we had no radio at that time. After an hour or two, he would say in his clipped way, "I have to turn the radio off, or it will run the battery down!" We never could understand what he meant by this.

Later on, Mr. Watt bought a large, elaborate console radio, which ran on batteries. But Watt and Babe couldn't enjoy their radio, because those batteries ran down so often. Each time, Mr. Watt had to go all the way to Monroe to buy new ones. Finally he decided it wasn't worth the effort to keep the radio running. In disgust, Mr.Watt ripped the radio guts out, hauled the varnished carcass to the barn, and used the beautiful wooden box as a feeding trough for his cows. And there it stayed for many years until it disintegrated.

Years before I was born, Old Man Watt's older children and my father and his siblings were about the same age, and living on adjacent farms. Although the Busbice/Rusheons were good neighbors to the Smiths, they tended to look down on them as backwoodsy and uneducated, and they didn't care to associate too closely.

So it came as a shock to the Busbice/Rusheons when their younger sister Pauline eloped with Allen Smith, Mr. Watt's oldest son. When word got around, we heard that our Uncle Elton said, "No, I can't believe that. Pauline would never marry such a sorry fellow."

One day in the wintertime, Old Man Watt Smith came to visit Uncle Emery and Aunt Ivie. They were all sitting in front of the fireplace, and unknown to Mr. Smith, Emery had installed a butane gas heater in the fireplace.

Mr. Smith chewed tobacco and dipped snuff. He was seated about ten feet away from the fireplace and as was his usual behavior, he reared back and spat a long stream of tobacco juice into the gas jets thinking it was a wood fire. His aim was good but when it hit the red-hot grate, it splattered a bit and made a frying sound. Aunt Ivie was taken aback and secretly horrified. She jumped up and said, "Oh, Mr. Smith, let me get you a spittoon." Mr. Smith replied, "Oh no, Miss Ivie, don't go to no extra trouble for me, I can hit it from here."

At the end of the harvest season, a small group of farmers were discussing the results of their efforts and describing how they had cultivated their cotton and how well their strategy had worked. Uncle Emery had had a good year and produced ten or twelve bales of cotton for his efforts. He also had the deserved reputation of being one of the best farmers in the community.

After Emery finished explaining his cultivation and fertilization program, Mr. Cockerill disagreed with almost every point, and proceeded to tell him how he should have done it. Emery thought for a minute then asked Mr. Cockerill, "Neal, how many bales of cotton did you make this year?" "Tut, I made one bale," he replied. Emery responded with this comment, "Well thank you, Neal, but I don't take advice from a one-bale farmer."

Ivy Brooks was a farmer of small physical stature. The Gee Whiz Harrow, for cultivating cotton, was invented in the 1930s and it was a very heavy implement and difficult to maneuver. Like everything the farmer did, cultivation was done by hand and powered by a mule or horse. Farm equipment using gasoline engines had not reached that far into the backcountry. Quite a few local farmers had bought a Gee Whiz harrow and liked it, and Ivy decided to follow the crowd. After a short time Ivy discovered the weight of the harrow was too much for him, since it had to be picked up at the end of each row while the mule turned around. After each day of harrowing he was completely "stove up", as we said then, meaning sore and exhausted.

Soon Ivy decided that he and the Gee Whiz Harrow should part company, and he notified other farmers that his harrow was for sale. When asked about his relationship with this implement, he remarked, "Whoever invented the Gee Whiz Harrow had *damn* little to do!" He and the G.W.H. never met again.

Uncle Emery told and retold the story, making sure that this statement of Ivy's remained part of the Busbice lore.

My Uncle Emery could see the humor in most situations and not just tell funny stories but tell stories funny. He had a knack for enhancing segments of the story in just the right places to give it pizzazz. Much of the lore now being perpetuated by our family came from the many stories Emery loved to tell.

One such story involved Emery and our neighbor Luther Kilpatrick at the end of a foxhunt in the fall of the year. Emery and Luther had been hunting all night and just before daybreak they happened upon a persimmon tree. Since both of them were hungry, they began feeling around in the dark for the ripe, moist persimmons that had fallen on the ground. Suddenly, Luther began spitting, coughing, and cursing. "What's the matter Luther?" Emery asked. Luther replied, "I picked up a pig turd and ate it, thinkin' it was a persimmon." Emery was splitting with laughter while Luther continued spitting and cursing and pleading with Emery not to tell anyone about the embarrassing incident.

However, the joke on Luther was too good for Emery to keep it secret and he began telling everyone he saw about it. To try and save himself from embarrassment, Luther began telling the story as if it had happened to Emery. Regardless how it happened, the moral of the story as Emery put it is, "Don't ever eat 'simmons in the dark."

Harold Holton was the youngest member of a large family and his mother passed away when he was very young. None of his older siblings were academically inclined and neither was he. He failed each of the first three grades at least once and when he got too big for his desk he dropped out of school, because he was embarrassed to be in class with the younger children. Either compulsory attendance was not in effect in the mid-1930s, or school officials at the Eros school looked the other way.

Harold liked auto mechanics and, when he grew up, Morris Stuckey hired him to work in his garage. Harold was a good mechanic but had much difficulty doing the necessary paper work, so Morris took care of that responsibility.

Eros was about twenty-five miles from Monroe, the nearest big town. When anyone asked where we were from, residents of our area would usually tilt our heads in the direction of Eros and reply, "Out 'ere at Eros," meaning out from Monroe. Some people would slur the word Eros and it sounded like "Earse".

When the Korean War broke out, several young men including Harold were drafted into the Army and were required to report to the Shreveport induction station for processing. Harold and Earl Nalley were called to report at the same time, and Harold was in line just ahead of Earl.

Harold took a seat at the desk and gave the clerk his name, age, and religion upon request. When the clerk asked him where he was from, Harold jerked his head toward Eros and slurred, "Out 'ere at Earse." The clerk seemed a little puzzled and asked again, "What town are you from?" Harold again replied, "Out 'ere at Earse." The clerk looked more puzzled or stunned than ever so he asked, "How do you spell it?" Harold didn't read or spell, so he replied nonchalantly, "I don't have to spell it, I live there."

The frustrated clerk looked up at Earl for help, so Earl stepped in and provided the necessary information. Of course, Harold was rejected by the Army and he returned to his beloved hometown out 'ere at Earse and continued fixin' 'em cars.

I like to think we had a unique blend of people in Eros. All residents, plain and eccentric, were embraced and accepted in our community. And observing all these folks fostered my sense of humor.

~8~

"I Am Thine, O Lord"

The economic hardship of the Depression resulted in diminishing tax revenues, which caused the federal government to cancel the pensions of many disabled veterans. Daddy was one of these. This was perceived as a government betrayal. Veterans organized a march on Washington to lobby Congress to have their benefits restored. Although he was unable to afford the trip to Washington, Daddy helped organize a group that represented our area. There were many discussions of this issue on our front porch. The demonstrators in Washington were known as Cox's Army, and were turned back from the U.S. Capitol by General MacArthur and his regular army troops, which included Lt Dwight D. Eisenhower. There was much publicity about the event, and feelings ran high in the country.

Seven years later, my father decided to run for political office. The only campaign literature he had printed was a calling card inscribed, "O.O. Busbice for Police Jury, Ward One – Give a World War Veteran a Chance". That was a powerful message since there were only about three World War I veterans living in Ward One and all of them were considered heroes.

In our rural community, campaigning consisted of going door to door to every home, attending political rallies, participating at cake walks and pie suppers, and getting out the vote.

Ward One was unique in that nearly all of its citizens were related. Today people would probably joke that the DNA is all the same in the greater Eros community, and at that time it would have been very close to being correct. This was a mild concern because people didn't have a handle on Daddy's family background. His family had moved to this tiny settlement at the turn of the century. No family or friends lived nearby. No one really knew the family's background. Busbice was no ordinary name and some people were skeptical of anyone who was not "one of us".

My mother was mildly opposed to politics because of the ethical problems involved, and she mistrusted politicians. But she went along with my father's decision. In the late 1930s and early 1940s there were no Republican voters in our area so Democratic candidates who won the primary were automatically elected in the general election. As a result there were no partisan politics, just Long and anti-Long. Since Huey Long was assassinated in 1935, his brother Governor Earl Long dominated the political scene from 1936 up until about 1960. Earl was more colorful than Huey but not as clever. My father was firmly in the Long camp.

We held a straw vote on all the candidates in my fifth grade class. On election night, January 16, 1940, my parents gave my brothers and me permission to go to the Eros Box (precinct) to watch the poll workers count the votes. Every voter that day had marked a paper ballot and placed it in a box with a slot cut in the top to keep it confidential. When time came to count the votes, the precinct chairman brought in the full ballot boxes and opened them up one at a time, and called out the results as five poll workers marked them down on their tally sheets. After four upright marks and a hash mark on the fifth count, each of the five poll workers would yell out, "Tally!" in unison, if they had counted correctly. If any one of the five didn't yell "Tally," the chairman had to go back and recount the last five votes until all were in agreement.

That process went on until after midnight. To me, this was exciting -- especially when various candidates would come by and check on how they were doing vote-wise and tell every one the latest news about who was ahead in other precincts. Talk about politics was very interesting to me as far back as I can remember. I got caught up in all the hubbub and prognosticating, conferencing, and friendly side betting going on around me. I decided someday I would like to be the candidate, generate all this excitement, and earn everybody's respect.

It was a thrill when the precinct chairman announced that my father had won by a large majority. Daddy was very popular and he won handily. Eros was the largest precinct and by the time its votes were counted, other precincts had reported their results and daddy was unofficially declared the winner.

There was no one with much political clout living in Hog Hair and consequently, that geographic area was usually the last in Ward One to receive public road maintenance. Road maintenance was one of the major responsibilities of the Police Jury (the governing body of Jackson Parish) and when Daddy was campaigning for that office, he had promised the voters in Hog Hair that he would correct that situation.

When he was elected, true to his word he made every effort to provide good service to the Hog Hair constituents. After a few months passed and his road crew had worked on the roads in Hog Hair, Daddy was attending a school function at Eros High School. Several of his constituents were also in attendance. Among them was Mr. Reese, a vocal resident who had been critical of former police jurymen about a lack of service to Hog Hair. Before the program started, Mr. Reese walked up to the group that had gathered in the back of the auditorium to talk politics with Daddy. As he approached the men he didn't say, "Excuse me," or any thing else, but he interrupted their conversation and belted out in a very loud voice, "Mr. Oates, I want to thank you," and all heads turned in Mr. Reese's direction. At this point, Daddy said, his spirits lifted because it was unusual for Mr. Reese to compliment elected officials no matter what services they had rendered to Hog Hair. But Mr. Reese hastened to continue and said, "Mr. Oates, I want to thank you for what you did to improve the roads in our area since you were elected, *although it was mighty little.*" Daddy said he found himself elated then deflated in just a few seconds, but instantly he and his friends saw the humor in the exchange and all had a good laugh.

Every Sunday, Daddy loaded us all into the school bus and drove a roundabout route through the community to pick up anyone who wanted to go to Oak Grove Baptist Church. Daddy served as song leader, deacon and superintendent of the Sunday school. By the time we arrived at church the bus was full, and sometimes people were standing in the aisle. Daddy did this just to be a good neighbor, and he never charged money. But he did take fifty cents apiece for gas when he drove a busload of people twenty-five miles to shop in Monroe each month.

The church had a membership of about thirty families. Before the service, men and women congregated separately in clumps in the churchyard, and in the men's groups you could hear a lot of talk about politics. The women talked mainly about babies, canning, and cooking. All the discussions broke up when someone came to the front door and invited us into the church.

When it came time for Daddy to lead the congregation in the song service, he walked up to the front of the church and instructed everyone to turn to page fifty so we could sing his favorite song.

I Am Thine O Lord
By Fanny G. Crosby and W.H. Doane

I am thine, O Lord, I have heard thy voice
And it told thy love to me.
But I long to rise in the arms of fate
And be closer drawn to thee.

Chorus:
Draw me nearer, nearer, nearer blessed Lord
To the cross where thou hast died
Draw me nearer, nearer, nearer blessed Lord
To thy precious bleeding side.

After the first hymn he took suggestions from the congregation. We sang standbys like "What a Friend We Have in Jesus," "Standing on the

Promises," "Washed in the Blood," and "Bringing in the Sheaves." He liked best the songs that had a strong beat and moved along, energizing people. "Sing out!" Daddy would exclaim. "Sing like you mean it!" He had a warm tenor voice (like mine), and he liked to embellish with harmony on the last chorus.

We had an Amen corner, where the deacons, including Daddy, sat. Occasionally the older deacons boosted the preacher's esteem by inserting an "Amen" or two during the sermon. Senior deacon J. Noble Taylor had a special place in that corner, where a knot had fallen out of the wooden floor. J. Noble chewed tobacco, and he used that hole for a spittoon. Nobody but J. Noble ever wanted to sit in that spot. Daddy used to tease Momma that she must be related to him, because her mother's maiden name was Noble.

Cousin Bobby and I were fascinated by the Amen corner and the characters that inhabited it. We were tickled by the snuff-dippers and the tobacco-chewers using the hole in the floor. Because of our tendency to see the humor in everything, Bobby and I weren't allowed to sit together in church. As in school, if we sat near each other we usually got in trouble for giggling. Once we started giggling it was almost impossible to stop.

At least once a year on a Sunday after church, Momma and Daddy would take us all to the Hasley Cemetery in West Monroe, to lay flowers on the Connella graves. As I grew older, I began to ask questions about our relatives buried there and how they died. Momma told me that her mother died of cancer. She said that my grandfather was killed. When I asked who killed him and why, she said, "Jim Faust killed him in an argument." I had never heard the name Jim Faust before. Later she told me Jim Faust was her sister's husband.

Occasionally we visited the graves of my Rusheon grandparents at Salem Baptist Church.

Daddy and Uncle Emery, were the beneficiaries of my cousin Lancelot's generosity when he drove them to Georgia in his new 1940 Chevrolet. Daddy and Emery had not seen their childhood home in forty-two years. The trip was a gift from Lancelot for their helping him through college.

My cousin Lancelot was teaching agriculture in 1940, and he was the first Busbice ever to graduate from college. Uncle L.B. and Uncle T.O. both had master's degrees but their surnames were Rusheon.

Daddy's contribution to Lancelot's college career had been to hire him every summer to take charge of our watermelon work crew. We had more than ten acres in watermelons. When Daddy was away on a watermelon-selling trip, the four or five boys he left behind worked in the melon patch under Lancelot's direction, selecting the melons for the next trip and piling them under brush so they wouldn't ripen too fast in the hot sun. When Daddy returned the melons would be ready to load for his next trip, and Daddy selected the best worker to accompany him as a reward.

When the Japanese bombed Pearl Harbor on December 7, 1941, I was twelve, in the seventh grade, and not too aware of what that cowardly act meant and how it would change the world I lived in. Before long everyone I knew was dedicated to helping in the war effort to defeat Hitler, Tojo, and the Axis powers. This was one war, and the only one during my lifetime, where I heard no dissension. I knew only that everybody was united and pulling together in concert with the United States and all of the allied countries to win the war as quickly as possible to preserve democracy for freedom-loving people.

I couldn't wait to volunteer to do my part, but I was too young to enlist even if my mother would let me. My heart was overflowing with pride for America and I made a secret vow that if our country's freedom was ever threatened again, I would be the first to volunteer.

The war changed much of our daily life. Many of our male teachers were drafted, and some of the women went to work in munitions plants, where they could earn twice as much. The superintendent of schools asked Momma if she would come back to teach. Momma was eager to do so, but this presented a conflict: there was a regulation that prohibited both spouses from being employed by the same government agency – in this case, the school system.

But my father was an innovator and a finagler, and well-connected with the political machine in Jackson Parish. On the Q.T., before anyone was aware the situation was developing, Daddy convinced the board of education to transfer his school bus contract to Uncle Emery. Two or three men who had wanted the school bus contract were incensed that Daddy had outfoxed them. The funny part was, Emery couldn't drive, and had to hire Daddy back as a private employee to drive his bus. This freed Momma to take the teaching job.

As the days went by there was a lot of fear as to whether the mainland would be hit next. Otis Jr. had joined the service in late 1940 for a one-year hitch designed to attract young men and build the military, in the event the United States would be pulled into the war in Europe. Before his year was up, Japan bombed Pearl Harbor and brought us into the war. The Army then transferred him into the regular army to serve for the duration. When Junior came home on leave, he and Connella went out honky-tonking with Cousin Lancelot and friends. Connella observed how the girls would flock to Junior in his uniform, and he decided to enlist too.

In World War I, Daddy had taken his basic training at Camp Shelby, Mississippi. In World War II, both Junior and Connella were assigned to the same basic training center.

Junior was hospitalized with a spot on his lung while in basic training, and because of the gas shortage Daddy hitchhiked to Camp Shelby to see him. On the way he picked up Connella, who was stationed at Jackson Air Base in Mississippi. On the highway south of Jackson they had some trouble getting picked up by motorists. Connella was in his uniform, and he suggested that Daddy stand fifty yards back, so drivers would think they were picking up a single serviceman. But when cars stopped, Connella explained that he was with his dad and they were trying to go visit his sick brother. Then the drivers usually agreed to take them both.

Junior recovered, and his spot was determined not to be tuberculosis, which doctors had feared.

In 1942 a big scrap drive was launched throughout the country. To do its part for the war effort, my school sponsored a local drive for scrap metal. The principal, Mr. Raley, appointed Temple as co-chairman for this effort. It was a lot of fun scouring our farm for old plowshares, worn out tools, and anything else made of metal that we could spare, and taking them to school, weighing them and heaving them up on top of the growing scrap metal pile. Students were awarded special colored ribbons based on the amount they had contributed. Our scrap metal drive was a huge success and it made all of us feel patriotic.

Connella took advantage of the scrap drive to make a little profit out of our unused terracing machine. Connella sold that big machine for scrap iron, without informing anyone. Then he shipped out to do his duty for Uncle Sam in the Army Air Corps. No one noticed the machine was gone until Uncle Seaborn wrote Daddy from Texas, asking to have the terracing machine sent to him.

Junior fought in North Africa, France and Italy. Connella served in the southwest Pacific. My dad fretted a great deal about their safety; he knew what dangers they faced. We in the family could tell that Daddy was worn down with worry.

Since Daddy was a World War I vet, many of his friends dropped by and wanted to discuss what their sons were going through, from basic training to battlefield. On our front porch they talked about the war and shared their worries, discussing the world situation and how it would affect people like us.

Daddy didn't like to talk about his war experiences, but if pressed, he would. Daddy said after one battle, the Germans had retreated. Daddy was assigned to take a message to another unit, and he had to cross the field where dead and wounded were lying. One injured German soldier was on the ground, holding up his canteen and pointing to it, asking for water. Daddy didn't know what to do; he had been instructed to watch out for any tricks by the enemy. So he reluctantly passed on by. His instincts as a human were contrary to his orders as a soldier. He was sickened by it, but he had to follow his orders and complete his mission. Each time he told this story, the regret was clear in his voice. When asked if he had ever killed a German, Daddy would reply, "Not to my knowledge."

As in most wars, meat was a scarce item for the troops in 1918. Everyone was kidding about eventually having to eat horsemeat. Holding forth on the front porch swing, Daddy told a story about Army food in France. He thought he detected a little difference in the taste of the meat one day. He asked the server what kind of meat that was, and was told it was beef. After a week of "beef," Daddy went to the Noncommissioned Officer in Charge of the mess hall, asked him outright, and the NCOIC admitted it was horsemeat. The French were happy to eat it since no other meat was to be found. Daddy told us, "Even after I learned it was really horse, I didn't turn it down."

He said that on one occasion when the battle got hot and heavy, he did not think that he or any of his buddies would survive. Daddy stopped a second or two and offered up a short prayer in which he asked God to spare his life, and if he lived, he would produce sons to help win the next war to preserve freedom for America if it became necessary. He then remarked, "I have two sons serving now in battle areas on both sides of the world and several more sons who may have to serve if the war is not over quickly."

Eventually six of Daddy's seven sons served in the military, three of whom saw duty in battle zones – Otis Jr. and Connella during World War II, and Temple in the Korean War.

Junior was awarded the Purple Heart on the island of Corsica when the Germans bombed a hospital where he worked as a laboratory technician. He was just leaving work and was about a hundred yards from the hospital when the bomb hit and a flying piece of glass hit his face just in front of his ear, leaving a big scar.

The war hero in our family was my cousin Lannie Mack. He was best buddies with Junior; they did a lot of things together, including raising hell sometimes. Daddy and Uncle Emery were challenged trying to keep them out of mischief and on the straight and narrow. After high school, Lannie Mack had joined the Civilian Conservation Corps -- the program instituted by President Roosevelt to build and maintain parks and recreational areas throughout the United States and provide work for young men in an era when unemployment was extremely high.

Lannie Mack left the CCC and joined the Marine Corps when war in Europe seemed inevitable. He was stationed at Pearl Harbor during the bombing by Japan on December 7, 1941, but he was uninjured. Later he lost his left arm in the battle of Iwo Jima. It was his unit that raised the flag on Mt. Suribachi, Iwo Jima.

After the war, Bobby and I were passing through Monroe on our way back to college and we stopped to see Lannie Mack. He took us out to lunch in his truck, which he managed to shift, steer, and maneuver with his one arm. He was always reluctant to tell war stories, but in response to our questions, he told us the story of how his arm was hit by a mortar shell just before the storming of the hill, so he missed the final moments at the top. Lannie Mack was remorseful that he had let his Marine buddies down by not being there for the final push. But he felt very proud to have served in the Marines.

Daddy had been healthy and active all of his life until he had his first heart attack in 1943. At that time, Monroe did not have oxygen tents for heart patients. There was no air conditioning, and the July heat must have been oppressive.

He rested at Riverside Sanitarium and was placed on medication for two weeks. My mother was permitted to sleep on a cot in the same room with him. Daddy was scheduled to be released the next day, when he experienced another massive heart attack at five o'clock in the morning. He called out Momma's name and she in turn called the nurse, then rushed to his bedside to give him a hug, and he was gone.

My father passed away on July 15, 1943. He left nine children. I was only fourteen at the time. My mother was still at the hospital with him and Helen was home taking care of the family when Uncle Emery came to notify us that Daddy had died.

I could hear Helen sobbing from the next room. When I came out she gave me a big hug. I was in shock; I don't remember shedding any tears at that time. I do remember going back to my room and lying down on the bed and trying to sort it all out in my mind.

What should I do? Should I go wake up my brothers and tell them? – no, Helen was in charge and would do that. But how could I banish this helpless feeling? I stayed in bed until Helen called us to breakfast, and my thoughts strayed to the future. It was probably very selfish of me, but my first thought after the initial shock was, "There goes my college education." My parents had given me so much encouragement to make good grades so I could attend college and become a teacher. I had my heart set on it and I resolved right then that I would make it one way or another.

Otis O. Busbice, Jr.   *Connella A. Busbice*
Helen Fay Busbice   *Temple A. Busbice*

C. LeMoyne Busbice   Billy A. Busbice
Bernarr G. Busbice   Marilyn Kay Busbice

My two oldest brothers, Junior and Connella, were fighting in North Africa and Guadalcanal and unable to come home to attend Daddy's funeral. They were notified of Daddy's death via the Red Cross.

Since Daddy was a member of the governing body of Jackson Parish and had been very active in the community all his life, his funeral was very well attended. The procession to Hasley Cemetery in West Monroe stretched for more than a mile.

Upon his death, the Police Jury adopted a resolution commending Daddy for his service.

When God Called Daddy Away
  By Wayne Busbice
  Pub. Old Home Place Music

My daddy was very young at heart
With all his children he would play
We would all run to greet him when he came home at night
But God called Daddy away.

Chorus:

When God called Daddy away
I listened and I heard Daddy say
Be good to your mother, your sisters and brothers
And we'll all meet in heaven someday.

When God called Daddy to his new home up there
I was then very young
But I'll never forget his kind gentle face
So proud of his daughters and his sons.

~9~

Education Comes First

Dying at the young age of fifty, Daddy was the first of his adult siblings to pass away. This caused a huge problem for my mother, since my father and his siblings had never divided up the original farm property. To add to the problem, our new house had been built on an undivided parcel of the farm. We literally didn't have a home we could call our own.

After Daddy's funeral I wandered out to the back porch of Emery's house where all my aunts and uncles were gathered. I heard Aunt Mae Belle exclaim in anger, "We have got to remember we are all brothers and sisters. We must all stick together and share equally in the farm." The discussion stopped when they noticed me. But in retrospect I realize they meant that Momma would get an equal share even though, as a Busbice, Daddy was considered Grandpa's stepson, and not entitled to an equal share by inheritance law.

To acquire some of the original farm, Momma bought out some of the aunts and uncles, and others very generously donated their shares in the undivided property. (After I became an adult, I bought a couple of parcels for Momma. I never intended to ask for repayment. However, upon her death, we found a promissory note signed and notarized requesting that I be reimbursed from her estate for these purchases.) This process gave her 140 acres and the farm was subdivided to give Momma the parcel that included the home site. To have title to a home and surrounding property relieved her mind considerably.

This was the first public exposure of the complications with the names Busbice and Rusheon and why Daddy's brothers and sisters carried both these names.

We resumed our lives without Daddy and sorely missed him. After everything settled down, Momma was offered an opportunity to finish out Daddy's term on the Police Jury that had a little more than a year to run. Momma declined the offer because she was teaching sixth grade at Eros school and the school board had transferred Daddy's school bus contract over to her name. My brother Temple, at fifteen, was a very good driver so Momma asked permission to allow him to drive the bus. The request was granted with the proviso that she be present on the bus each day to provide adult supervision. Momma was also left with running the farm and caring for the family.

Uncle Emery stepped in and took charge of managing the farming activities in addition to keeping up with his own farm operation. He was a good, hardworking man, and he took a close interest in our lives. He gave me personal advice and attention that was very valuable and comforting. Uncle Emery used to tell me, "Get all the education you can. I was only able to get as far as the fifth grade. You could really say that I only have a third grade education, since I was allowed to go to school only on rainy days. My daddy kept me home to work on the farm."

Also, Momma's bachelor brother, Uncle Allison, had come back to live with us to help out and provide day-to-day supervision to ensure that my brothers and I completed our assigned tasks. Allison was an avid reader and kept up with the war news.

Uncle Emery and Aunt Ivie

When the uncles were not directly involved with the farm chores, Momma gave Temple the unofficial position of our leader; he was to report to her about any difficulties. This worked fairly well, but on occasion we younger brothers were not completely cooperative. Like any boys our age, we resented being bossed by a brother just a few years older than we were.

However, Daddy's death brought my siblings and my cousins closer together in shared work on the farm. One example was in the fall of 1943. Just before his death, Daddy had made a bumper crop of cotton. My mother was having a difficult time getting it harvested so we could be enrolled in the new school term before we got too far behind.

Momma had five boys left at home. She promised us, plus cousins Donald and Bobby, that if we would pick a bale of cotton a day for four days, she would let us take the school bus to Chatham to see the movie on Saturday night. This was a nearly impossible challenge: we each had to pick an average of 200 pounds a day for four days straight. (Two hundred pounds of cotton picked by one person in a day would place you in the top ten percent of adult farm workers in our community, a status achievement.)

We made it, and we were overjoyed to go to the movies. It was a rare treat, especially since gas was rationed and not allowed for recreational driving. As luck would have it, Bob Hope, Bing Crosby and Dorothy Lamour were starring in "The Road to Morocco".

In one hilarious scene, after Bing Crosby discovered he could make good money by selling Bob Hope into slavery in Morocco, Hope asked Dorothy Lamour, "How could my best friend do this to me? As a slave, they could make me pick cotton." That line was very meaningful to us tired boys sitting in the Busbice row.

Cousin Donald was about three years my senior. We spent a lot of time together cutting firewood and pulpwood for sale during the summer months when we were through working in the fields. Wood was plentiful on our farm and our parents gave us the timber. All we had to do was saw and split the wood, and find a buyer willing to pay our price. During these work periods we sang a lot of duets to take the boredom out of our activity. Cutting wood was very hard work in the Louisiana summer, but we made what we thought was a lot of spending money from these projects. In those days, parents didn't have money to give their kids an allowance. We had to earn our own spending money.

Donald was the oldest of the kids in my age group, and therefore he usually assumed the leadership role. He was never at a loss to plan fun things for us to do. Generally we would choose up sides and have a corncob war until someone got hurt a little and then we would switch to robbing wasps' nests in the barn until someone got stung, usually Bobby or me. This would bring a scolding from our parents.

Donald loved to fish on Scothorn Branch and he taught me where and how to catch fish. We would fish a while then go in swimming a while, and on occasion look for Indian arrowheads on the hill just above the branch. We worked a lot and played a lot and never had time to get bored.

On a bright moonlit night Donald and I were poisoning cotton in the Bonnet House Cut to kill boll weevils. We were using arsenic powder in a cloth bag and shaking it as we walked along so the poison dust would settle on the cotton leaves and cotton squares from which the boll develops. When the boll weevils and cotton worms ate the leaves and punctured the squares, the arsenic poison killed them, which saved the harvest. It was very important to poison at the crucial time to catch the insects at the correct stage of their development. And it had to be done at night so the dew would fix the arsenic on the plant.

Donald had brought along his dog, Boss, and I had our family dog, Mag, with me. We were going up and down the cotton rows working and visiting at the same time while the dogs ran around chasing rabbits and any other animals they could find. All of a sudden about ten feet in front of us, Mag began to growl angrily and shake something violently in her mouth. We stopped dead in our tracks because we knew that Mag liked to kill snakes of any kind and we suspected she was attacking a rattlesnake. This particular location was noted for its abundance of rattlesnakes. After the violent attack was over, Donald and I walked to the scene of the attack and sure enough, Mag had killed a huge rattlesnake that would have bitten us had she not interceded. Unfortunately, Mag suffered a couple of bites on her throat and head and she soon began to swell. Before long she staggered away weakly through the cotton patch, never to be seen alive again.

Two or three months later, my brothers and I were searching through the woods for litered (cured) pine logs to burn in the fireplace, when I came upon Mag's decaying carcass where she had selected a spot in the limbs of a fallen tree to finish out her last days on earth. I stood there a few minutes thanking her for giving her life to protect us. I called my brothers over to see her and pay their last respects to our beloved family pet. Donald and I firmly believe that her heroic act that night in the cotton patch saved one or both of us from meeting an untimely death.

Becoming a freshman at Eros High School was no big deal, as I just walked upstairs in the same school building I had been attending since grade two. Academically, I tied with Charlene Barnes for the highest grade point average that year. Momma was very proud but she made it clear that if I worked a little harder, I could be first in my sophomore year and not have to share the honors with anyone else. Charlene moved away during that summer so I surmised it shouldn't be too difficult for me to be first in my class without working too hard. Actually, the competition was not that difficult. Out of about twenty classmates, there were only about five or six students who were considered college bound.

I was the only freshman to make the varsity basketball team at Eros High School, and generally I was the high scorer. An away game was scheduled with Okaloosa High School and Miss Moffet, an Eros teacher for decades, drove our team the twelve miles to the other school. (Buses could not be used because of the wartime gas shortage.) We were the underdogs by a large margin.

As soon as the game started I made two long shot baskets. Flustered, the Okaloosa team called time out, and Miss Moffet came over to our bench to say, "Good work, Wayne! You boys win this game and I'll take you all to Monroe next weekend to see 'Thirty Seconds over Tokyo'." This was a big incentive for all of us, and somehow we won the game in an upset.

This was in 1942 and the whole country was in a patriotic fever. The movie was about Col. Jimmy Doolittle's raid on Tokyo from the deck of an aircraft carrier – the first time bombers had ever been used in this way. The raid was successful, but many of the airmen in the B-25s were captured or killed. However, the fact that United States bombers could reach Tokyo was a huge morale builder for Americans. Col. Doolittle's courage, and the movie portraying it, inspired me to want to become a military pilot.

I blush now to think that another factor in my career decision was that Van Johnson was the leading man in the movie. Van was a good-looking, rugged, freckled redhead, like me. Many times in my teen years teachers and others had accused me of looking a lot like him: "Did anyone ever tell you that you look just like Van Johnson?" So it seemed attainable that I could be a pilot too.

I really enjoyed playing basketball and I spent a great deal of my time and energy working out with the team and competing in official games during my sophomore year. I continued to be the top scorer. We lived five miles from the school and after team practice and official games, I had to walk home because gas was rationed during World War II and there was very little motor vehicle traffic on the road. When the occasional car or truck came by though, I could count on a ride because in those days people in the country always stopped and offered a ride to anyone walking. I tied with Golda Hessler for academic honors at the end of that school year. Both years, my cousin Bobby was right behind me academically. My mother was still proud of me and encouraged me to dig a little harder the next year.

My sister Helen had been salutatorian of her high school class and won an academic scholarship to Northwestern Louisiana University, and I always looked forward to the times when she would come home on holidays and spring break. On occasion, she would bring a girlfriend home with her and I enjoyed listening to them talk about college life. By the time they returned to college, I would have developed a crush on her girlfriend. I also enjoyed the time Helen spent trying to teach me how to dance to the popular records she brought home with her. The only records we had at home to play on our windup Victrola were country and western, and square dance music.

Helen talked to me a lot about girls' attitudes and boy-girl relationships. I will be forever grateful for the time we spent together because she shared a lot of things that gave me insight into female psychology and the dating game.

At the end of my sophomore year, I was voted the Best All-Around Male Student of the school, beating out Temple by one vote. There was some good-natured ribbing at my house about this event. Temple was very popular and had the lead in the junior-senior play that year. LeMoyne was president of the Future Farmers of America.

In spite of the fact that I was doing well academically and involved in many school activities, including sports, 4-H club, serving as an officer in the Future Farmers of America, and a member of the school's parliamentary procedures team, my mother felt that the school was not doing a good job preparing me for college. She pointed out that I needed to earn an academic scholarship to defray college expenses. During the war years qualified teachers were scarce and schools were employing uncertified teachers out of necessity. Eros High School was a small school and had reduced its course offerings to the bare minimum, with no electives, to meet the standard requirements for graduation.

Momma worked out a plan with Uncle Elton, my father's brother, to have me live with his family and attend Mangham High School in order to be better prepared for college. This type of arrangement was customary in the Busbice family. Cousin Lancelot had lived with Uncle L.B., who was principal of Greenville High School, to finish his high school work. Cousin Lois came to live with us to attend her first year of college. Later my brother Billy went to live with Uncle T.O., who was principal of Haughton High School.

Final arrangements for my move to live with Uncle Elton and Aunt Eva's family on Boeuf River were completed after the first six weeks of my junior year. My agriculture teacher was disappointed with the decision and asked my mother and me to reconsider, and so did the principal and my basketball coach. All lamented the fact that they were losing a good student and athlete, combined with the fact that my mother was a teacher there so it was not good PR for the school; but they all agreed that it would probably be in my best interest. I had mixed feelings about leaving my family, my friends, and especially my cousin Bobby, who I considered my best friend. I felt very comfortable about who I was, being popular among my friends and looking forward to playing on a winning varsity basketball team.

Through winning a 4-H crop and livestock judging contest, I had won a trip that summer to participate in a statewide agriculture judging competition held at Louisiana State University. This was very rewarding, and was considered quite an accomplishment. It was an exciting trip for me to spend a week in Baton Rouge and make new friends who attended other schools. It was hard for me to leave my comfortable niche at school and home, but soon Uncle Elton, my father's brother, came in his pickup truck and spirited me away to a new family, new school, and a different life.

~10~

New Home on Boeuf River

In the old days, Aunt Eva's relatives had lived on a farm next to Grandpa Rusheon's property. When sixteen-year-old Eva came to visit her kin, she and her cousin wandered down to the plum thicket on the property line to pick some fruit. Elton Busbice noticed her, was impressed and introduced himself. He started dropping by to visit, and invited the two girls to a singing evening at his house. Now everybody in the area knew that Elton's family was musical, and that they sometimes invited the neighbors over to listen.

After dark on the appointed day, Elton and Oates arrived to walk the girls the half-mile to their farm. Eva had two surprises that night: one, Elton claimed her for his companion, although she had expected to pair up with Oates, whom she admired; and, two, there really wasn't any singing planned.

That was the beginning of Elton's courtship with Eva, and they were married within the year.

By the time I was in my teens, Uncle Elton and Aunt Eva had a large cotton farm on Boeuf River near Mangham, about fifty miles from my home. Their household was much like the one I was raised in. They had eight children: Lois, Hollace, Kenneth, Verlon, Joyce, Thaddeus, Shirley, and Bruce. Also Mildred McAndrews, my age, was a foster child who had been living with the family since her mother had died when she was very young. Lois, Hollace, and Verlon had left the nest by the time I arrived to join the family.

Hollace, who was very bright, had joined the Navy and was sent to a special program at Harvard to become a commissioned officer. He was very impressive in his uniform when he came home to visit. Luckily for me, Hollace couldn't fit into his old shoes anymore, so I inherited two pairs from him, and was very glad to get them. They were the nicest shoes I had ever owned.

I shared a room with my cousin Thaddeus and took my place on the farm doing chores and farm work as a responsible member of the family, similar to what I had been doing on our home farm. The living conditions were also like my home near Eros with no electricity, no running water and no indoor toilet facilities. However, there was a hand pump installed in the kitchen so we didn't have to go outside to draw water for drinking, doing the dishes, bathing and cooking. And the family values were the same. We worked hard, tried to excel in school, and got along well with each other.

All my friends in Eros had warned me that I would be homesick and would want to return home after a few weeks. I was sure that this would not be a problem, and I was surprised when I became very homesick. In about two weeks I hitchhiked home for the weekend.

After that, I got back home regularly by taking the bus on Friday morning to school, walking about a half mile to the highway, hitchhiking twenty-five miles to Monroe, walking across the bridge over the Ouachita River to highway 13, hitchhiking twenty miles to White's store, and walking the five miles home from there. I usually got back to school on Monday in time for the end of the first period after hitching to Monroe, spending the night with Connella and his wife Jeweldine, and hitching back to Mangham. Neither Momma nor Aunt Eva liked my skipping school, but they tolerated it since my grades remained good.

On my first visit, I asked Momma about returning home to live but she encouraged me to give it more time and to try to stick it out a little longer. Before long the homesickness abated, primarily because my new family was quite interesting and made me feel that I really belonged there.

Cousin Thad and I became very close and enjoyed each other's company. One day I was bragging to Thad that I could do wonders with a slingshot. I pointed to the barn door that had a baseball-sized hole in it to pull a chain through for fastening. "Thad," I said, "just watch this. I'm going to use that hole for a bullseye." I stood fifty feet away, took careful aim, and put that stone right through the hole. Then we heard the sound of breaking glass. Uncle Elton had stored his winter supply of syrup in glass jugs inside the barn. It took us a long while to clean up the mess of syrup and hay from the barn floor. Thad was impressed so I didn't let on that it was purely a lucky shot.

In addition to our outdoor activity, Thad and I played a lot of table games with Aunt Eva and my first cousins, Kenneth and Shirley: card games, checkers, Chinese checkers, and dominoes. Sometimes Thad and Kenneth and I played cards with Aunt Eva while the girls gossiped in their rooms. Bruce was only six years old at the time I moved in and occasionally we played fish and other kids' games to include him. Bruce was a live wire and always smiling and jovial. After supper, Thad and I would join Joyce and Mildred in the kitchen after they had cleaned up the dishes, and we talked about school, boyfriends and girlfriends. We did our homework on the kitchen table if we hadn't finished it during study hall at school. There was a lot of kidding, joking and telling the latest stories going around at school.

Shirley, Uncle Elton, Aunt Eva, and Bruce

When I had been living with Elton and Eva's family for about a year, Uncle Seaborn and his grown children and grandchildren came to visit. It was a thrill the day Seaborn's son Pershing, on leave from the Navy and wearing his uniform, took us teenagers to a movie in his block-long Buick.

As usual in my family, during the three-day visit the adults often secreted themselves in a separate room to talk for hours. We all understood not to interrupt, or the conversation would come to an abrupt stop.

My cousin Joyce and I, born only one day apart, were great pals. After the visitors left, Joyce and I talked about what we observed. I asked her what she thought all the secret meetings were about. Joyce pulled me into a quiet hallway and told me, "I think I know, and I'll tell you, but it's a deep secret and you must never tell anyone."

She told me that her brother, Hollace, had listened at the door on a previous visit, and heard the grownups talking about our Grandpa Rusheon killing a man once, in Georgia. And that was the reason the family had to move to Louisiana. Grandpa came here first as a young man, changed his name to Rusheon, and then sent for his family. She said he was our real, not step grandpa, our real name was Busby, and all our aunts and uncles were really full brothers and sisters.

This was a bombshell to me. I listened in shock and disbelief. That would explain why we didn't know anything about our Grandpa Busbice who had supposedly died in Georgia – there was no such person.

After Joyce finished, I told her I didn't believe it. "Don't you think we'd know by now?" I asked. She assured me it was true, but that everyone was sworn to secrecy.

I was electrified. Could this be true? I wanted to talk to Hollace, but he was away in the Navy, so I couldn't ask him. I was determined to get to the bottom of the story.

Later, I would tell this incredible story to Bobby, my confidant. We both decided Joyce must be mistaken; this could not be true. But meanwhile, real life on the farm took over.

One of the first things I remember being different about farming on Boeuf River was that the arable land we had to cultivate was flat, hardpacked, black, rich alluvial soil. Our farm near Eros was hilly and consisted mainly of sandy loam, which was much easier to till but had to be conserved by terraces, contour plowing, planting winter cover crops, and strip farming. At Uncle Elton's place on Boeuf River, soil conservation required keeping drainage ditches open to allow excess water to run off and prevent ponding.

Another major difference in farming there was sharecropping. Uncle Elton had four families, one black and three white, who owned no land of their own and were sharecroppers for him. Traditionally, landowners would assign a portion of their cropland to families who owned no land, and would divide the cotton crop profits at the end of the year based on a pre-arranged agreement. But Uncle Elton's method was unique and very successful. He gave each of them a tenant house for the family to live in, a garden spot of their own; he furnished the seed and fertilizer, mules and equipment, and the sharecropper furnished the labor.

The four sharecroppers worked the land as a team together with my Uncle Elton and me. My cousin Thad did the minor chores. This was the first time I was accepted as a worker on equal footing with the adults on someone else's farm. Uncle Elton's method was more inclusive and more productive than other farmers in the region. Instead of performing more like an overseer, he set up a system for all to work together, share and share alike. Uncle Elton's leadership ensured that the crops were cultivated and harvested using approved practices.

In general, the tenant received one-half of the cotton produced and my uncle received one-half. Uncle Elton was very fair and evenhanded with everyone. We all felt like one big family.

At mid-morning, the sharecroppers' wives took turns bringing hot coffee to us in the fields. Showing off a little, I'd tell Uncle Elton, "I'll just keep plowing, because I don't drink coffee." After a while I recognized that the work team was having a great time talking and joking while I was still working. I resolved then and there to learn to like coffee.

Coffee was the beverage of choice for nearly everyone in Louisiana. During World War II when gasoline was rationed and cars were scarce, people walked to their neighbors' houses to socialize, and you'd hear someone say, "Come on in – the coffee is just waiting for you, hot, saucered and blowed."

My love for coffee was muted when I went to college in Cajun country and the only coffee served was very dark, rich, and loaded with chicory. It gave me indigestion, and I developed a lifelong love of tea, instead.

The essence of sharecropping during the Great Depression had been the freedom of both parties to accept or reject any proposed arrangement. There were many options based on how much land was available to be worked. Mr. Dorsey, the black sharecropper on Uncle Elton's farm, told me once that sharecropping was going out of style because there were too many "ups" in the program. I asked him what he meant by too many "ups". He said, "Well the first thing in the morning you wake up, then you have to get up, next you have to gear up, then you have to start up the day's work, and at the end of the year, you have to settle up, and there is always a f--- up, then you have to move up." When mechanization became full-blown in the South during the middle of the twentieth century, sharecropping became obsolete.

When I was twelve years old, I had learned just enough about the guitar that I could accompany myself when I was singing. So, I had decided to write a song. It was the first song I ever wrote, entitled, "You Told Me a Lie". I had imitated the country music that I had heard on the radio and on records. Early country songs were about momma, the old home place, trains, lost love, and broken hearts. They were very emotional and pulled on your heartstrings. I can't remember all the verses, but my first endeavor went like this:

I am oh, so lonely tonight
And the stars are not shining in the sky
But when you left me I knew outright
That you told me a lie.
Chorus:
You told me a lie
And now I sit and cry
You didn't treat me right
And now the sun gives no light.

I was living with Uncle Elton two years after I wrote this song and I was attracted to the pretty daughter of a sharecropper on his farm. I was too shy to show my interest in any way. Mainly, I didn't want to be teased about it by my girl cousins.

I was friendly with this girl's family, named Lovelady, and they invited me to bring my guitar on one of my visits to their house. I played a few songs, then I mentioned, "That last song, I wrote myself." They replied, "No, no, somebody else must have written it. That sounds as good as the songs on the radio." I insisted I had written it, and I basked in their approval. The daughter was impressed too. This was a powerful incentive for me in my music.

In contrast to my own family, Uncle Elton and Aunt Eva attended church only occasionally. Wartime gas rationing was partially the reason.

There were numerous black churches around because black people in Boeuf River made up about forty percent of the population. Black people centered their social activities as well as their religious doings on their church. Attending Sunday services for them was an all day affair. If you walked past their church around eleven a.m., you could hear the choir using the "lining" technique: one person would speak a line, then the choir and congregation would answer, singing the same words, without instrumental accompaniment. I really enjoyed listening to them and found a few excuses to walk by their church.

When there was a death in a black family, the funeral home held the deceased until rites could be performed the next Sunday, regardless of the day of death. This practice was a holdover from slavery days when Sunday was the only available personal day for blacks.

Occasionally we visited my uncle Joe Rusheon, who had a cotton farm and lived directly across Boeuf River from Uncle Elton. There was a ferry about a mile down the river to take people and horse-drawn vehicles across. In the fall of 1945 we got word that Uncle Joe had gone squirrel hunting to celebrate the end of the cotton harvest. While climbing high up into a tree to retrieve a squirrel he had just killed, Joe fell to the ground. When he didn't return home, a group of friends went out looking, and they heard Uncle Joe yelling deep in the woods. He was unable to move, because his broken ribs had punctured a lung. The immediate problem was finding a way to get Joe to the road so an ambulance could pick him up. They brought in a tractor with a trailer half-filled with cotton to ease his ride.

At the hospital, tests seemed to indicate that a heart attack actually caused his fall. Uncle Joe lived only a few days in the hospital and died of his injuries. Uncle Elton and Aunt Eva took in Aunt Inez and their three very young children, Jerry, Cookie, and Jack, until arrangements could be made for them. Uncle Elton arranged for them to receive welfare and to rent a tenant house. (I would become good friends with my cousin Jack in later years.)

The academic program at Mangham was very good and I felt I was getting better instruction from the teachers there. I was installed as a member of the National Honor Society at the end of my junior year.

There were no varsity sports programs at Mangham at this time because the school had donated all of its athletic equipment for football and basketball to the airbase Selman Field, in Monroe, to help out with the war effort. Several of my friends and I were very anxious to play basketball, so in the early spring I asked the principal if we could establish our own team and play some of the neighboring schools. He agreed and gave me the keys to the athletic storeroom in a small abandoned wing of the school. I was astonished because the room had been declared off limits to all students and there seemed to be a mystery about it. Doug McKay, a good friend, and I went to the room and, sure enough, we found enough good basketball uniforms to suit out about eight players. I asked Doug why the room had been placed off limits, and he said, "Come here, I want to show you something on the front of this door." He pointed out a bullet hole in the door about five feet off the floor. He told me that about four years earlier a senior girl had committed suicide in that room and the bullet went through her body and made the hole in the door. He said there had never been an official explanation as to why the student had committed suicide, but the unofficial story was that she had become pregnant and couldn't face her parents with this shame. It was a great shame to have a child out of wedlock, and according to the mores of the community, there was no redemption.

Doug and I were very excited to have permission to organize a basketball team and enter the Richland Parish's varsity interscholastic program. We had no coach, but the principal allowed us to work it out among ourselves. Parents and teachers drove us to nearby schools to play official games and I was selected as the captain of the team. We had about equal wins and losses, but we had a great time.

One weekend in 1945, Aunt Eva took several of the kids to Monroe to shop and visit her mother. On the way back home it was getting dark and Aunt Eva asked me to drive the old Dodge pickup, which always seemed to be in need of repair. (In order to produce military vehicles for the war effort, no automobiles or trucks were built during the war years, 1941 to 1945. Everyone who was lucky enough to own a car or a pickup had a difficult time keeping it running and getting tires for it. This was a real hardship on farmers who had to get their crops to market and their cotton to the gin.)

It was a very dark night and we were nearing a dead-end intersection on the gravel road when a hobbled mule jumped right in front of me. I slammed on the brakes and swerved to miss the mule but the brakes failed and the headlights shorted out. It was so dark I couldn't see a thing but luckily we were only going about five miles an hour by this time. I was feeling helpless behind the wheel with no lights and no brakes, and Joyce and Mildred screaming, "We're going in the ditch! We're going in the ditch!" We continued across the dead-end intersection and landed in the ditch with the front end hitting the embankment. Aunt Eva was sitting in the middle next to me and Mildred was sitting on the passenger side with Joyce in her lap. Thad, Kenneth, Shirley and Bruce were riding in the truck bed in the back, huddled under quilts and blankets.

No one was hurt except Joyce who bumped her head on the windshield, cracking the glass and putting a big bump on her head. An auto mechanic friend happened by and pulled us out of the ditch, found the short in the headlights and fixed them so I could see to drive. He told me to drive the two miles to our house very slowly and if I had to stop, put the truck in a low gear. We made it home okay but a little shook up.

The next day Uncle Elton had a mechanic fix the lights and brakes. Later, he took the truck to Monroe and had the windshield replaced. Everyone was understanding, and no one blamed or scolded me for the accident. The funny part was the truck landed in the ditch right in front of a billboard with the message IF YOU DRINK DON'T DRIVE AND IF YOU DRIVE DON'T DRINK. Of course no one was drinking, but my cousins and friends at school had a lot of fun teasing me about the incident.

I was doing chores in the barn with Thad in April of 1945 when Shirley came running up to tell us Aunt Eva wanted us to come to the garden. As soon as I got to Aunt Eva, we saw she was very upset. She told us President Roosevelt had just died. Our family admired the president so we were very sad, and also concerned about the future of the war and our brothers who were in the service. We discussed our new president, Harry Truman, and our hopes that he would be able to carry on the good work Roosevelt had begun. For the rest of the day, the uncertainty of the future hung over us and we just dragged around at our chores.

I returned home at the end of the school year to help out on the farm. LeMoyne, Billy, Bernarr, and I made the crop for the family in the summer of 1945, with the help of our uncles, Emery and Allison. My youngest sister, Marilyn, was old enough by this time to help Momma with the work around the house.

Bernarr, Momma and Marilyn. Momma's nest was getting smaller

That summer was the beginning of a lifetime of performing. LeMoyne and I played for several country dances in the community. LeMoyne played the fiddle and I accompanied him on the guitar and did the lead singing. We were only sixteen and seventeen and inexperienced, but people seemed to like us.

Now that the war in Europe was over, Momma had to give up her teaching position since many former teachers at Eros were returning home and reclaiming their jobs. She had to give up the school bus contract that year because Temple had moved away and LeMoyne was soon to join the Air Corps, leaving no one at home old enough to drive. Billy was leaving to live with Uncle T.O. near Shreveport in order to finish his high school program at a better school. Momma was getting by on a small widow's pension from the Veterans Administration, funds from the sale of the cotton crop, and wages she earned substituting for the Eros postmistress. Money began to be even scarcer around our house.

When I left to return to Mangham High School, only Bernarr and Marilyn remained living at home with Momma. Since there was no one left to carry on the farming, Momma rented out part of the farm.

My social life picked up considerably in my senior year and I began dating several girls. Chapman (Sonny) McKay and I had become best buddies and we did a lot of double dating because he was dating Mildred. Joyce, Mildred and I were seniors and we supported each other in sharing information about people we were dating. I would share gossip about their boyfriends that I picked up in the locker room, and they did the same for me. We made an intriguing game of it, and took pleasure in surprising our dates with personal information that they had thought was secret.

Returning to school in the fall of 1945 I learned that our coach was back from the war, and I looked forward to playing both basketball and baseball under his tutelage.

Mr. Jones was a good coach and we had a winning basketball season. The coach appointed me captain of the team and again I was the highest scorer for the year. We won second place in the Richland Parish league and I made All Parish Forward.

I established a very close relationship with Coach Jones. During official games I could always tell if he was pleased with the team's performance: if we were doing well he would yell, "Okay! Red!" (I had been given the nickname "Red" for my hair, soon after I arrived at Mangham High School.) If things weren't going well, he would just say "Red!!" – meaning, I want you and the team to get back out there and keep your heads up, keep your eye on the ball and do what I taught you! During one exciting game we beat our rival, Rayville High School, by only two points and I was high scorer for the game. The next day the sports section of the local newspaper carried a report on the close game. In it the reporter stated that Rayville would have won if it hadn't been for that "orange-headed, bowlegged boy from Mangham."

Many years later in 1996, at our fiftieth high school reunion, I saw the coach for the first time in forty-five years. As he approached the restaurant he noticed me at the door, and yelled across the parking lot, "Okay!! Red!!" When he and his wife approached me, he turned to his wife and said, "You remember Red, don't you? When he played for me, he was all over the court like a cat." It was a great thrill to see the coach again and have him recognize me even though I had gray hair instead of red.

In baseball, we played only a few games and had a mediocre season. I played first base and sometimes switched to second base. My batting average was just fair.

The newspapers in the area carried the results of all of our sports activities and I caught the attention of the head coach of Northeast Louisiana College, who sent a representative to talk to me about attending Northeast on a general athletic scholarship. But I had made up my mind early on that I wanted to attend Southwestern Louisiana Institute, now known as the University of Louisiana, and study to become an agriculture teacher, so I declined the interview with the coach.

My oldest cousin, Lancelot, who became an agriculture teacher, influenced my career decision. He was the first one of our generation to graduate from college and this impressed me very much. He earned an academic scholarship to Louisiana State University and worked very hard in his spare time to pay for his education. Observing his seriousness of purpose and strong work ethic gave me incentive to follow in his footsteps academically and professionally. He was one of my early role models. Lancelot was very competitive in everything that he did. He usually was the top student in all of his classes until he graduated from high school. When we were doing farm chores, such as picking cotton, he made it clear that he would not allow anyone to pick more than he did.

Others besides Lancelot influenced my choice of career. My mother and two of her sisters were teachers. On my father's side, two aunts were teachers and two uncles were career educators.

Mangham HS Honor Society, 1946. Foster sister Mildred McAndrews, second from left in bottom row; Wayne, bottom row right

At the end of my senior year, my classmates elected me Best All-Around Male Student. Mildred was elected Best All-Around Female Student and Joyce won the lead in the senior play. Uncle Elton and Aunt Eva were extremely proud to have three of the top graduating students living in their household. I also served as president of the Honor Society, treasurer of the Future Farmers of America, business manager of the yearbook, and reporter for the senior class.

Momma was able to attend my graduation. She was very happy with my high school success and very thankful to my aunt and uncle for their support and assistance. On graduation night, I received an academic and work scholarship to Southwestern (now University of Louisiana), and the Veterans of Foreign Wars award for leadership and scholarship.

My high school principal, Mr. Judd, and several of my teachers encouraged me to take a scholarship to attend Louisiana State University in Baton Rouge, major in law and get involved in politics. I declined that scholarship for several reasons: one, I didn't know any lawyers and I had no concept about what a law career would entail; and two, I had made my decision in the eighth grade to become an agriculture teacher because educators had always served as my role models; and three, money was scarce because of our family situation and Southwestern had also given me a work scholarship. And the two scholarships combined would pay my tuition, room, board and laundry. Even with the scholarships offered by LSU it would have been beyond my financial reach. Momma had reached the bottom of the barrel of her resources and simply couldn't provide any more money for my education. With the Southwestern decision, the only expenses we had to face were clothes, transportation and an allowance.

My summer fell into place, as well. My best buddy Sonny McKay was dating Mildred. His father, Mr. McKay, owned a service station and convenience store, which required tending seven days a week. Mr. McKay asked Sonny and me to take over the business for the summer, so he could take a rest. The offer included my living at their house in Archibald, near Mangham.

After a summer of double dating with Sonny and Mildred in Mr. McKay's car, I was college bound and eager to pursue my next challenge.

~11~

College Days in Cajun Country

My trip to college was a long eight-hour, two hundred mile ride. The Trailways bus stopped in every small town on the way. Momma didn't have the money to accompany me, and I didn't know anyone at the school. I arrived in Lafayette on September 18, 1946, carrying two worn-out suitcases and wearing a hand-me-down suit.

I walked a mile from the bus station to the campus of Southwestern, and on my way I was greeted by several upperclassmen, football players who had reported to school early for practice. (I had come early for freshman orientation.) I was standing there struggling with my suitcase while the friendly upperclassmen asked a lot of questions about where I was from, what high school I attended, what was I going to major in and things like that. When I said I was from Eros, in north Louisiana, they replied, "Oh, you're a Yankee."

But we seemed to be getting along great until one of the football players asked a guy named Spike if he had brought along his hair clippers. Spike answered in the affirmative and approached me with a friendly grin as he explained that all freshmen were required to have all of their hair cut off. He also made it clear that I could go downtown and have a barber take care of cutting all my hair off or he would be happy to give me a fifty percent discount. At that time I had thick wavy red hair and as Spike was cutting my hair the other students were cheering, and some were faking moans and groans as each lock fell to the ground. Although it was a little traumatic, it was in good fun.

Hazing freshmen was still allowed in those days, and it lasted all year. After my haircut, I was informed that I would have to go to the bookstore and purchase a beanie, write my new identity "Slimy Dog Busbice" on the front in big letters, and when any upper classman asked me what my name was I was required to reply, "Slimy Dog Busbice, SIR!" in a loud voice.

Freshmen girls were required to wear the skullcap but didn't have to cut their hair. Male upperclassmen were not allowed to haze female students and upper class females were not allowed to haze male students. We were required to do small chores for any upperclassmen when requested – fetch things, carry books and sit with them during football games and serve drinks and snacks. However, they were not allowed to interfere with class attendance or library work.

During homecoming week we had to build a big bonfire and yell cheers in Cajun style – "Yea rouge/yea blanc/yea bulldogs/allons!" (Yea red! Yea white! Yea bulldogs -- let's go!) The school mascot was a tough looking bulldog named Gee and school colors were vermilion and white. After the bonfire burned down we were required to run the gauntlet between two lines of upperclassmen who would strike us with their belts.

When people asked me, "Where are you from?" I would reply, "Eros, Louisiana." That naturally elicited a response, "Where the hell is that, I never heard of it." Since nobody had ever heard of Chatham, Frantom, Hog Hair or Jumping Gully, the settlements around Eros, it was complicated and boring to explain. So my cousins, siblings and I devised a description.

"First, take a map of Louisiana and locate Monroe in the north central part of the state, then follow state Route 13 southwest about twenty-five miles and you will find Eros. Turn left at the school and follow the dirt road about three miles then grab a vine and swing in on it the last two miles." If they had not been listening very closely, that last part would pique their interest and bring forth a grin. And they never forgot that part of the directions.

Eros remained a small obscure town, but I would get a little sensitive when people refer to me as an Erosian, which sounds just like "erosion", and I would hastily correct them and say, "I'm an Erosonian."

College was my first exposure to Catholics and to Cajuns. The first thing that caught my attention was that almost everyone spoke Cajun French to each other and English when addressing me. If I hadn't known better, I would have sworn I was in a foreign country. This was culture shock on a major scale. Cajuns so dominated the landscape that they joked about the three Cajun presidents: Thibodeaux Roosevelt, Woodreaux Wilson, and Hebert ("ay-bare") Hoover.

There were no dorm rooms available on campus due to the large number of ex-GIs returning to college. However the college had made arrangements with the city of Lafayette to rent surplus barracks at the municipal airport – a defunct Army Air training base -- about three miles from campus. A converted Army bus was to shuttle students there and back every thirty minutes until nine p.m. I told the registration clerk that this would present a hardship for me because my work scholarship required me to work three meals a day in the dining hall.

The room assignment clerk seemed sympathetic to my plight and promised to request a transfer to the campus for me as soon as possible. I was afraid I wouldn't be able to make my work and class schedule.

Because I was living off campus and working three shifts in the dining hall, I couldn't find time to register for my classes. I would get in a crowded line and just before I could move up halfway it would be time to go to work. I began to panic because I knew time was running out to register. I finally decided to ask the dean of men, Glynn Abel, for assistance. He immediately put me at ease and stated, "I'll see that you get registered and I will ask the dietitian to excuse you from work if we don't finish in time for your next shift." He took me directly to the registrar's office and walked me through the process personally. From that day forward I never passed his office without saying hello, and Dean Abel always stopped when we met on campus, to ask if everything was all right with me. I was surprised by the kindness and compassion this busy man showed, and I resolved to be more like him. I still admire him for making a slimy dog feel comfortable.

Fortunately, two weeks after my arrival I was transferred to a campus dormitory, complete with a housemother and four students to a room – all males, of course. Coed dorms were not even imagined. Our white stucco building was located at the south end of campus, nestled between the poultry lab and farm, and Vet Village. The crowing roosters or crying babies woke us up every morning so we didn't have to worry about being late for class.

During my freshman year, the college installed three Navy surplus modular metal barracks and I chose to live in one of those. The Navy barracks, supervised by a housefather, were open bay in plan. We used standalone wooden lockers to arrange a large room-like area with space for four to six boys.

Lafayette was in the heart of the Cajun country and one night during the Mardi Gras celebration, all the freshmen boys had to go downtown wearing skullcaps and pajamas, make a long line by holding hands, and do a snake dance down Main Street singing and shouting school cheers. The police had closed Main Street to vehicles for this activity. Hazing was not allowed during class time and after the first nine weeks, most upperclassmen lost interest in it but we still had to wear our skullcaps.

World War II had just ended, and about seventy-five percent of the male students were veterans attending school on the G.I. Bill. You could always tell the veterans because enlisted men dressed in their fatigues and dungarees, and former officers usually attended classes in suit and tie. Veterans frowned on the hazing scene even though they were exempt from the hazing shenanigans. Veterans also didn't believe in social sororities and fraternities, and by the time I graduated hazing and participation in Greek letter organizations all but disappeared. Academic, professional and sports clubs were very popular. I joined Sigma Alpha Gamma, a professional agricultural club and the college FFA designed for future agriculture teachers.

In my junior year I became an officer in Sigma Alpha Gamma, and two of us were assigned to meet with Dr. Joel Lafayette Fletcher, the college president, to invite him to our annual banquet. When we entered Dr. Fletcher's office it was evident he had done his homework because he said, "Hello, Wayne, I understand you are from Eros." I was taken aback and impressed that he even knew about my hometown. I asked him how he knew about Eros, and he replied, "There is a very soft spot in my heart for Eros, because that is where I met my wife-to-be when I was a young man working as a traveling salesman. She was working at the Eros bank when it was a good sized little town." That episode gave me a little more status among my peers.

Legend had it that Dr. Fletcher was very interested in increasing the number of agriculture students because southwest Louisiana led the state in production of rice, sugar cane and yams. Louisiana State University was the agricultural and mechanical college established by the Smith-Hughes Act of 1917. Under the Act, LSU received federal money to teach agricultural education and it preferred to maintain that status as the only authorized vocational agricultural program in the state. It was said that Dr. Fletcher was instrumental in convincing the state board of education to grant Southwestern the right to train vocational agriculture teachers.

My work scholarship required me to work thirty hours a week as a busboy in the O.K. Allen dining room (named after an unpopular former governor who was a protégé of Huey Long) for the first two years.

My cousin Bobby spent his first year in college at LSU in Baton Rouge. But then Uncle Emery had a heart attack, money was even scarcer, and tuition at Southwestern was cheaper, so in our sophomore year Bobby joined me there. As work crew supervisor of the busboys in the dining hall, I was able to get Bobby a job, and from then on we were inseparable throughout college.

I was transferred to work in the library circulation department. I didn't really enjoy busing tables because it felt demeaning, but the library work seemed to have more status. One thing I did like about both jobs was getting to know and serve other students. There were only about five thousand students on campus but another five thousand commuted every day. I got to know hundreds of them because of my contacts at my workstations.

There was very little time to study or socialize. My mother sent me two dollars a week for an allowance that took care of my toiletries and one movie on the weekend.

When I felt sorry for myself, I remembered Lancelot. When he was in college at LSU, he had to stay at school during school breaks, lacking the money to go home. The cafeteria was closed, and food was hard to come by. Lancelot showed his initiative by fishing in the campus pond with a string and a safety pin, and catching fish for his dinner.

Skullcaps – beanies - played an important role in saving me money. After that long bus ride to college the first day, I learned from other students that hitchhiking was an effective alternative means of transportation to travel back and forth to visit my family. A student wearing a college tee shirt or a skullcap rarely had trouble getting a ride. Since no automobiles were made from 1942 to 1946, transportation was a real problem, and people made an effort to help students whenever they felt it was safe.

Some of our friends and relatives were concerned about Bobby and me hitchhiking 200 miles from college during the school breaks. One reason for their concern was that at the end of World War II, some criminals put on surplus military uniforms to hitchhike for the purpose of robbery, car theft, or even murder. So many people stopped picking up anyone except college students.

There was a protocol on the side of the road. You never got in front of the guy who was in line before you. So while waiting for another car to pick us up, Bobby and I sang duets, talked with other guys hitching, and bought candy bars and Cokes for lunch at gas stations.

Bobby and I actually enjoyed the experience of catching a ride with a stranger. Only twice in all our college years did we ever take more than one day to make it home. There were no interstate highways yet. So very early on, we learned to never get a ride that didn't take us to Alexandria, LeBeau, Monroe, or straight to Eros. In a podunk town, no one would stop to pick us up. If we had to spend the night somewhere, we'd have to sleep in a hotel lobby since we had no money for a room. We could easily get a ride from Lafayette to Alexandria; then from Alexandria to Monroe, and from Monroe to Eros. Then we walked home on gravel roads the last five miles. When we got to Monroe, if we had fifty cents in our pocket we bought a bus ticket to Eros, for the simple reason that few drivers wanted to go to Eros.

Once, I was traveling alone on the bus to Eros when a man sat down with me. We chatted awhile, and then he noticed a Mexican man sitting two seats behind us. He said to me, "See that Mexican sitting back there? Well, I'm from Texas, and back home we make our Mexicans sit in the back with the coloreds. Let's go back there and throw him out." I was horrified, and it took a little persuading to convince him that I would not help him do that.

It's true, there was a sign in the front of the bus stating, "Whites sit in front, coloreds sit in back". One day when Bobby and I were riding the bus, the driver stopped to pick up an elderly black woman. She was crippled, probably with arthritis, and had trouble getting into the bus to begin with. She proceeded very slowly down the aisle with great difficulty, trying to get to the back. The passengers were getting restless and impatient as the driver waited for her to be seated. As she got about halfway, a black lady in the back seats called out to reassure her, "That's okay, auntie, you jus takes yo time, cuz you's got mo time than you is money." This broke the ice and all the passengers chuckled.

Once a man and woman stopped to pick us up. The four of us had a nice conversation, and we soon realized the woman was another hitchhiker. After the driver stopped and let the girl off at a little town, Bobby and I mentioned that it was unusual for a woman to be hitchhiking. The driver told us, "I try to help anyone I can. After she got in the car, I realized she was a prostitute. That's why I stopped and picked you guys up, for my protection."

In 1948, there were no air-conditioned cars by today's standards. Some cars had crude air coolers: a system involving a water tank that attached to the car window and blew cooled air into the car. We thought that was a wonderful innovation. From then on, Bobby and I refused to hitch a ride in any car without an air cooler.

In May of 1947, I joined the U.S. Naval Reserve. Several of my newfound college friends in my dormitory were Navy veterans and were members of the Naval Reserve Organized Surface Division that conducted military drill once a week at the former Army Air training base where I had lived for my first few weeks on campus. They encouraged me to join their unit. Bobby and I became seamen apprentices and attended drill every Wednesday night. (We were called "Wednesday night warriors" by our college mates). We began learning a new language, Navy jargon. Left became port, right became starboard, floor became a deck, rear became fantail, forward became fo'c'sle, wall became bulkhead, front and back became fore and aft and so on.

Since we were issued a full complement of Navy clothing in our seabags, we were able to wear Navy dungarees and shoes to class like the veterans. The many campus veterans preferred to wear Army fatigues or Navy dungarees to class instead of traditional dressy casual college attire. Navy dungarees didn't carry any rank insignia so it didn't violate any military rules. With our new navy togs, we became right in style. This was helpful since our parents didn't have to purchase so many clothes for us. The real morale builder was the fact that we were paid thirty-three dollars every three months for attending unit training assemblies. This was big spending money for us and we would take in a movie on the weekend and occasionally have a beer or two with the guys.

Bobby and I both were assigned to train as radio operators. I spent my first two-week summer training cruise in the Caribbean on a destroyer as a gunner's mate. When there was an all-hands call to man battle stations to practice defense, I was assigned as a first loader on a 40mm gun positioned approximately at amidships. The tactical training squad launched an unmanned airplane drone and we tried to shoot it down. My regularly assigned duty was manning the intercom, with headphones, on the bridge in the Combat Information Center. An instrument on the ship's bridge automatically calculated the distance from our ship to the other ships in the convoy. I reported this information every two minutes to the Officer of the Day, and he relayed it to the ship's captain if one or more of the ships in the convoy was getting too close or straying away from the others.

My job was four hours on and four off, around the clock. I was gratified to be involved in the operation of the ship—I could hear the captain's orders and discussions. But it was very tedious to have four hours of constant attention to the instruments, and then only four hours to eat or sleep – your choice.

I got sick as soon as the training cruise left New Orleans for Guantanamo Bay, Cuba. The water was very choppy at the mouth of the Mississippi, as we approached the Gulf of Mexico. We were all in our dress uniforms lined up on the forecastle standing uniform inspection. Several of us had to break ranks and throw up over the side rail and we stayed there for a while. The inspecting officer came over to us after dismissing the rest of the troops. He walked up to my buddy beside me and said, "It looks like you are pretty weak, Sailor." Whereupon my buddy pulled himself up on the rail, gave a huge heave over the side, and replied, "Sir, I don't know what to say except that I seem to be throwing it as far as everyone else." The officer just smiled a little, patted him on the shoulder and said, "Hang in there," then walked away visibly trying not to laugh out loud.

I was as sick as anyone and couldn't hold down any food or water, which caused me to lose twenty pounds in the four days it took to reach Guantanamo. There didn't seem to be any way I could get relief from the seasickness. However, being seasick didn't excuse me from duty. It is difficult to describe the illness except to say that on several occasions while heaving my guts over the side, I seriously felt like just jumping over the railing and ending it all.

While in port we went on maneuvers to the other side of the island to practice more gunnery activities. We were there two days and by the time we got underway again heading to Jamaica, I was completely over my seasickness and felt exhilarated in the sea air. Since I felt better, I had a great time visiting Jamaica and was intrigued with the natives and their lifestyle. A lot of small boys were running the streets begging for candy, money, and gum. Some offered to arrange a date with their "sisters", but we had been warned on the ship to stay away from the girls on the street and the red light district because of the potential for contracting a social disease.

I took a second summer navy cruise in 1948 cruising the same area as before, only we entered the Gulf of Mexico via Sabine River out of Lake Charles, Louisiana. Sure enough, I got seasick again and the experience was a replay of the first cruise.

Back in college, every three months after collecting my seaman's pay I felt rich and splurged on going to a restaurant, or to the L'Acadian, a local college hangout, to have one or two beers with my buddies. This occasional social diversion made me feel special for a few hours and gave me something to look forward to.

I was working thirty hours a week and taking twenty to twenty-two credit hours per semester, and taking classes through every summer. Special permission from your advisor was required to register for more than seventeen hours. But to graduate early, I had to double up on courses. Each semester, I presented my advisor a registration form with seventeen hours on it and got it approved. Then I added another course to the form before turning it in to the registrar. Only once -- an occasion when I had signed up for twenty-two hours -- did the registration clerk question the number of hours, because I was on a work scholarship. But I pointed out the course was required, and the form was signed by my advisor, so she let it pass.

Generally for every three weekly lectures one lab was required. Labs were not regularly scheduled but were set at times convenient for the professor, and it was impossible for me to make all the lab classes I was supposed to attend. I made a decision to continue with the lab classes I could manage, and get a friend to cover at the ones I couldn't attend by answering for me in roll call. Since the classes were so crowded with veterans, roll was called by number instead of name. I simply gave my number to a friend to call out. This was tricky because professors were aware of this practice, and sometimes would call out a question for say, number 28 to answer. If I were number 28 and had "responded" to the roll call, but was not present, my friend was left with egg on his face. A couple of times this did happen, but most professors understood the problem and were able to make light of it.

Because of my hectic schedule, and because I broke up with a girlfriend back in Mangham, I became very depressed. In a letter to my mother I complained about how difficult my life was, and that I was considering dropping out, or transferring to a college closer to home. My usually positive attitude had turned defeatist.

Momma tried to make me feel better by sending an anonymous poem, entitled "Words". This poem made me realize that only I could solve my problems. In addition, I couldn't bear to disappoint my mother. Her two oldest sons dropped out of college to go to World War II. My sister Helen finished college, but Temple and LeMoyne were not interested. I was my mother's grand hope for the future, that one of her sons would finish college. I put this poem away and read it often.

Forty years later, when I had a recording company, I would set these words to music, add a chorus, and record the song with Bobby, Bernarr, and my son John. I published it on an album called "Stained Glass Bluegrass".

Words
  By Wayne Busbice
  Pub. Old Home Place Music

A careless word may kindle strife
A cruel word may wreck a life
A bitter word may hate instill
A brutal word may smite and kill.

Chorus:
So 'til the day that Jesus comes
Each word you speak should help someone
It'll be so sweet when this earthly race is run
To hear Him say, "A job well done!"

A gracious word will smooth the way
A joyous word will light the day
A timely word may lessen stress
A loving word will heal and bless.

Because of World War II, no updated text books were available to rely on and professors would tell us as we entered new classes, "If you bought a textbook for this class, you may as well throw it out the window – it is no good and I will provide you with all the information you will need to pass this course." During my last three semesters I was fortunate enough to work in the circulation department of the library and was able to check out a few textbooks that were essential references in my major. To my recollection, I purchased only one textbook while working on my bachelor's degree.

My method of studying was to take copious notes in class, then quiz and be quizzed by my classmates as we walked back and forth to class, at our workstation in the dining hall/library, and preparing for bed at night. Before final exams several of my classmates and I would squeeze in an hour or so for group study and a round table discussion. Each of us would take responsibility for a certain segment of the subject matter.

My degree work progressed along at a slightly above average level and I told my mother and former teachers at Mangham High School that I was sacrificing my usual quality of work for quantity so I could finish early. They usually advised against my plan but I was determined to graduate in record time.

In my senior year, I was under intense pressure because of my schoolwork, my work schedule, and trying to help my brother Junior get readjusted to college and lick his alcohol addiction.

After the war Junior had difficulty adjusting to civilian life. He tried very hard to overcome his alcoholism and thought that if he rejoined the service he could get help and make a better go of it. Serving an additional year or two in the Air Force did not help with his problem or made any progress in his career, so he was invited to leave the service with an honorable discharge. I was a junior when Junior enrolled at Southwestern as a sophomore under the G.I. Bill.

During his short stay at Southwestern in 1948, I tried very hard to help him. Rightly or wrongly, I felt responsible for him, especially when he was under the influence. I spent a lot of time and energy trying to figure how to help him reject drinking, and what I could do to make him change.

Word got back to the dean of men that Otis Jr. was not adjusting well, and at times was creating a disruption in the dormitory. The dean met with my brother and the two agreed that Junior should withdraw from school so he could get help. He returned home about two weeks before the Thanksgiving holidays and interviewed for several jobs in Monroe; he was hired to manage a service station.

When I returned home for the Thanksgiving holidays, Junior told me about his plans and seemed very excited and upbeat about working out his problems and embarking upon a career. He asked me if I would go to Monroe with him the next day to take care of some personal business and see a first rate movie. I was very tired from the trip home and declined so I could get some rest. I took a long nap during the morning and around lunchtime I decided to go meet him at the theater at two o'clock. I caught the bus to Monroe and arrived at the theater on time but I did not see my brother. I watched the movie and returned to Eros on the bus. I noticed that there was a ball game being played in the high school gym that was about a half mile from home.

I asked the bus driver to let me off at the school and as I walked into the gym I saw people staring at me and whispering to one another. I didn't understand what was going on until a friend of the family came over and asked me if I had been home within the last hour. I told him that I had not. He told me that Junior passed away that afternoon at home with what appeared to be a massive heart attack.

The friend took me to the house and there were a lot of people present including the coroner and the undertaker. I almost went into shock when I saw my brother stretched out on the couch appearing to be asleep and actually looking healthy. I noticed that his arm was hanging a little off the edge of the couch and the thought came to my mind that if I could just straighten it out and place it back firmly on the couch, he would come back to life. I began to feel dizzy and Mrs. Bates, my former English teacher, put her arm around me and made me sit down. and put my head between my legs to prevent me from passing out and falling. My palms were sweating and I noticed that I was white as a sheet. I was nineteen and I was the only immediate family member on the scene.

My mother was in Dallas, Texas, to attend the wedding of my brother, LeMoyne. Connella lived in Falls Church, Virginia, Helen in Dallas, Temple in Monroe, and Billy was away in college at Natchitoches. Bernarr, was living on the farm with Aunt Ivie and Uncle Emery and helping them care for the stock while Uncle Emery was recuperating from a heart attack. Marilyn, was staying with a classmate for the weekend while Momma was in Dallas. Friends began notifying everyone at this juncture.

Uncle Allison had discovered Junior sitting on a stool in front of a vanity, appearing to be asleep with his head resting on his arms. Allison walked over to my brother, pushed him on the shoulder to wake him up, and to his surprise his body slumped to the floor.

The coroner decided an autopsy was required because my brother was only twenty-seven years old, and his death might be service connected. Someone was able to get my mother on the telephone to give permission to take him to Shreveport for an autopsy. I was the only one available to accompany his body in the ambulance.

One of my uncles, either Emery or Ted, gave me a few dollars so I could get a room in Ruston, on the way to Shreveport. By this time it was too late to have the autopsy performed that night. The funeral home director and I left Ruston early the next morning. I didn't sleep a wink. I was pale and must have looked awful because the ambulance driver kept asking me if I was okay. I assured him that I was a little shaky but would be all right.

We drove a hundred miles, and for the entire trip every time we passed a liquor store I had the urge to yell "Stop!" to the driver so I could run over, pick up an axe or a bat, and break every whiskey bottle in the joint.

After the autopsy, the doctor asked me if Junior was a heavy smoker or a heavy drinker. I replied yes to both questions. He said the autopsy revealed that Junior had arteriosclerosis, and the aortic arch had calcified and burst causing instant death. The coroner stated that alcohol and tobacco were contributing factors.

Otis Jr. was buried on Thanksgiving Day in Hasley Cemetery in West Monroe beside our father. All family members were able to return home for the funeral and that was a sad, sad Thanksgiving Day.

I can imagine how difficult it must have been for my mother to lose her firstborn, who had so much promise, so early in his life. We were an upright family, and in addition to the normal grief, my main feeling about his death was a sense of shame for his alcoholism. Momma rationalized it after the funeral: "I blame the Germans for his death as much as if they had killed him on the battlefield."

In Junior's baby book, my mother penned this on June 5, 1921: "All of Daddy's sisters, brothers and folks were there to see Oates Jr. They were expecting a big fat baby and were terribly disappointed when a tiny 8½ pound boy was unwrapped. But when he grew to 20 lbs. at four months old they thought there never was such another."

By this time the reader may wonder why Otis spelled his name differently than my father. My father spelled his name Oates, pronounced "Oat-ess". Junior changed the spelling of his name from Oates to Otis when he started college. The professors pronounced his name "Oats" as in "he's feeling his oats." He didn't relish having his name pronounced like a popular grain crop.

When Otis Jr. died suddenly, everything seemed to come crashing down on me. I returned to college with his death constantly on my mind. I remained pale and fragile and lost twenty-five pounds. My friends kept asking me if everything was all right. Of course I said everything was fine, but I continued to drift deeper into depression and nervous anxiety.

I noticed that every time I took a deep breath I had chest pains. My mind played tricks on me and I started to believe that I was having heart trouble, and would die soon with cardiovascular disease like my father and brother. I was so convinced I would die soon that I would not go anywhere without a friend, even walking home at night from my job at the library, for fear that I'd die on the way and no one would find my body.

This continued until I went home for Easter vacation. Momma noticed right away that I had lost a lot of weight and that I was withdrawn and definitely not my usual self. I broke down and confessed that I thought I had heart disease because of my constant chest pains. She sent me to our cardiologist immediately. He gave me a thorough examination and declared that I had pleurisy – not heart disease. It felt like a huge weight had been lifted off of my shoulders, chest and mind.

I began a quick recovery and vowed to quit smoking and never to drink coffee or alcoholic beverages in order to protect my health.

Bobby and I were experts at helping each other keep up our spirits through the rough times. We had a little game going with the professors regarding our last name. It didn't look like any name they had ever seen, and since we were in Cajun country they just assumed it was French. We would let them try a couple of times, i.e., "Buz'-bee cee?" "Bush-ice?" or "Buz'-bu'-ce'?" Then the professor would look up puzzled and we would sound off in unison, "Guess again!" and that would bring loud chuckles from our classmates. The professor would usually start shaking his head and then we would pronounce it for him. The usual reply was, "Thank you, I have never run across that name before." We knew that for sure.

During our senior year while taking a health education course required for all prospective teachers, Bobby and I were seated next to each other in the instrumental music classroom. Our professor was Mr. Brown who was a former athletic director and somewhat of a curmudgeon. He would come in with an armload of books and reference materials and throw them down hard in a boisterous motion on the closest music stand, then adjust the stand to the proper level. Bobby and I decided that on the final exam day we would play a trick on him. We placed a music stand in position where he usually lectured and loosened the adjustment key so it would collapse if weight was placed on it. Sure enough, Prof. Brown came in as usual and plopped his books down hard -- naturally it collapsed to the floor with a loud noise – books and papers crashed to the floor and went everywhere. All of the students laughed out loud and the professor wasn't pleased. Bobby and I got the biggest laugh and we couldn't stop giggling. Prof. Brown grumbled something like, "Looks like we have a prankster or two in this class, but I usually get the last word in this course." Bobby and I went into the final test with one point shy of an A but when the grades were posted, we each made a D -- the only D I ever made in college. The professor was true to his word and neither Bobby nor I challenged him.

In the semester just prior to graduation, I received a legislative scholarship from my state representative that paid for my cap and gown, graduation invitations, class ring and miscellaneous fees. At that time I was able to improve my social life by dating and attending campus dances.

Approximately 670 students graduated in my class of 1949. At a ceremony in the basketball gymasium, Dr. Fletcher read off the names of the graduates from behind a podium, while on the floor the dean of the appropriate department handed out a diploma, gave congratulations, and shook the hand of each student as he walked by. Dr. Fletcher also congratulated each graduate as he or she passed. But when it was time for the agriculture graduates, Dr. Fletcher left his podium and came down to floor level to announce the names. Dr. Arceneaux, Dean of Agriculture, handed out the diplomas and the handshakes, then presented each graduate to Dr. Fletcher for another round of personal congratulations and handshakes from him. It was apparent that Dr. Fletcher was very gratified to see his efforts come to fruition, that so many young men and women were going out to teach agriculture and home economics.

I completed my requirements for a Bachelor of Science degree in two years and eight months and was barely twenty. I took much pride in my achievement. To my great sorrow, Momma could not afford to come to my graduation. She had given me more encouragement and moral support than any one else. I give her unequivocal credit for ensuring my college success.

Armed with my college diploma, I returned to my hometown of Eros and was ready to set the world on fire.

Wayne, a college senior

Patterns: Music, Teaching, and Politics

Jobs were scarce in Eros, but fortunately my former principal J.D. Koonce, who was now serving as the Jackson Parish superintendent of schools, hired me as an agriculture teacher.

My assignment was to work in the Institutional On-the-Farm Training program with returning World War II veterans who were training to be farmers through financial assistance from the G.I. Bill. I moved back in with my mother for the first time since I was fifteen.

I liked my job because I knew most of my students, who were several years older than me. I received instant respect since my charges knew Lancelot, who was teaching agriculture in the parish, Daddy and Uncle Emery. They all had good reputations as excellent farmers, and my students assumed that I had learned the important, practical farming practices from them. Otherwise, I would have had to prove myself before they would take instruction kindly from someone several years their junior with "book larnin'". Very few of my students had graduated from high school.

Since I was only twenty, my mother had to sign all of my legal documents, in particular the note to purchase a new car. The car was required for my job since I spent most of my time traveling around the rural roads visiting my students on their farms.

The car gave me an opportunity to date and socialize in nearby Monroe, which helped because Eros was so isolated. I dated my former high school sweetheart in Mangham again, but we learned that we had grown apart over the three years I had been gone.

Cousin Bobby graduated a semester after I did and we ran around together. I was more than ready to spread my wings. I'm afraid I overdid it somewhat. I missed a lot of sleep but really enjoyed myself.

In the fall of 1950 there was a local and state election, and the political leaders in Ward One asked me to help get out the vote for our side. I had a new 1950 Ford auto so I was asked to transport certain voters to the polls. I was given twenty dollars from campaign funds to pay for my gas. One staffer asked me to go pick up a couple about five miles away but when I checked in with the party leader to keep him informed of my activities, he said "Don't go there, they are against us." This gave me cause for concern and I didn't feel right about the conflicting instructions.

I pondered over it for a while and decided to go get the couple anyway because, I reasoned, they had a right to cast their ballots. As it turned out the husband was against our candidates but had forgotten to update his registration, but the wife had updated her registration. She was supporting our candidates and voted for them. I reported this back to the party leader and he said, "Good work" – so every thing worked out in the long run.

I was asked to go get another lady and bring her to the polls, but to first take her by the general store to do some grocery shopping. When we entered the store the owner said "Go pick out what groceries you need and bring them to the register when you finish." I was a little suspicious so I observed closely what happened next.

Mrs. F. took the groceries to the register, the owner bagged them up and handed them to Mrs. F. and said, "No charge, you know our arrangement is the same as before." Mrs. F. said. "Yes, I do," and thanked her. Then I placed her groceries in the car and drove her to the polling place. In my innocence, I found this a little disturbing because I felt I had been unknowingly drawn into an illegal activity.

As I saw it, Mrs. F. was bribed for her vote, never mind that her vote was probably against the ticket my family supported. Later I talked this over with Uncle Emery, who was a poll worker, and he said there was really nothing I could do because it would be their word against mine and, "Besides," he said, "I happen to know Mrs. F. is a strong supporter for *our* side." In other words, Minnie F. got her free groceries and went to the polls and voted the way she pleased.

It disturbed me to hear about another incident at the polling place. There were several residents who came to vote who could not read or write, and they were assigned a poll worker to assist them with the process. A certain poll worker took the voter into an adjacent room where Uncle Emery was stationed, and he overheard the poll worker ask, "Who do you wish to vote for, for governor?" The lady responded, "Sam Jones." The poll worker said, "See these two blocks beside the candidate's names? Since you want to vote for Sam Jones, just mark an X in the block by Earl Long's name to cancel him out." In essence, she was actually voting for Earl Long instead of her real choice. The poll worker continued on down the ballot, instructing her in the same manner that resulted in tricking her to vote for his choice of candidates. Uncle Emery reported the incident to an official, but I don't know the outcome.

Everything seemed to be going well during my first year as an employed adult and getting established as a productive member of the community. I was inducted into the Masons, led the singing at Eros Baptist Church, played on the town baseball and basketball teams, became active in local politics and played in a local country band with my brothers LeMoyne and Bernarr for country dances.

Jamming in the living room: Wayne, LeMoyne, Billy, Bernarr

One autumn night Allen Crowell, Bernarr, Billy and I played a gig at the Rest-A-While nightclub, a honky-tonk in Monroe. I was unaware that Allen drank and couldn't hold his liquor. Customers kept buying him drinks as was customary for the band, and Allen was pretty well under the weather by the end of the evening. He promptly fell asleep on the back seat of the car as we were driving home.

As the driver, I didn't drink any but missed my turn on the outskirts of town because we were laughing and talking about how well we were received by the club audience. It was after midnight and since there didn't appear to be anyone else on the streets, I ran a stop sign in my haste to get back on the right street. Suddenly, a police car appeared and pulled me over.

There were two police officers in the patrol car and they were very nice to begin with, asking a few questions about where we lived and what we had been doing. They explained that they were just giving me a warning because they had an "audience" in the townspeople and they needed to keep them satisfied. At that statement Billy made a smart remark, "Audience? I don't see any audience and I don't hear anybody clapping." Then the policemen got serious and one asked, "Have you boys been drinking?" About that time

Allen, sleeping in the back seat, awakened and he slurred, "Why, of course not!" He admonished them, "These are Miz Fay's boys." Then he slumped and promptly passed out again.

The officer decided to give me only a five dollar ticket for running a stop sign since he could tell that I, as the driver, had not been drinking. Because of the flak he got from my passengers, I felt lucky that it was not more severe.

My brother Bernarr was still at home attending high school. He was beginning to develop what would become his outstanding talent playing the mandolin that would lead to his music career as Buzz Busby. During that year Bernarr and I began playing clubs in West Monroe and Monroe with several other local musicians.

One night, we were visiting a country music club in Monroe on South Grand. Bill Nettles and the Dixie Blue Boys were playing, known for their smash hit "Hadacol Boogie" -- written about a popular energy tonic. The Dixie Blue Boys asked us to play a few numbers while they were on a break.

We made a good impression, and at the end of our session two well-dressed gentlemen came over and asked if they could join our table. (We could tell they were different because no one we knew went around in a suit and tie.) Of course we invited them to sit down and they introduced themselves as representatives of the Singer Sewing Machine Company. They went on to say they enjoyed our music and they were searching for a guitar-mandolin duet with good vocals to perform as an opening act throughout the South when they made public presentations of their sewing machines. It all sounded very tempting but I explained that Bernarr was still a senior in high school and that I had just finished college and was now a teacher. This offer had immediate appeal but didn't seem to me to be a permanent career for either of us so I passed up the opportunity.

A Tragic Love Affair
By Wayne Busbice
Pub. Old Home Place Music

On a farm in dear old Dixie
Where the snow white cotton grows
That's where I met my darling
And I learned to love her so.

Oh she had the sweetest dimples
And her lips were sweet as wine
Her smile was like an angel
And she promised to be mine.

I left her in the springtime
To search for wealth and fame
She promised to be waiting
When I returned her love to claim.

Well I traveled the wide world over
But my search was all in vain
I kept dreaming of my darling
I could hear her calling my name.

When I returned to claim my sweetheart
They told me she had gone
To live up there with the angels
Now heaven is her home.

In my breast I'll hold her memory
Till we're joined together up there
And now this ends my story
Of my tragic love affair.

~13~

Grounded – How You Like That?

President Truman determined that communism must be stopped, declared a "police action" (war) in Korea, and activated the draft board, which informed Bobby and me that we were eligible for the draft immediately. We decided we would prefer to serve in the Air Force instead of being drafted into the Army or activated with our Navy unit; so along with Billy, who was still in college, we hastened to the Air Force recruiting station. The three of us joined the Air Force in August of 1950.

Billy, Bobby and I reported to Lackland Air Force Base in San Antonio, Texas, for basic training. I was surprised to see the extent of segregation in the city of San Antonio: not only were blacks not permitted to use the public pools but neither were Hispanics. Blacks and Hispanics all had to use one pool, and whites another. But there was no segregation on military bases. This was my first time living and training with anyone other than Caucasians and I welcomed the experience.

We had one private there, about five foot six, a comical looking guy, very friendly and outgoing, named Private Gonzales. Gonzales was a natural comedian and was very popular.

We were marching along one day after being out at the firing range for a couple of days, and in the hot September weather our fatigue uniforms got a little out of shape. Pvt. Gonzales was slightly bowlegged and by this time his uniform was very rumpled. Suddenly, the drill instructor called us to a halt to check our uniforms; we were approaching the main part of the base and he wanted his troops to look sharp. When he came back and looked at Pvt. Gonzales he observed that his uniform was a disgrace. The drill instructor got right up into his face, looked him directly in the eye and yelled, "Private, I want you to stand at attention when I am inspecting the ranks!"

Now there were three acceptable responses to any reprimand: "Yes, Sir!" "No, Sir!" and "No excuse, Sir!" But Gonzales didn't crack a smile, he just looked straight ahead in a military manner, and said, "Sir, I am at attention. It's just my fatigues, – *they're* at ease." And he said it loud enough that all fifty people in the flight could hear him and the drill instructor was taken aback when we all laughed out loud – and that was against the rules too – so the drill instructor decided he would just calm us down and move on. He just chewed us out for not maintaining our military bearing and making him look bad in the eyes of fellow drill instructors – who were very competitive about the discipline and spit-and-polish of their troops. But in a parting shot he told Gonzales, "Get those fatigues in the laundry right away so they can stand at attention, too!"

While at Lackland, we were given a battery of tests to determine our aptitude and ability to be successful in a specific military career field. As it turned out Bobby, Billy and I qualified in many areas the Air Force could use at the time. The three of us had a conference to determine if we could agree on a specialty that would keep us together for our entire four-year tour. We were pressed for time to decide, but we narrowed it down to either radio operator or radio technician. I chose radio operator and I hoped to be assigned to a B-29 in order to get flying time. Evidently they signed up for radio technician. We were all disappointed and they accused me, and rightly so, of not paying attention to what we agreed on. But it was too late to make a change and we were separated. Soon I was shipped to Keesler AFB, Mississippi and they were sent to Scott AFB, Illinois.

My training began in October at Keesler AFB and went well. After a few months I learned how the service operated. With typical perceptiveness I decided I would be happier as an officer and that instead of being a radio operator on a B-29, I would prefer to be the pilot. It was generally felt in the Air Force that, "If you're not a pilot, you're not s—t."

So I decided to apply for air cadet training and specialize in multi-engine aircraft in order to qualify for B-29s. I knew I had motion sickness and had been told by World War II airmen that I would be less likely to become airsick on a large plane.

I flunked the spatial relations part of the test and was disqualified. That was a blow to my ego but my commander encouraged me to apply for officer candidate school and become an administrative officer. I took his advice and filled out an application, passed the exam and waited to be called. In the meantime I completed the radio school ranking second in the class, and that gave me the right to choose my assignment. I was getting excited because I was sure I would be able to select B-29 duty. Wrong.

The day before graduation my friend and classmate James Adams, who was number one in the class, got the B-29 slot and the next twelve airmen who finished in the top twenty-five percent of the class were notified to report to the hangar for instructions regarding our future assignment. The master sergeant greeted us with a big smile and informed us that we had been selected to enter a very important, prestigious career field.

It turned out we had been selected to be in Security Service (SS). The training and future duties were classified and couldn't be discussed. The only thing the master sergeant was permitted to share with us was that our assignment would require us to wear civilian clothes and live off the military base, probably in a hotel room or on a small island out in the Pacific. We would be able to write one letter a month to our parents and correspond with no one else. We were given a few days to go home for a visit and explain to our parents what was in store for us and prepare them for what was to come.

When upon return to the base we began studying Russian code, I realized what I was getting into. However in about two weeks I received my orders to report to officers candidate school at Lackland AFB at San Antonio, Texas on July 1, 1951.

All of my buddies in the SS promised to keep in touch with me when they received their permanent assignment. Sadly, I never heard from any of them again. I suppose that Security Service prohibited them from doing so for their own safety, and so there would be no chance of blowing their cover.

When I arrived at Officer Candidate School (OCS), I was greeted by an upperclassman, who informed me I had been assigned to Easy Flight. I thought he meant an "easy" flight and I smiled and said, "Oh, yeah." He thought I was being flippant and it didn't take but the twinkling of a Form One (discipline slip) to wipe the smile off my face and make me snap to attention: "Chin in! -- chest out! -- look straight ahead!"

The six months following was filled with rigorous physical military training combined with academic and leadership instruction and exercises. Only college graduates could qualify for officer training so they crammed all of the military academy requirements into those six months.

During my training in OCS, several of my buddies decided to apply for pilot training and they suggested I join them. This time I passed the test and physical with flying colors. This boosted my ego considerably and I couldn't wait to pin on my second lieutenant bars and begin flying into the wild blue yonder.

I graduated in the class of 51D near Christmas time and was scheduled to report to Greenville AFB, Mississippi for pilot training. Again, my mother couldn't afford to attend the graduation and commissioning exercises. However, my brother Temple came to my graduation. Temple was in the Army at that time and stationed at Ft. Smith, Arkansas. He received an autographed dollar bill from me, as tradition dictates for the person who gives the new officer his first salute.

Lieutenant Busbice in pilot training

I reported to pilot training at Greenville AFB, Mississippi, in January of 1952. We had quite a few foreign military taking basic flight training with us by international agreement, as well as troops from Puerto Rico and Guam. At times there was a language barrier between our American instructors and some of the foreign students.

One day we had a foreign student who was going up for his first solo flight, and of course, he was a little apprehensive. After he had been gone a while, a radio message came through to the tower from his aircraft, "Mayday! Mayday! Come in tower!" Tower replied, "What's the problem?" The student pilot responded in a heavy accent, "Have oil on windshield and don't know what that mean!" At the time, his pilot instructor was in the control tower. He answered, "Don't panic, just look at the instruments and see if the oil pressure gauge is in the green," -- meaning it's okay. The pilot responded frantically, in his accent, "Yes, oil pressure gauge in green." The instructor replied, "Well, just bring it on in and we'll check it out; there doesn't seem to be anything serious if the pressure gauge is working fine." The student pilot said, "Not sure, not sure! You sure everything okay?" The instructor replied, "Yes, don't panic, just bring it on in and we'll take a look at it."

By the sound of his voice, the fledgling pilot felt that his concern was not being taken seriously. Soon he called back in a panic, "Mayday! Mayday! Oil on windshield, oil gauge not in green and falling fast -- HOW YOU LIKE THAT!!?" The answer came back from the tower, "It's okay, you're near the field and you'll be all right. Just come straight on in now and you should not have any trouble landing. I can see your aircraft from here." The student pilot, although flustered, was able to land and everyone breathed a sigh of relief. But the story made the rounds of the base and "How you like that!?" was soon a catchphrase.

When my basic flight program at Greenville AFB began in the T-6 aircraft, I would get a little airsick on take offs and landings. I managed not to use my barf bag for a couple of weeks, then we began practicing stalls and tailspins and that made me considerably sick; but I hung in there and my problem was improving because we were flying every day. Then weather moved in and we couldn't fly for about four or five days.

The very next time we went up the instructor had me practice tailspins over the Mississippi River, count the spirals, and pull out of it on the third or fourth spin, using the river to help keep count. Right away, I began getting very sick and on the second exercise I reached for my barf bag and filled it up. The instructor had to take over the controls. After we landed the instructor asked if I thought I should continue flight training. When I begged, he agreed to give me one more chance, but to no avail -- the next day was a repeat performance.

I was sent to the flight surgeon, and then to the Air University in Montgomery, Alabama, for a series of tests to determine if my problem was psychological or physiological. The flight surgeon there counseled me to resign from flight school because it was apparently not psychological. He asked me what I really wanted to do. My reply was, "I really want to be a pilot." He explained that it may be possible to condition a person with true motion sickness to overcome it temporarily, but if there was a long delay between flights the problem would return. I was devastated, since this was the first time in my life I had failed to accomplish something I really wanted to achieve.

My future was in the hands of Air Force personnel at this point. A few days later I got my orders to report to Craig AFB, Alabama to fill the slot of base education officer. I was pleased because this was compatible with my background, education and experience. My duties were to help the base personnel improve their educational standing by arranging correspondence courses from the USAF Institute of Technology, University of Alabama, University of Maryland and local colleges so personnel could obtain a bachelor's or an advanced degree. I also administered General Educational Development exams for individuals who were seeking a high school diploma.

My other duties included base exchange officer -- managing the BX, bookstore officer, postal officer and photo lab officer.

My graduation from Officers' Candidate School at the end of 1951 had come with a two-week furlough. My brother Connella and sister-in-law Jeweldine extended an invitation to me to spend Christmas with them at their home in Falls Church, Virginia. Connella and Jeweldine were eager to introduce me to "the girl next door," their neighbor, Margaret Woodward.

Margaret and I seemed to have a lot in common. We were both born in the South, had rural backgrounds, an interest in history, and were Southern Baptists. After a very short courtship during which we rarely saw each other while I attended pilot training, we wed on May 17, 1952, filled with the hope and promise of young love.

Our son, John Wayne, was born on July 21, 1953, at the Craig Air Force Base hospital in Selma, Ala. That day was one of the happiest in my life. When I went to the hospital to see him for the first time, I went to the nursery and viewed at least twenty newborns through the glass, but had no difficulty in picking him out as my son. It is not true that all newborn babies look the same. He was beautiful and we named him John Wayne after his maternal great-grandfather and me, not the movie actor.

Baby John was only a week old the day I left for Francis E. Warren AFB, Wyoming, to attend a three-month course in supply services, for additional training for my BX position. I had been in Wyoming for just a week when there was a ceasefire in the Korean conflict. Consequently, reserve officers on extended active duty like me were given the choice of signing up indefinitely or requesting a release from active duty.

Margaret and her parents implored me to get out of the service and try to find suitable employment in the D.C. metro area. When I talked to my superiors, they encouraged me to stay on active duty and make a career of the military. I firmly believed that upon their recommendation, I would become a regular officer, which would have brought more tenure, status and benefits than serving as a reserve officer.

I was torn. I enjoyed the life of an Air Force officer, but because I was anxious to be with my family and get to know my baby boy, I opted to request a release from active duty. Had I stayed in the Air Force as a regular officer, my career and future would have been assured. But I felt strongly it was more important to put my family first and take my chances in the civilian world.

My brother, Connella, had already encouraged me to consider moving to the Washington D.C. area to live because career opportunities were much better there than in Louisiana. Additionally, since one of my duties as base education officer was coordinating University of Maryland correspondence courses, I had given a lot of thought to enrolling in the University of Maryland to work on my master's degree upon discharge.

I made my decision: Washington D.C. it would be. Immediately upon our move to Falls Church, Virginia, I enlisted in the District of Columbia Air National Guard, a Reserve of the Air Force, in order to earn extra money for my small family. We were headquartered at Andrews Air Force Base.

Three Thousand Miles Lonesome
  by Wayne Busbice
  Pub. Old Home Place Music

I left my heart with someone I love so
I kissed her tears and said I had to go
Now I realize that she is the only one,
And I'm three thousand miles lonesome.

Chorus:
Yes, I'm three thousand miles lonesome
I'm payin' for the wrongs I have done
She's not to blame, I know that I'm the guilty one
And I'm three thousand miles lonesome.

We're too far apart for her to hear me calling
But my love for her is still falling
My dreams at night are always of the same one
That makes me three thousand miles lonesome.

~14~

Master Teacher

Moving north and looking for a job was a shock. I looked around the crowded Washington area and said to myself, "Nobody here knows my daddy." The family I came from in Louisiana meant nothing here; making my way in the world was up to me. After I'd been there awhile I realized most people my age didn't have their daddies, either.

I visited the Veterans Administration to sign up for my master's degree on the G.I. Bill. After I'd filled out the ton of paper work required, the counselor asked why I listed my ultimate objective as a master's. I said I didn't know if I wanted to try for the doctoral degree and if I did, I would apply for eligibility after I finished the master's program. He explained that the form I was filling out was the only request for stating my final objective and could not be modified later on. I gave it about two seconds thought and changed my objective to obtaining a doctor's degree. I often think how much I owe that counselor for encouraging me to consider that alternative, because I had no inclination at that time to pursue a doctoral program, much less complete one. It would have cost more than I could afford to pay for out of pocket.

I enrolled as a full time graduate student at the University of Maryland majoring in Rural Life and Education with minors in Educational Administration and Guidance Counseling. And I applied for a teaching job at Adams Teachers Agency. It didn't take long before I was hired by Montgomery County Public Schools in Maryland, contiguous to Washington. I was unaware that I had lucked into the most prestigious school district in Maryland and in the entire Washington metropolitan area.

I began teaching fulltime in October, 1953. This career move made it necessary to drop several classes at the university and become a part time grad student.

My new job was a twelve-month position teaching agriculture -- my certified career field -- at Gaithersburg High School. I commuted across the Potomac River from Virginia to Gaithersburg and to the University of Maryland for university classes for two years until we bought a house in Rockville, Maryland, which made it much easier. Margaret was employed at the National Institutes of Health in Bethesda. My mother-in-law Grace Woodward was the caretaker of our son, John, during the day.

The Gaithersburg school was a combination junior-senior high school with grades seven through twelve and an enrollment of approximately 1000 students. The agriculture department had been neglected for several years before I came, and there were only twenty students enrolled in the agriculture program. The adult farmer program was growing by leaps and bounds. The principal and vocational-technical supervisor wanted to relieve the current Ag teacher to work full time with the adults, and charged me with the responsibility of building up the enrollment in the all-day program. The Gaithersburg chapter of Future Farmers of America (FFA) ranked near the bottom of the list in the Maryland FFA organization. Therefore, I was also given the task of improving the status of Gaithersburg FFA in the state rankings. While I was working on building up the agriculture enrollment I taught one class of general science and one class of general math.

For the first two years I taught at Gaithersburg High School I struggled in my job. I was very frustrated when students didn't progress as rapidly as I thought they should. I woke up every morning depressed, and hated to go to work. In the spring of my second year I made a commitment to myself that I would teach one more year and if I didn't like my job then, I would seek other employment.

I was continuing my part time university courses working on a master's degree and I discussed my concerns with several professors. Each of them kept telling me that it appeared that I was getting frustrated because I was too strict and my students were not progressing in their course work as fast as I would like for them to. I felt that I was a failure as a teacher. They recommended that I not give up the high standards I expected them to achieve but that I should just relax and concentrate on "teaching the students instead of the subject". I had been taught that concept all through college and it hadn't sunk in. Apparently I needed to really think about making more effort to connect with each student personally. When I put that concept into practice, the students began to appreciate me more, worked harder and progressed more rapidly.

Vocational agriculture was offered in the ninth through the twelfth grades. I made a request that the school administration add an eighth grade pre-vocational class to help encourage students to continue in agriculture in ninth through twelfth grades. With the agriculture teachers in the small towns of Damascus and Poolesville, I developed the curriculum for this program because there was none in existence. Many students wanted to continue in the program, but parents of college-bound students felt that their children should take only college preparatory courses. Generally, students who enrolled in vocational agriculture were tracked in non-

129

college preparatory classes. This was a valid point so I asked the principal to grant me permission to offer a college prep agriculture program for students who wished to go on to college.

Within three years I had an enrollment of more than seventy students. About thirty percent of those students were in my college prep agriculture program and this fact prompted the academic departments in the school to give more recognition and acceptance to my students and the agriculture and FFA programs as a whole. From then on the Ag department and FFA programs enjoyed a higher status among my colleagues.

By the end of my fourth teaching year, my students had established the Gaithersburg FFA chapter as the top chapter in the state by winning top honors in public speaking, dairy judging, milk judging, beef cattle judging, land judging and in nearly every other competitive contest at the state level. On one occasion, they won top honors in the national Hoard's Dairyman judging contest. Several of my judging teams won trips to regional judging contests competing with other Middle Atlantic States.

In 1957, I was selected to chaperone the state FFA delegation to the national FFA convention in Kansas City. There I had a special breakfast with other FFA advisors and former president Harry Truman, who was our special guest. This was a big thrill as Truman has always been my favorite president, based on his leadership style and overall accomplishments. He gave the major address at the convention and talked about his background as a dirt farmer, and the importance of the U.S. Constitution.

Teaching agriculture in the school's alfalfa field

By this time I loved my job and felt very comfortable in my career. Due to the recognition of our Ag program at the state level, I was recommended to receive the designation of Master Teacher by Montgomery County

Public Schools. This required a master's, five years experience in the classroom, and outstanding performance.

In general, most teachers felt that vocational programs were not as important as the academic subjects. This was a minor discriminatory issue compared to two other serious practices that I encountered as an educator. Discrimination against women in the workplace was still being practiced in the field of education. This was a carryover from the Depression years. During the war years, women proved their value in the workplace, doing all kinds of jobs. The G.I. Bill gave many veterans the opportunity to attend college and many of them were encouraged to choose teaching as a career. Of course most teachers at that time were women, so school districts that wanted to have a balanced staff began to offer men higher pay grades in order to recruit them. The main rationale for paying men higher salaries was that men traditionally were the breadwinners and needed more pay to support their families, whereas women were basically supplementing their husbands' income.

This inequity created a morale problem among faculty members. It was considered patently unfair by men and women teachers alike. The Montgomery County Education Association and the Maryland State Teachers Association set about to correct this unfair practice of paying women less than men for doing the exact same job. Progress was slow, but the first step was a provision to pay heads of household equal pay regardless of gender. After a few years in this mode, women were given equal pay for comparable jobs in the field of education. I was an active member of both educational organizations and fought hard to help bring these changes about. Morale improved immediately after this was corrected, and it resulted in a much more friendly, collegial atmosphere in the schools.

Segregation was the most undemocratic, egregious practice in public schools when I began my teaching career. The Supreme Court eliminated the right to practice segregation in public schools by its 1954 ruling in Brown vs. the Board of Education. Implementation was to proceed "at all deliberate speed." Many state governments were reluctant to implement the court's decision. The country was divided, and politicians built careers on opposing integration.

Montgomery County handled the process of integration very smoothly. A plan was drawn up and integration began slowly in 1956 by enrolling a few minority students in all-white schools the first year and increasing the enrollment gradually. After a few years, all the black schools were closed and both minority students and minority teachers were fully integrated without a major incident. It took many years for some states to comply.

131

When President Johnson signed the 1964 Civil Rights Act, he turned to an aide and said, "We [the Democratic Party] have just lost the South for a generation." Southerners who could not accept integration bolted from the Democratic Party. In places, segregation continued in more socially acceptable ways by shifting government support to private schools.

In 1956 I was getting established in Maryland and owned a home there, but my heart was still in Louisiana, where my mother and most of my brothers and sisters lived. I visited Momma in Eros for two weeks every summer.

I missed my mother a lot, and I decided to write a song about my feelings. I had only gotten as far as the first or second verse one Saturday morning. I was working on the song with my guitar, figuring out words and music, when my brother Temple telephoned, to tell me that Momma was in the hospital with viral encephalitis. This was totally unexpected, because Momma had been in good health. I asked Temple if I should come home, and he replied, "If you want to see her alive, I think you should come."

Bernarr and I drove eighteen hours straight through, with his wife Pat and Margaret in the car, and we were able to join all of our brothers and sisters at the hospital in time to see Momma.

Two weeks after my return to Maryland, I was called back to Eros for the funeral. My mother died at age sixty-two on Nov. 12, 1956, the day after her birthday.

Momma had unequivocally requested a private funeral, telling Billy and his wife Tommye Jean, who had been living with her, that this was her wish. But when I got there, as the last child to arrive, people who knew her and loved Momma were lined up in the yard and all around the house, hoping to get in to see her and pay their respects. Her neighbors, former students, members of her church, and people who knew Momma as postmistress were begging for a public funeral in the church.

Helen explained to me that the family had put it to a vote, whether the funeral should be public or private. It was a tie vote until I arrived. I voted to have the church funeral, and allow Momma's many friends to attend. This upset Billy, who felt strongly about carrying out Momma's final wishes.

I Want to See Mother Again
  By Wayne Busbice
  Pub. Old Home Place Music

Tonight here alone it seems I can see
A place that's so dear to me
I haven't seen the home folks since I can't remember when
And I want to see Mother again.

Chorus:

Well, I want to go back to my home on the farm
I want to be with Mother to shield her from harm
I'm tired of ramblin' and livin' in sin
And I want to see Mother again.

When I left home I heard Mother say
Now son, don't stay too long
But time has passed and my memory grows dim
And I've got to see Mother again.

Recitation:
As these thoughts raced through my mind, I decided to return to the old home place that I once knew so well.

As I stepped upon the front porch I turned and gazed upon the familiar places and landmarks I knew so well that brought joy to my heart when I was a boy. The scenes of my childhood were once again before my eyes and it makes me feel proud to know that I was brought up in an atmosphere of true family love and devotion. While still engrossed in my thoughts of the past, I became aware there was no one there to welcome me home--- and even though my heart cried out for Mother I guess I knew she was gone.

Well my mother has gone to that beautiful shore
She's gone to be with Jesus, to suffer no more
When my Lord calls me from this world of sin
I know I'll see Mother again.

I taught agriculture at Gaithersburg High School from 1954 through August of 1959 and during that period of time there were great sociological changes taking place. When the Supreme Court ordered desegregation of schools, the decision had a major impact on housing. Busing was initiated in order to facilitate integration, since blacks and whites lived in separate housing developments and school areas. In the Washington, D.C. area, we saw an explosion of the phenomenon known as "white flight". Some unscrupulous real estate firms encouraged the trend by becoming "blockbusters". This meant buying a large, expensive house in a white affluent neighborhood then offering reduced or free rent to a large black family so the white residents would sell out cheaply and move to the outskirts of town. As whites fled, their houses sold for bargain prices.

As this flight escalated, many of the farmers in my school area began selling their big farms to real estate developers, which had the effect of reducing the number of students interested in enrolling in agriculture. I realized that family farming in Montgomery County was on the wane, and I would have to move farther out in the rural areas of the state if I was going to continue teaching agriculture. My principal, Robert A. Gibson, whom I greatly respected as an outstanding educator, had encouraged me to consider counseling or administration as a future career.

I began to give serious thought to moving to another phase in my education career. I wanted to stay in the Washington area so I could continue my military service at Andrews. And I was enjoying songwriting and performing occasionally.

~15~

"Back Home in the Air National Guard"

I was a lieutenant when I attended my first Air National Guard summer camp, held at Otis AFB on Cape Cod in Hyannis, Massachusetts. Since it takes three fighter squadrons to complete an Air Force Wing, when the D.C. Air National Guard attended summer camp, fighter squadrons from New York and Maryland joined us to give our 113th Tactical Fighter Wing a full complement of troops. As the advanced detachment camp supply officer, it was my responsibility to locate and secure all the supplies and materials we needed to run our two-week training program. The summer detachment commander, Col. Myers, was a hard-driving individual and he wanted everything done yesterday to make sure everything was in good order when the main body arrived.

Some barracks were not ready for occupancy because there were inoperative showers and commodes in two latrines and the plumbers had not been able to get them ready in time. Col. Myers sent 1st Lt Barnes from the Baltimore unit, who was acting as the unit supply officer for the Maryland group, to draw their supplies from HQ (me). Lt. Barnes was assigned to take a few men, check out the tools he needed, and dig two slit trenches for the men assigned to the inoperative toilets. (A slit trench is about eighteen inches wide and about two feet deep, constructed in the trees or outside areas. The men had to pull down their pants and straddle the trench to use it). When Lt. Barnes gave me the forms to sign I noticed he had not filled in the block indicating his position. I asked Barnes, "What is your title?" He replied that he didn't know because this project was not in his job description". So I wrote "Lt. Barnes, Slit Trench Project Officer" and I handed him his copies.

Lt. Barnes was taken aback, and it was an awkward moment. He didn't relish the idea of having Slit Trench Officer as a duty on his permanent record. But he knew I meant no disrespect, and we were all a little batty, working under stress of trying to open up a field that had been in mothballs for ten years.

Col. Myers really was a hard driving, effective officer and he could get things done that seemed impossible. He didn't allow any complaining and he wasn't too well liked because he seemed more interested in accomplishing the mission than appeasing the troops. Of course, this is the military way.

This was my first introduction to the Air National Guard method of operations. Also, it was my first time to meet James Coles, a fellow lieutenant. We became fast military friends and later civilian friends since we both eventually became secondary school principals in Montgomery County, Maryland.

Jim was assigned as the food services officer for summer camp, in charge of the mess hall. We had an initial meeting with Col. Myers after every officer had a chance to assess the area of his responsibility. We reported our findings to Col. Myers at the staff meeting regarding the problems we uncovered and what needed to be done. Lt. Jim Coles reported, "The mess hall hasn't been in operation since 1945. Hardly anything works, everything is rusty, and the facility needs a complete overhaul." Col. Myers asked, "When do you think you will be able to serve your first meal"? Jim replied, "I think I can be ready in about three days, Sir". Without changing his expression, Col. Myers promptly replied, "Lt. Coles, you will serve breakfast tomorrow morning at oh-six-hundred without fail."

We were all a little shook up by that exchange, because we knew what was coming when it was our turn to report. Basically, we all stated, "There doesn't seem to be anything we can't handle, Sir." With that, Col. Meyers said, "Let's get it done gentlemen, meeting dismissed." Jim Coles kept his workers on duty all night and his food service staff served breakfast the next morning as ordered.

My Air National Guard unit deployed to Savannah, Georgia for many of our two weeks' summer field trainings. I would leave at five a.m. to drive down highway U.S. 1 and U.S. 17 to Savannah. This was before I-95 was built, and U.S. highways went through a lot of small towns, so it was an accomplishment to get there in one day.

Integration was a significant issue in the Air National Guard at that time, and we had just integrated our unit. Heretofore we had been an all-white unit. Our military unit at Andrews AFB had a smooth transition to integration and we were very proud of that fact.

When it was announced in the Savannah newspaper that the DC 113th Tactical Fighter Wing's black members would be sleeping in the same barracks with whites at Travis Field in Savannah, the local Ku Klux Klan was upset and requested a permit to march. They dressed all in white. The rule at that time was that the KKK could parade, but had to show their faces – they could not wear the hood over their heads. The Klan conducted a march through Savannah, then formed a convoy of autos and pickup trucks, driving out ten miles to Travis Field, and up and down throughout the base to make their point. The convoy didn't stop or create any incidents so essentially it was a peaceful demonstration.

The regular military had been integrated since the late 1940s, but Travis Field was a civilian-owned contract campsite for Air National Guard troops to conduct summer training. There had been little or no integration at any level in Georgia to this date. Since civilians living around the base were allowed to purchase membership in the pool, black troops were prohibited from swimming.

When my friend Lt. Jim Coles heard about that rule, he decided to make a statement. Jim was a tall, well built, attractive black man in good physical condition. This ban on blacks using the pool didn't go over too well with him, so he went to the barracks, put on a swimsuit, strode up to the pool and ignored the lifeguard's protestations. He marched right up to the diving board and gave a loud Tarzan yell, beat his chest, dove in and swam to the other end, climbed out, turned around, took a bow and waved, with all eyes on him. It was an Olympic size pool and Jim swam the entire length underwater. Some observers worried that he was in trouble because he didn't surface until he reached the end. He left the pool area quietly with all eyes popping but no one challenged him.

The next year the military and the campsite commander had worked everything out and the pool was no longer segregated. Our visiting D.C. troops could relax.

Because beaches in the Savannah area had not yet been integrated in the 1950s, Tybee beach had been designated as a white beach and Atlantic and Hilton Head beaches were designated "for colored only". Jim Coles and Jim Turner were required to use the segregated beaches and I felt bad for them because at Andrews AFB in Washington there were no restrictions. When they returned after a weekend at the "colored" beaches, I asked them how they felt about the situation and how they got along with the people there. They said, "We went straight from the base to the beach on a bus and we met a lot of people who were very friendly. They went out of their way to make us feel welcome. Actually, we felt more comfortable there because everybody we met had been under segregation for years and it is just a way of life here in Georgia."

Our wing commander was Gen. Willard W. Milliken, a good man. He was the kind of person who had a seriousness of purpose with everything he did - he was firm but fair and strictly military. Gen. Milliken always gave a hundred and ten percent, and wanted everyone else to do so.

Milliken was an Iowa farm boy who came up the hard way. During World War II he volunteered for pilot training. He'd always wanted to be a pilot, but he washed out on some technicality on his first effort. He was determined, so he went to Canada to join the flying sergeants program, and was shipped overseas after winning his wings. He was doing a great job as a fighter pilot in combat, so he got released from the Royal Canadian Air Force and applied again in the U.S., where he was accepted as a pilot. He went on to become a triple ace for the U.S. and a war hero. He took the 121st fighter squadron to Korea as their leader, rejoined the D.C. Air National Guard, and soon became the commander.

Gen. Milliken ate, slept, and dreamed military missions and exercises. The troops used to joke behind his back, "He wants the best unit in the worst way, and that's maybe what he'll get." Everyone respected him, but he was not the kind of guy who'd go to the bars at summer camp, slap the troops on the back, and live it up.

At one of our summer camps Gen. Milliken received a call from the Pentagon that high-ranking military brass were planning to visit our unit to observe the quality of our training. Milliken decided on the spur of the moment to hold a parade in their honor. He hurriedly left his office to get things organized. The first officer he ran into was Captain Jim Coles. He explained the situation to Jim and said, "I need a color guard for this parade and in the interest of urgency, I am asking you to form one. And have them prepared to perform at a minute's notice." Jim arranged the color guard and sent word they would be ready – to just let him know the date, time, and place and he would have them there.

The visitors came the next day and when the parade started Gen. Milliken was quite surprised and bemused at the same time because every one of the members of the color guard was black. After the parade, Milliken sent for Jim, who reported in his class A uniform and gave a sharp salute. Jim wondered if he was going to get a chewing out or a pat on the back for providing the snappy color guard for the parade. The general started his conversation with, "Captain Coles, I don't quite understand what happened at the parade, but the next time I ask you to form a color guard, I don't mean a colored guard." Jim replied, "Sir, you asked for a color guard and those men were the only qualified ones available on short notice." Milliken dismissed Capt. Coles with no further discussion. Although the general was suspicious, Jim had no intention of trying to make a statement or embarrass anyone, especially the general – it was merely a coincidence.

We always had a big party at summer camp and Gen. Milliken would drop by for a few minutes but he was a little standoffish – he was the top man and he didn't want to get too familiar with the troops.

I wrote a lot of songs about the Air National Guard, and one of the songs was about him. Fellow officers kept encouraging me to sing it for him. One evening one of my buddies said, "Milliken is coming over to the Officers' Club later and you have got to sing that song about him – he'll probably get a charge out of it." I said, "Okay, but I don't know if I'll get demoted or sent to the guardhouse." I played the guitar and sang my song to the general to the tune of "My Bonnie Lies Over the Ocean".

Back Home in the Air National Guard
   By Wayne Busbice
   Pub Old Home Place Music

In peacetime I'm gonna make colonel
I'll go where it's not very hard
Where you don't have to have any talent
Back home in the Air National Guard

Chorus:
Back home, back home
Back home in the Air National Guard—Zoom! Zoom!
Back home, I said back home,
Back home in the Air National Guard.

In '50 he was a lieutenant
He put his nose to the stone and worked hard
And now he is ou-our commander
Back home in the Air National Guard

The general seemed a little embarrassed, but everyone got a good laugh out of it. By this time we had walked outside. As we talked and milled around, the general complained about the mosquitoes and left a little early. Then my buddies said, "Oh Buzz, you'll be called into the office in the morning in your class A uniform." (Everyone I know named Busbice has been called Buzz at some time or other.)

In the military when you were summoned to the commander's office in full dress uniform, you could expect to be disciplined in some way. But Gen. Milliken took it well, and actually he asked for a signed copy of the first record I recorded.

"Back Home in the Air National Guard" was a spoof on our own officers and men, and it was written in a humorous vein to keep our morale up, because it seemed to us that every time we got in a shooting war, the Pentagon would call up the Reserves, the Air National Guard and the

Army Guard to do the fighting. We thought the regulars seem to miss a lot of the front line action.

I recorded the song, and it was played on jukeboxes at summer camp. My picture was in the town newspaper as well as the base newspaper, playing the guitar sitting under the wing of an F100 fighter plane.

At ANG camp near Tomah, Wisconsin, a couple of years later, I was raising a glass at happy hour in the officers' club when I heard some familiar singing. My buddies recognized the music, and together we went out to find a dozen pilots in their Maryland Air National Guard flight uniforms, gathered on the screened porch. They were drinking beer and serenading the neighborhood with my song.

While I was busy establishing a career in teaching, working on my master's degree at University of Maryland, and putting in monthly duty weekends in the Air National Guard, in the 1950s my brother Bernarr moved to Washington to work for the FBI.

~16~

"Lost" .

My brother Buzz loved bluegrass like it was a religion. Once he mastered the mandolin, the only thing he really cared about was music.

As boys, Buzz and I had a thing going, teasing each other about which style was best to play at gigs -- he wanted to play bluegrass. I wanted to play country, because when we played at clubs, people couldn't dance to bluegrass music -- the tempo was too fast.

When selecting songs to play at private parties, I would sing songs from Hank Williams, Roy Acuff, and Bob Wills' western swing. Buzz always wanted to add a Bill Monroe or a Flatt and Scruggs number, like "Blue Moon of Kentucky". I prefer a traditional rendition of country songs like "Lovesick Blues" by Hank Williams, or "Walking the Floor over You" by Ernest Tubb. As rock and roll started becoming popular, I was disappointed because it dominated the airwaves, displacing good country and western programs. I never did learn to appreciate R&R.

Country music stations played both kinds of music, country and bluegrass, along with western swing, known as country and western. They were all considered the same genre.

Elvis Presley got his start touring with Hank Snow's Grand Ole Opry group. Bluegrass fans didn't particularly want Elvis to be on the same show with Hank because they thought rock and roll was bastardizing country music. As rock and roll grew in popularity, young people, especially, started requesting R&R songs to be played at parties or clubs. When we were playing a gig, people would come up and request "Blue Suede Shoes," "That's All Right, Mama" and other rock songs Elvis had popularized. We replied that we didn't do R&R, we played only country and western. R&R was radically different from the country genre – but eventually Elvis won everybody over.

As a result, country stations became rock stations and it was tougher and tougher for country music artists to get airplay. Listeners were loyal to the country sound but they were being pulled into the rock era. Ultimately the stations reclassified the music they played as rock and roll, country, western, bluegrass, mountain music, old time-y and folk. This proliferation of the different kinds of music became a boost to hootenanny, which is a

141

combination of folk, country and bluegrass. The hootenanny craze lasted a few years and produced popular artists like Peter, Paul and Mary, Joan Baez and Pete Seeger, before it faded and various styles of rock music took over.

Top-billed country music singers now don't sing traditional country: they sing rock music with a country voice and country-style lyrics. The industry is much more sophisticated – recording artists have to be able to read music! But country and bluegrass is experiencing a comeback. I remained a bluegrass fan because it remains roots music and it will never fade completely.

What distinguishes bluegrass from country? Bluegrass artists do not use electric amplified instruments. Their bands use only acoustic instruments including banjo, dobro, fiddle, standup bass, regular guitar, and mandolin. There is occasionally an exception to this rule and that is the use of an electric bass to help keep the rhythm smooth and even and give the sound depth, especially when performing on an outdoor stage. Acoustic instruments – those without any amplification -- keep the music pure and produce a high-pitched, lonely sound, usually peppy, twangy and fast. (Bluegrass musicians exaggerate a little of that, just to make it authentic.)

In Washington D.C. Buzz got acquainted with the musical Stoneman family. Pop Stoneman, who was an early recording artist for Victor records back in the 1920s, had a smash hit entitled "The Sinking of the Titanic," that brought him national and international acclaim.

The Stoneman family of over a dozen children was from the Blue Ridge in Virginia and most of them played in the band. They became regular performers at the Grand Ole Opry in the late 50s and early 60s. Scott Stoneman, the son, was arguably the best fiddle player in the country. When Scott played at the Grand Old Opry for the first time, he got six encores – unheard of.

Buzz and Scott Stoneman were about the same age, and they teamed up to play clubs together. Buzz took the stage name Buzz Busby and used it for the rest of his life.

Mac Wiseman interviewed Buzz and Scott to play with him on his daily WBMD radio show and clubs in Baltimore. Buzz and Scott had made a gentleman's agreement that if only one of them was offered a job, he would not take it. It had to be both of them playing for Mac as sidemen, or neither would play. Both the young men were excellent musicians, and Mac hired both of them. Mac Wiseman's smash hit was on the Dot record label: "I Still Write Your Name in the Sand".

Buzz met and fell in love with Patricia Harriet Padgett, a girl from Riverdale, Maryland. They married on January 7, 1953. At Pat's urging, Buzz decided to return to Washington, where he was already well-known and in demand at local clubs.

Now Buzz was playing a lot of gigs and introducing bluegrass to an enthusiastic Washington audience. Buzz was noted for his tremolo style of mandolin playing, and few in the world could keep up with him. People marveled at his playing and couldn't get enough of it. He fanned his hand so fast on the mandolin strings that it was just a blur. People wanted to hear his kind of music, but nobody else was playing it. Buzz's style of bluegrass caught on like a frenzy in Washington. All his friends, including me, encouraged him to put out a record for greater exposure.

Buzz had his own weekly radio show with Pete Pike on WGAY in Silver Spring, and on WINX in Rockville, both in Maryland; and on WARL in Arlington, Virginia. I was teaching school four miles away in Gaithersburg, and sometimes I'd stop by the WINX studio unannounced to be an impromptu guest on his show, and join the band as vocalist in a gospel number. Buzz never used a script; his live radio shows were spontaneous.

In 1953, Buzz wrote the song "Just Me and the Jukebox", and thought it had potential. So he had a demo made on a 45rpm disk. He was living in an apartment on East Capitol St. in Washington, and he invited me over to listen and give my opinion. I agreed that the song had promise, and suggested he record it. Mac Wiseman also thought the song should be recorded. Later Buzz wrote "Lost", which he liked even better. But with his rapid success during the next few years, he was too busy with radio, club, TV, and constant show dates to concentrate on a recording career.

Buzz organized and began booking his own band, the Bayou Boys, in 1954. Within only three years he became the undisputed top bluegrass artist in the Washington, D.C., area. He was only nineteen when he gained professional recognition as the leader of the top musical group. In that short time, Buzz and the Bayou Boys won the National Country Music contest at Warrenton, Virginia, and performed on national radio shows at the WWVA Jamboree in Wheeling, West Virginia, the Louisiana Hayride in Shreveport, Louisiana, and the New Dominion Barn Dance in Richmond, Virginia.

Buzz and his band had the first daily live country/bluegrass show on television in Washington. It was carried on WRC, an affiliate of NBC. The show ran for twenty-eight weeks and was immensely popular -- partly because Washington was home to many transplants from the Blue Ridge mountains who grew up with country music, but primarily because up until then homegrown music had been available only on radio. I visited Buzz a few times when The Bayou Boys were playing at a club in Bethesda. Mike Seeger, Pete Seeger's younger brother, also dropped by to sit in on a session regularly. Buzz and Mike backed up my singing on their mandolins.

FEATURING THE FOLLOWING BLUEGRASS GREATS:
Buzz Busby, Scott Stoneman, Charlie Waller, Don Stover, Carl Nelson,
Pete Pike, Tom Morgan, Eddie Stubbs, Donnie Bryant, Porter Church, Smiley Hobbs,
and many others...

Buzz's down-home manner and his intense mandolin tremolo backed by enormous talent had made him a star. He played often on the same stage as Elvis Presley, Johnny Cash, Jerry Lee Lewis, Johnny Horton, George Jones and other luminaries.

Buzz Busby and the Bayou Boys were regularly featured on the Louisiana Hayride – second in popularity only to the Grand Ole Opry. While living in Louisiana, the group discovered the pace was very relaxed compared to their hectic schedule in Washington, D.C. Buzz had time to concentrate on his recording career, and released a 45rpm on Jiffy records, an independent label. "Lost" was selected to be the A Side, and "Just Me and the Jukebox" on the B Side. Top notch bluegrass musicians on the A Side included Buzz on vocals and mandolin, Charlie Waller on guitar, Scott Stoneman on fiddle, Don Stover on the banjo, and Lee Cole on bass.

Side B featured the same musicians except Dobber Johnson replaced Scott Stoneman on the fiddle.

Just Me and the Jukebox
  By Buzz Busby
  Pub. Jiffy Publishers

There's people all around me the night life is so gay
I'm reminded of you as I listen to the jukebox play
It tells me of our wasted love and how you've been untrue
Just me and the jukebox to tell my troubles to.

Chorus:
Just me and the jukebox to pass the time of day
Just me and the jukebox who knows the price I pay
A glass of wine to ease my mind since we've been apart
Just me and the jukebox who knows my broken heart.

The wine it flows so freely to ease my aching brain
The jukebox tells me how you've caused all our grief and shame
The gay nightlife you've chosen instead of a happy home
Just me and the jukebox, who knows I'm all alone.

We were all surprised when "Just Me and the Jukebox" got a lot more airplay than "Lost". "Just Me and the Jukebox" was more commercial. It had a honkytonk flavor. The song spoke the language of the down-home country boy, and the beat was compatible with a dance tempo, unlike the traditional bluegrass tunes.

On the other hand, "Lost" had the customary high lonesome sound and also a haunting character, with an unusual arrangement. It starts off with a slow, high-pitched lonesome sound, then breaks out into a fast pace that carries the listener right along with it into a frenzy. Disk jockeys said "Lost" grabs your attention and you can't help but listen. Buzz once said that he felt bluegrass had a spiritual quality, and that inspired him to write "Lost" using a different approach. Jerry Garcia of the Grateful Dead liked "Lost" so much that he and Peter Rowan used it on their show dates in the 1970s, and placed it on their album, "Old and In the Way, Vol. 2". Garcia called it the best bluegrass song ever written.

Buzz had found a unique niche for his music. Eddie Stubbs, the WSM announcer known as the Voice of the Grand Ole Opry, had this to say about

Buzz's music in the liner notes of a retrospective 1950s CD ("Buzz Busby: Going Home," by Starday Records):

Buzz Busby and the Bayou Boys on Starday Records represent the high lonesome sound of bluegrass at its absolute highest level of intensity. No one, not even Bill Monroe or the Stanley Brothers at their zenith, ever recorded anything with more passionate heart, soul, and pain than "Lonesome Road", "Cold and Windy Night", and "Where Will This End". The legendary Scott Stoneman, one of the most soulful fiddlers in bluegrass, recorded some of the best and most intense work with Buzz on these recordings. When it comes to this style of bluegrass, this is as good as it will ever be done.

The same album carried this tribute by Marty Stuart, Grand Ole Opry star and master mandolinist:

Buzz Busby and the Bayou Boys are the poster boys for that old song, "The Wicked Path of Sin". Their music comes from the darkest regions of the soul. It personifies the high lonesome sound of bluegrass. They scream with terror as they cry out from the depths of the unknown. It is the most wicked bluegrass music ever made this side of heaven.

In Louisiana, the band members missed the Washington style of living and they all decided to return to D.C. after about a year. Soon after their son Timothy was born, Buzz and Pat decided to split up.

In the summer of 1957 Buzz and the Bayou Boys were working gigs regularly. Many of the original musicians had been replaced, but they were still a tight, professional group. Buzz demanded perfection from his sidemen. After each show, the group stopped in at their favorite watering holes to meet and greet their fellow musician friends and have a beer or two. After a night of drinking after their Fourth of July performance, Buzz fell asleep in the back seat of their car. The driver suddenly swerved and crashed head-on into a utility pole.

Buzz was pronounced dead on the scene by medics. But on the way to the hospital, the technicians were able to re-start his heart. He remained in a coma for two days and was hospitalized for over a month. The other men who had been in the car were treated and released.

I visited Buzz at Prince George's General Hospital after he awakened. He continually asked me, "Am I going to live or die?" For some reason he thought I knew the answer. I tried to assure Buzz he was going to make it. I told him to relax and be quiet, and everything would be all right.

During Buzz's long convalescence, which lasted over six months, the Bayou Boys needed to work. They re-organized under the leadership of Bill Emerson, the banjo player, who had driven home separately the night of the accident. They named the new group the Country Gentlemen, which became nationally and internationally famous. Later, the Country Gentlemen spun off into the Seldom Scene and other groups. In the beginning, they continued playing in the style Buzz had popularized.

Bill Emerson later went on to join the Navy to play with the U.S. Navy Band Country Current, and became its leader with the rank of chief musician. The Country Current tours the U.S. as a recruiting tool. Bill is considered one of the top banjo players in the country.

Meanwhile, rock and roll was replacing country and bluegrass on local stations. Buzz couldn't seem to get straightened out. He became addicted to alcohol and faded away from the music scene.

Lost
By Buzz Busby
Pub. Jiffy Publishers

Since you turned me down all I do is ramble round
Now I don't care what happens to me
My heart was young and gay; since the day you went away
Now life has no meaning to me.

Chorus:
Lost, lost, lost,
Lost in this world without you
Lost, lost, lost,
Lost in this world without you.

Those love words you said to me still haunt my memory
It seems you're on my mind both day and night
The lies that you told still torture my soul
Love was blind, I guess I couldn't see.

Many of the musicians in the Washington area idolized Buzz for his talent, but they didn't particularly want to be around him when he'd been drinking. His friends would call me to say, "Buzz is great, and I love him like a brother, but he's been at my house two or three days and I can't get him to leave. I would like to bring him over to your house and maybe you can sober him up."

I became a surrogate father to Buzz and tried to keep him on the straight and narrow but to no avail. He just couldn't seem to get it together, ending up in jail periodically and serving two short prison sentences. As a result of one incident he ended up in Pineville, the same mental institution

147

our Aunt Laura had died in. After a few weeks he decided he didn't want to be there, so he escaped out the window in the time-honored manner of tying the bed sheets together. But before he reached the ground the sheets gave way and Buzz fell and injured his back, which gave him lifelong problems.

Buzz always hung around with the guys who were down on their luck. They looked up to him for his talent and boosted his ego. I've often thought Buzz might have done better in his career if he had hung around with a better class of losers, as the joke goes.

After Buzz's light dimmed in popularity, he slid down further professionally because of his drinking and unreliability. He became a disk jockey in Leonardtown, Maryland, where he and his band played in local clubs. While living there he was drinking and taking a prescription diet pill called Benzedrine, known as bennies or pep pills. When he needed a refill, his doctor was reluctant to continue his dosage and gave him a refill for a smaller quantity, with a warning for Buzz to cut back.

By this time Buzz had become dependent on the pep pills to do his job as disc jockey at the daily radio station as well as to perform at the club three or four nights a week. When the doctor wasn't looking, Buzz took one of his blank prescription pads from his desk. He filled it out, forged the doctor's signature, and took it down to the pharmacy to have it filled. The pharmacist recognized it was not the doctor's writing and called the police. Buzz was arrested, put in jail and charged with attempt to obtain diet pills using a forged prescription.

I talked to a lawyer in Leonardtown who was kind enough to investigate the charges at the courthouse. He said in his opinion Buzz didn't need legal representation. He had no record at that time and the charges were not that severe -- basically forgery. The lawyer advised that considering the charge Buzz should throw himself on the mercy of the court.

Leonardtown at that time was having an upsurge of drug incidents and authorities were under pressure to do something about it. When the trial date came, the charges had been changed to "obtaining narcotics on a forged prescription" instead of the original charge of "attempt to obtain diet pills on a forged prescription". This elevated the charge to a narcotics violation, much more serious than forgery. Buzz pleaded guilty as advised, and was sentenced to two years in prison at Jessup, Maryland. Buzz knew he was guilty of forgery and he was under the impression that that was what he was charged with.

Dressed in my Air Force major's uniform, I visited Buzz in prison. The guard at the sign-in desk looked surprised, and asked me, "Major, do you have someone serving time in here?" I said, "Yes, Bernarr Busbice is my brother." The guard shook his head in disbelief. "I can't believe that, and you a major in the Air Force. I'm a retired chief warrant officer, and that doesn't make any sense to me." I admitted it was very embarrassing.

When I got to Buzz, he explained that he had been treated unfairly and he begged me to get him out. He insisted that he had not obtained narcotics or any substance and the only thing he had done was forge a prescription for diet pills. I agreed I would investigate and help if I could. But I said I would not lift a finger if the charges were accurate.

As I left the prison, I asked the warrant officer for his advice, giving a synopsis of what Buzz had told me. The guard explained the most serious aspect: the record had been tabbed as a narcotics case. He said if that was allowed to stand, it would follow Buzz the rest of his life and cause a myriad of problems for him in the future.

I asked the guard if I should start by seeing the warden. He doubted the warden would see me because I didn't have any evidence to present, only hearsay. Instead, he recommended that I conduct a thorough investigation by going to Leonardtown and talking with the doctor, the pharmacist and the judge to get all the facts. He advised me to ask the judge to write a letter to the warden if I could convince him that errors were made. I thanked the guard for being candid and willing to help a fellow officer.

The next day I asked for a day of leave from Andrews, drove the two hours to Leonardtown, Maryland, and located the courthouse, the doctor's office and the pharmacy.

I was dressed in my class A uniform, dress blues with ribbons, for effect. I decided to start with the doctor and when I arrived at his office he was seeing patients. I walked in and told the receptionist that I wished to have a personal conference with the doctor when it was convenient. I fully expected that I would not get an audience with him until he had finished with all his patients. To my surprise, he asked the receptionist to show me in.

At first, the doctor seemed anxious and defensive. I apologized for coming in without an appointment but I only had one day off to visit Leonardtown to try and find out what had happened to my brother. The doctor explained that he had been unaware that Buzz had taken a prescription pad from his desk until the police came by later that day and asked him to identify the forged prescription. He was very forthright, friendly and cooperative.

I proceeded to the drugstore to talk with the pharmacist who had turned Buzz in. The pharmacist, too, was very friendly and cooperative and explained the routine he had followed in handling the matter. I was convinced by this time that neither of them were out to get Buzz or were a part of a conspiracy to trap him as Buzz suspected.

I next went to the courthouse to see if I could possibly get a chance to speak with Judge Dorsey, the presiding judge at Buzz's trial. I explained to the judge's secretary who I was and why I was there and asked her to see if the judge had time to discuss the case with me. Surprisingly, she returned and said the judge would see me now. By this time I was congratulating myself for making the decision to wear my uniform.

Judge Dorsey was folksy and down-to-earth, and he seemed eager to help. I summarized what I had done and what I had learned from everyone I had talked to. I explained that my major concern was that Jessup prison records indicated that Buzz was guilty of obtaining narcotics with a forged prescription. Judge Dorsey brought out two very thick law books and showed me the paragraphs that pertained to the case and they were contradictory about the classification of benzedrine. One reference indicated that benzedrine was an amphetamine and the other indicated that it could cause dependency or be addictive like a narcotic. Judge Dorsey stated that the prosecutor went with the narcotic reference. I pointed out that Buzz did not obtain anything but only attempted to secure an amphetamine via forgery.

I asked the judge if he would be willing to write a letter to the warden indicating that the prison record should be corrected. I was very pleased when the judge agreed to write to the warden and state that he, the judge, would have no objection if Buzz were released on probation. This got the ball rolling and everything began to fall into place. The warden accepted the judge's recommendation, and contacted Governor Tawes of Maryland, who agreed to release Buzz provided that Buzz could show he had a place to live and steady employment. Our brother, Billy, a high school coach, agreed to take Buzz in to live with his family in Louisiana; and a long time family friend, Willard Kilpatrick, agreed to give him a job at his Ford agency in Jonesboro.

A further condition of Gov. Tawes' was that Governor Jimmy Davis of Louisiana would accept him as a parolee in the state. Buzz knew Jimmy Davis personally from the days on the Louisiana Hayride, when Buzz and the Bayou Boys performed with him. Visiting bands would back up Jimmy, a former country music superstar, who wrote "You are My Sunshine." Buzz and the Bayou Boys had played for him several times, and they had developed a mutual respect. Naturally, Governor Davis agreed to allow Buzz to live in Louisiana.

Our family was very pleased for Buzz and hoped he could change his ways while living where he was born and raised. It worked well for a time but when he had served out his probation he decided to return to the Washington area to live. There he reverted back to his old lifestyle.

These were dark days for Buzz and a very stressful time for me. Luckily, his close buddies kept me informed of his antics so together we could prevent him from putting himself in harm's way -- which was not an easy task. When I tried to counsel him on improving his life, Buzz admitted, "I started at the top, and worked diligently until I reached the bottom." Buzz's friends had hundreds of stories like this, and we all felt that he wouldn't live to be forty. Buzz felt the same way and sometimes said so to me.

Buzz suffered from long term illness in his later years. He battled diabetes and Parkinson's disease. But he still performed occasionally, and he continued to receive honors and recognition for his contributions to bluegrass. In 1978 Buzz's rendition of "Mandolin Twist" was included in Volume 14 of the U.S. Folk Music in America Series, as a part of the Library of Congress Bicentennial Program, and is kept in the Library of Congress Archive of Folk Song. The album notes expand our understanding of his music:

This brilliant mandolin piece is a medley incorporating standard bluegrass banjo tunes – Earl Scruggs' "Earl's Breakdown" and "Flint Hill Special" and Sonny Osborne's "Sunny Mountain Chimes."... the melodies call for a glissando effect, created by tuning the mandolin strings down and back. The "chimes" are played by touching the strings at their harmonic points...Though he appears and records infrequently, [Busby] is, along with Bill Monroe, one of the most original mandolin stylists in the bluegrass idiom.

In the 1980s, Time-Life produced fourteen box sets, each containing three records, in a series titled Country and Western Music. Buzz and the Bayou Boys were featured on Album 12 of the series with "Just Me and the Jukebox". Buzz was the only bluegrass musician represented.

~17~

"Goin' Back to Dixie"

Inspired by my brother's success, two of my Air Force buddies offered to finance a record production for me as a novelty. They had heard me play for military functions and parties and at the officers' club at Andrews Air Force Base. I asked Buzz and his band to accompany me on the recording.

My first 45rpm was recorded at Circle Recording Studio, a few blocks from the White House. We chose Circle because it had a reputation for quality work. The studio had several hits including a record for Grandpa Jones, a Grand Ole Opry star.

I'd never been in a studio before and I was impressed with all the recording equipment. The technician had to determine the type of music so he could place us in the proper positions. I sang lead and played rhythm guitar, and was backed by a fiddle, piano, bass, and Buzz on electric guitar. We had to do a couple of takes so the recording engineer could establish the proper sound level for the instruments and vocals. I was very excited and suffered the usual stage fright, though there was no audience. After several takes we all got into the swing of things and my anxiety dissipated. We cut four sides that day, just in case the record sold well enough to release a second effort.

My record was released on the Ott label in 1957 and included two of my own songs: "Going Back to Dixie" backed by "I'll Love You Forever". To my surprise, it did very well.

I had been inspired to write "Goin' Back to Dixie" while driving to Louisiana to see my family in the summer of 1956 with Margaret, John, and Margaret's mother in the car. It was a beautiful, sunny day, I was feeling especially good, and I was on my way home to see Momma, so I began making up a tune to hum while we rode along in our '54 Chevy, traveling down Route 11 through Tennessee, Alabama, and Mississippi. After a while I sang out loud as I made up the words to go with it. Margaret and John and Mrs. Woodward liked the sound, and encouraged me, suggesting rhymes. My heartstrings were pulling me back to my roots; that made me happy, and I wanted to sing about it.

On our drive back home to Maryland, I worked on polishing up the tune and the lyric. As soon as we arrived, I got out my guitar and my tape recorder, and recorded it over and over until the song came together. This was all done by ear, since I never learned to read music.

Goin' Back to Dixie
By Wayne Busbice
Pub. Old Home Place Music

Headin' for the Southland on a sunny day
Goin' back to Dixie, goin' there to stay
To a little ol' country town down ol' Louisiana way
Yes, I'm headin' back to Dixie where the Cajun girls like to play.

I'm riding in a boxcar and it hurts my back
I'd rather be drivin' my old Cadillac
But I lost all my money, a gamblin' and ramblin' around
So I'm headin' back to Dixie, and there I'm gonna settle down.

I gambled in Chicago and down in Washington
When I reach dear ol' Dixie I won't even play for fun
I've learned my lesson well and my heart is in my mouth
'Cause I'm headin' back to Dixie to the deep, deep South.

Yes, I'm headin' for the Southland, when I draw my pay
I know I'll meet my friends all along the way
I'll meet them and greet them, and they will hear me say
I'm coming back to Dixie, and Dixie's where I'm gonna stay.

This record made the Top Ten in the D.C. metro area and number 60 in the nation, boosted by a lot of airplay by Don Owens and Tom "Tomcat" Reeder at WARL radio. Deejays classified my song as rockabilly. I figured the record probably did so well because it was a time of high mobility as southerners were migrating north for better jobs. I tapped into their nostalgia for home.

I did a guest spot on the Don Owens Show on Channel 5 WTTG TV in Washington. I also appeared on TV in Savannah, Georgia, while there for Air National Guard summer camp. Later we released the other two sides on the Ott label, of my own songs: " Tomorrow I May be Gone" backed with "Live Your Life With Care". The Ott label was a project of my Air Force buddies Wilbur Ott and Don Higgs. They hoped sales would be improved by buyers who confused Ott label with the very successful Nashville Dot label.

After my releases, Ben Adelman of Empire Records, who was recording Buzz's albums for Starday, invited me to work with him. At that time Ben Adelman was the recording manager for Jimmy Dean, Patsy Cline, and Roy Clark. I made a few singles and albums for Ben. Ben said to be successful, a musician had to follow the three R's: records, radio, and routing. Because of the interest in my records, especially "Goin' Back to Dixie," he thought he could make a career for me in music if I would quit my job and go on the road. But I told Ben that was too scary; my brother Buzz was a good example of why I would not want to go on the road.

Buzz had moved too quickly from obscurity to a TV show and success as the most popular musician in the Washington area. At the time of my conversation with Ben, Buzz was known for no-showing at his recording dates and stage shows. I could see the old saying was true: for every successful artist you can find ten who are on the skids. I was not willing to give up my career in teaching.

Another factor in my thinking was the payola scandal, which had recently turned the record industry upside down. In order to get airplay, record promoters had to grease the palms of popular disk jockeys. Only the major labels could afford to pay the price to have records promoted in big cities. This had the result of proliferating the small, independent record producers who could afford to pay the disk jockeys in smaller markets. It wasn't long until the intense competition resulted in charges of corruption and the record industry and the press began investigating. I just didn't want to get embroiled in that scenario.

Fading public interest in classic country music was another reason for my reluctance. At that time rock and roll had pretty much eliminated country and bluegrass in the public favor. It wasn't until Bill Monroe and a few leading bluegrass artists thought up the idea of bluegrass festivals during the hootenanny (folk music) rage in the 1960s that bluegrass artists were able to make a good living again. Traditional country never came back in a big way, but because of the festivals, bluegrass became a well-known roots music with a hardcore following of college kids and both city and country dwellers.

I recorded a few records under my real name but disk jockeys had difficulty pronouncing my last name correctly. Ben Adelman said we had to do something about that. He felt I should not use Busby to avoid confusion with my brother. Since I am of Scots-Irish descent, I suggested several names and Ben selected Red (from my old high school nickname) McCoy. We called my backup group the Sons of the Soil, to give the record a down-home farm flavor.

Ben Adelman re-recorded and released "Goin' Back to Dixie" on the Empire label. He agreed to record my original songs, have them pressed, and handle the publicity and marketing. The production costs just about equaled the sales receipts so I really didn't make any money.

About this time rock and roll pushed country music off the airwaves and many country and bluegrass artists were experiencing hard times. Most of the deejays classified my songs as rockabilly, which was really country with a little rock-n-roll thrown in. Long-playing records were replacing 45s so Ben had me make three LP albums, one for Mount Vernon Records from New York and two for Sutton Records of California. Most of them were original songs that I wrote and they made a little money. I really didn't care about that because I was having fun just recording and getting exposure for the songs I had written and having them published through BMI --Broadcast Music Incorporated.

I was willing to continue with my music locally as long as the effort would not interfere with my career in education. I was content to make a few records, play local gigs, parties, and the Montgomery County fair, and be what is known as a regional artist.

In 1961 commemorations of the beginning of the Civil War were being held all over the nation.

Washington had its own nearby battlefield, in Manassas, Virginia. There was to be a grand re-enactment of the first battle of the war, won by the South and called First Manassas by southerners. (Northerners call it Bull Run.) My son John and his cousin Glenn wore their Rebel soldier outfits when I took them out to the battlefield. Since my heart was still in Dixie, I wrote and recorded a song called "First Battle of Bull Run", on the Empire label.

My record got a lot of airplay on local country stations. I know of at least one teacher in Washington who used the song as a history lesson for her class, and she took them on a field trip to the re-enactment. The kids sang my song all the way there on the bus, and all the way back, complete with rebel yells.

First Battle of Bull Run
  By Wayne Busbice
  Pub. Old Home Place Music

Look away, Dixieland…

The very first battle of the Civil War
In eighteen sixty-one
Where the Yanks met the Rebels for the very first time

At the Battle of Bull Run.

They charged each other with thirty thousand troops
Available on each side
General Beauregard said, with a Rebel yell,
Yankee, we'll skin your hide.

At first it looked like McDowell's troops
Had the battle won
Then Jackson joined the Rebel band
And set the Yankees on the run.

The congressmen brought their wives along
To have a picnic and watch the fun
But Stonewall Jackson turned the tide
At the Battle of Bull Run.

He commanded his troops with a steady hand
As they began to fall
A brother officer made the remark
There stands Jackson like a stone wall.

Oh Stonewall Jackson was a mighty, mighty man
They called him Lee's right hand
He fought for what he thought was right
To preserve our Dixieland.

~18~

You're in the Schoolhouse Now

I was a counselor at Eastern Junior High for four years, before being promoted to the position of assistant principal and transferred to Broome Junior High School in Rockville, Maryland. Students at Broome were primarily from blue-collar families and ranked about equal to the national average in ability and intelligence. This gave me an opportunity to develop curriculum, make innovative schedules, and supervise the instructional program. I was also the boys' disciplinarian, which was the most challenging part of my assignment. The disciplinarian usually gets his name written in unflattering terms in the boys' bathrooms. However, I escaped that honor because the bad boys couldn't spell it.

It seemed I always had a few students in my office who dropped by just to talk, or who were sent by teachers for counseling. They were all curious about my middle name. The initial E was on my desk nameplate. I made a game out of it with the kids, and said, "You try to guess and I'll let you know when you're right." They were seated facing me at my desk, but hanging right behind them on the wall were diplomas for my bachelor's and master's degrees, all containing my full name in gothic print. The kids would come up with all the names they could think of, but nobody ever guessed Evon, pronounced Yvonne. And my secretary wouldn't give it away when she was asked, either. Each time they left my office I'd encourage them to keep guessing. "Don't give up," I told them.

In every school, some teachers stand out because of their self-styled philosophy in dealing with kids. Broome had a reputation of working very closely with students' learning disabilities. But Margaret Byrd was a dedicated teacher from the "old school" who ran her classroom with strict discipline. Occasionally some of her frustrated students would lash out.

Mrs. Byrd came down to my office and complained about one of the boys, who had just insulted her in the classroom. "Exactly what did he say?" I asked. She said, "He called me a mean ugly bitch. And as the disciplinarian, what are you going to do about that?" Mrs. Byrd didn't take any guff from anybody, the principal or anybody else.

She was very indignant, so I just looked at her without expression as I gathered my thoughts on how I should respond. After a minute, she demanded, "Well?! What are you thinking about?" Unable to find a diplomatic response, I gave up and said, "Well, you know, I think maybe

157

the kid's right." I braced myself for an attack. After nearly jumping out of her chair, Mrs. Byrd broke into laughter, and I joined in. After that episode we became very close friends, and Mrs. Byrd left my office laughing.

Everything went well and I was enjoying my tenure at Broome but toward the end of the school year the principal of Leland Junior High School in Chevy Chase requested that I be transferred there in September of that year. My current principal at Broome preferred to keep me, but he relented when the superintendent explained that I was to be groomed to replace the principal at Leland in a year or two. So I transferred to Leland JHS as assistant principal.

Leland was considered the most prestigious junior high school in Montgomery County and I had the privilege of working with embassy kids, senators' and congressmen's children. There were only four students in the school with IQs below one hundred.

Senator Tower from Texas had three daughters in our school, and when he wanted to take them on trips back home to Texas during the school year, he would call me personally to make arrangements, since I handled attendance. He was the only high-level official who did this; other dignitaries would have their wives or secretaries coordinate with the school for special requests.

All of the Tower children were very good students and served on the Student Council, which I sponsored. On a plane trip to Dallas to visit family, I was wearing my Air Force uniform when I was seated with Senator Tower. I introduced myself as his daughters' assistant principal and said I knew them well. I knew the senator was on the Senate Armed Services Committee, so when he looked oddly at my uniform, I quickly explained that since I was in the active reserve, wearing the uniform for travel was allowed, and was required to get a military-price ticket. Then the senator launched into a thorough discussion of his committee work to approve special funding for a Navy project.

Later, Senator Tower was nominated for Secretary of Defense under President G. H. Bush but was not confirmed because of rumors regarding sexual harassment during troop inspections. He died tragically in a plane crash in 1991, accompanied by one of his daughters.

Many of the affluent parents in Chevy Chase treated teachers as if they were their servants. And some of the teachers seemed intimidated by having to discipline children of famous parents. I was interested to note that although students from very affluent families predominated at Leland, they misbehaved just as often as any middle-class kid, but in more socially acceptable ways.

Secretary of Defense Clark Clifford's grandson was difficult to deal with, as was the boy's mother. Two teachers came to me one day upset about the boy, who was burning incense in a corner of the cafeteria. Because of their reluctance to be firm with him, I had to intervene. It was hard to make him understand why he couldn't do exactly what he pleased at school, since it was not explicitly forbidden by any rule he knew of.

One set of parents who were half-owners of the Philadelphia Eagles football team had a son attending school at Leland, and every time they flew to Paris or elsewhere on their many vacations the son would be left home under the supervision of the live-in maid. Most of the time he would arrive at school chauffeured in a Cadillac with a television in the back seat.

He was basically a good kid but every time he was left behind he usually gave himself time off from school. He was a genius at figuring out how to engage in bizarre behavior to get attention from his classmates. He would steal locks off lockers and hoard them for his "collection" to impress his buddies. He liked to steal a copy of each of his textbooks from other kids to keep at home. In this way, he didn't have to carry his books back and forth from school. When I caught up with him about this matter, he readily broke down and wept and had no explanation for his behavior, but his mother couldn't believe it. She requested permission to purchase an extra set of textbooks for him but the school board denied it. They contended that textbooks were purchased on the basis of enrollment and to sell any from the school's stock would result in a shortage for the students enrolled.

I recommended that the mother go directly to the publishers to order books privately, if she felt her son shouldn't have to be bothered carrying his books back and forth like everybody else. She ordered him a full set of books to keep at home.

In 1967 Israel attacked Egypt, instigating the Six Day War. At Leland, there was a precipitous drop in attendance – about a third of the students were absent. My job as attendance officer was to determine if a student was legally absent, or should be penalized in some way. When questioning them, I learned their justification was, "We are at war, you know!" I had to explain that the United States was not at war with anyone, and just because you're Jewish you can't stay out of school to support Israel.

In 1968 I enrolled in The American University in Washington, D.C., to get my doctorate in education administration. To meet my requirements for four fields of study, I chose Educational Management, Secondary School Administration, Counseling, and Psychology, and for my required tools of research I chose Education Statistics, and Testing and Evaluation.

There were many other graduate schools in the D.C. area but the American University was referred to as the "Ivy League" college in the metro area. Also, it was the only graduate school that didn't require doctoral students to attend full time during their last semester prior to graduation. Without this proviso and the G.I. Bill I could not have made it financially.

My philosophy professor was Dr. Burr, a direct descendant of Aaron Burr, and he was a real eccentric. He believed in ghosts and other beings that walked the earth. Once in a while he would stop lecturing and talk to these apparitions as they hung from the ceiling or walked through the classroom. He acted as if this were normal. Dr. Burr frequently explained to the class how Thomas Jefferson had been grossly unfair to Vice President Burr and had turned the country against him.

Tip O'Neill, former speaker of the House of Representatives, once said, "All politics is local." And I would like to add that I have encountered politics at every level of employment.

Although I had been promised the principal's job when my principal left Leland, someone else was placed in his position for political reasons. I was very disappointed but I was assured that it had nothing to do with me and I would get the next school opening. I was quite upset.

For different and valid reasons three more principal slots slipped through my grasp because of other forces at work, including a teachers' strike, minority integration of principal ranks, and experimental programs. Each time apologies were made and the superintendent continued to counsel me to be patient because, he said, "It *is* going to happen." I had faith in the superintendent and his staff and a good understanding of the politics involved.

It took three more years in which I was "often the bridesmaid but never the bride," but one day the associate superintendent stopped by my office to ask if I would be interested in being principal of Gaithersburg Junior High. He said, "I can assure you this time you will receive the appointment because the superintendent and the Board think you are the ideal person."

Gaithersburg Junior was the principalship I most desired, because I had taught at the senior high in Gaithersburg for six years and knew the faculty and community. I finally had achieved my goal at age thirty-five, and I was elated. I was once offered a position of supervisor in the school system central office, but turned it down. After that, I asked for a notation to be placed in my personnel file that I wished to remain a principal. I strongly believe my strength as an educator was working directly with students.

When I arrived for duty at Gaithersburg Junior, I discovered that about half the staff were teachers I knew from Gaithersburg High. If I hadn't taught in the community before, I would have experienced culture shock, coming from Leland. The student body was made up of children representing all levels except inner city families. We had suburban children, farm children, and city children, from blue collar and white collar families. Minorities numbered around twenty-two percent, compared to a total of only two minority students at my former school.

The median test scores at Gaithersburg Junior were equal to the national norms as measured by national standardized tests, although they were well below the performance of the Leland students. However, the demographics of the school area represented, basically, a microcosm of the United States. Before my arrival, Gaithersburg Junior High School had been characterized as a traditional school, devoid of innovative programs that used standard teaching techniques.

During my first year there I worked on gaining the confidence and support of the staff, students, and parents, which helped me make many changes. I instituted an instructional team concept (called school-within-a-school) that divided the students into groups of 120, to be managed by a team of teachers and one administrator and counselor, who could then meet and share teaching techniques and problem solving. I started a work-oriented curriculum program, which released some students for half a day of vocational training in local businesses after their classes. And I established a seven-period day to expand course options for developmental reading, Spanish, German, Latin, photography, dramatics, journalism, study skills, and agriculture.

Being an old Ag teacher, I recognized an opportunity to institute an agricultural program, since we fed into Gaithersburg High, which had a popular Ag program. I called it Environmental Agriculture so it could be a broader program. At that time no one in Maryland was teaching environmental Ag -- this program was the first one in the state in a junior high.

To do this, I solicited support from the state Supervisor of Agriculture, the University of Maryland, and the vocational technical supervisor of Montgomery County Public Schools. The program became popular, and other Maryland schools followed our lead. Virginia sent a state supervisor to interview me and observe our model. He returned and recommended it, and agriculture was ultimately begun in Virginia junior high schools too.

A school-based Mark Twain program was begun in 1971 as a pilot project to deal with children who were of average ability or higher, but were experiencing problems and not progressing normally in the classroom setting. Gaithersburg JHS was designated as a community school in 1974 and an aquatic center with an Olympic sized pool was built in 1976. This project – school and pool both available for public use after school hours -- was labeled a dramatic example of community-school planning and cooperation. It was the only such project in the state of Maryland at the time, and as far as I know, it still is.

When I first became principal, we had a student body of approximately 1000 students, in a facility built for 900. Within three years, because of the explosive development in the suburbs our student population increased to 1300. This required portable classrooms to be set up behind the school, but they still did not meet our needs for space. I scheduled classes in the cafeteria all through the day, except for lunch. One of the most creative classrooms I set up was a seventh grade science class in the band storage room. The poor science students had to work in a tiny closet crammed full of instruments. The instrumental music teacher was unhappy, but understanding.

Concomitant with the increased enrollment came more likelihood of vandalism. In a plea to the Superintendent of Schools for more classrooms, I told him that increasing the student population arithmetically increased difficulties geometrically.

I organized parent volunteers and cooperative teachers, and made a grid of the school. Initially I designated the halls with letters of the alphabet, A, B, C, and so forth. But when I presented it to the faculty and my plans for "Hall A" were met with laughter and jeering, I sheepishly recognized my mistake. I renamed them A Hall and B Hall, etc. I assigned teachers to cover each hallway and bathroom, and took the doors off the boys' bathrooms so any smoke could be noticed from the hallway. By these means we were able to keep vandalism to a minimum.

At the end of the 1976 school year, the Montgomery County Realtors' Association presented me with an award for having the least amount of vandalism out of more than 200 schools in the county. I also received kudos from parents, and an article in the *Gaithersburg Gazette*, a widely circulated suburban paper. I was proud of that and became the envy of my principal pals.

I greatly enjoyed my work at Gaithersburg Junior, and made lifelong friends. I continue to feel that Gaithersburg Junior is my professional family. And of course had I not been assigned to that school, I would never have met my current wife, who joined the staff after I had been there two years. While principal there, I received my doctorate from The American University, an Ed. D., in 1971.

I was fortunate to have an experienced, dedicated staff. Faculty and staff at Gaithersburg Junior totaled about 100. This group was in itself a small community, which was reflective of the greater community. We had a complete range of people with their own beliefs, ideas, lifestyles and character. I remember more than a hundred stories about memorable people in my school, but only a few can be told here.

The best teachers were apparent to the parents, the students, and the faculty itself. There was a natural aristocracy of merit and effectiveness.

Lucy Goldsmith was recognized by everyone as a teacher who could inspire any student at any level of ability. Many teachers came to her for advice on dealing with their most difficult pupils. Lucy was everyone's mother and beloved by all. The most intractable student would behave in her English class because her spirit shone through in everything she did.

Joe Rhinehart was a dedicated advocate for his students. Going beyond his regular English classes, he established a journalism program that won awards as number one in the state for several years. It was very rare to have a journalism program in a junior high. Joe basically pioneered the concept for the state of Maryland. He also sponsored a yearbook, the first one in the school, at my suggestion. I gave him all the funds from the yearbook sales to run his journalism program.

Probably because we both loved music, Ellsworth Briggs, the instrumental music teacher, and I had a natural bond. Elly had a unique friendly way of dealing with students in band and orchestra. Elly organized both the regular student variety show and the faculty-parent variety show that I initiated. The audience loved it when Elly and I did our act together, "Okie from Muskogee," in our string ties, cowboy hats and white buck shoes. We both sang; I played guitar and he played bass.

One young music student was teaching himself to play fiddle. Elly recognized that Eddie was very talented. Since Eddie had never played with accompaniment, Elly suggested that if we practiced with Eddie in the band room after school, we could teach him how to keep time. In this way Eddie could be showcased, with the two of us as backup, at the student variety show. The kids went wild when they heard Eddie's playing. He immediately became the most popular musician in the school.

That was his first time on a stage, but Eddie Stubbs later went on to fame as the fiddler for a national bluegrass band, the Johnson Mountain Boys, and is today working as the Voice of the Grand Ole Opry.

In ninth grade, Eddie was elected Student Council President. I arranged for him to make the morning PA announcements jointly with me. We established a good-natured, bantering format that set a humorous tone for the school day. The staff and students referred to this daily event as "The Wayne and Eddie Show".

Joe Haba was the epitome of a good school counselor. Students flocked to him just to talk things over. After I received my doctorate, the staff made an effort for everyone to call me Doctor Busbice instead of Mr. Busbice. One student ran up to Joe in the hallway and breathlessly said, "Mr. Haba, I'd like you to get me an appointment with Mister..uh, Doctor, uh…Mister Buzz-doctor!" Joe thought it was cute that she was making an effort. He told it around in the faculty room and Mister Buzz-doctor became my nickname.

Jinny McCauley was the principal's secretary and she had an immense and unswerving loyalty to me. She guarded my office diligently to protect my time and energy so I could accomplish more. Many people felt that she protected me too well; they referred to her as my first sergeant. Jinny was small in stature but big in power and performance. She was proud of standing up to any nasty person who invaded her territory, the front office. When an angry, out-of-control teacher broke the glass countertop in the office with his fist, five-foot-two Jinny looked way up at the towering man and said, "Now Mr. R., you're going to have to pay for that!" And he did.

Jinny had an excellent sense of humor and was loved and respected by everyone. She took a personal interest in anyone on the staff who had problems, whether at school or at home. Jinny had no fear, and kept the whole school laughing with her antics. For example, when passing out the operations manual at the first faculty orientation for the year (before the students arrived), she inserted suggestive – if not pornographic -- pictures in the manuals for her close friends.

My two assistant principals when I arrived as principal were Dr. Jim Toquinto and Tom Day. No beginning principal ever had such knowledgeable, experienced, effective and good-natured help in managing a school. Their contributions made my job a lot easier.

On the other hand, we had the normal problems of any organization.

One teacher was a kleptomaniac. When he was caught, I was able to save his job as well as keeping him out of jail, because he was at heart a good but troubled person. He got treatment, and I never heard that the shoplifting recurred.

One teacher had a problem that led him to sexually harass attractive teachers. He would grab a woman passing by in the hall, pull her into his darkened room, pin her to the wall and molest her until she could get away. This happened to several women. Times were different then; the public was not informed about such things, and for a long time no one reported him to me. But then I received complaints from several staff members at once. I reprimanded the teacher, and told him I would put a report in his file, but for the time being, the information would not go to the Board of Education. If I heard no more complaints for a year, the paper would be removed and no further action would be taken. If I *ever* heard another complaint I would recommend his dismissal. One year to the day he appeared in my office and asked for the report back. After receiving his assurance that his problem was under control, I returned the report.

Teachers are just like anyone else. They have life upheavals and midlife crises and problem marriages. There were several incidents of couples being discovered after hours in compromising positions in book closet, classroom, and on a health room cot.

At one time in my school I could count at least six couples having affairs -- and these are the ones who were married. I'm sure there were more I never heard about. To be fair, most of the people involved later divorced and married their lovers. As did I, later on.

We were a close-knit staff, and had many parties and after-school happy hours in local taverns. Many of our male teachers were very athletic and kept up long-running games of basketball and soccer in the gym, and jogging in the halls after school. They kept their gear in gym lockers. All were cautioned to keep their lockers locked, because some students had sticky hands.

Harry Huffer, a counselor, had lost two pairs of sneakers that way. Harry used indelible marker to put his initials on his next new pair of expensive sneakers. But they vanished, too. Soon thereafter, Harry was in his office counseling a disruptive student known for his volatility. Harry was sure the boy was wearing his missing sneakers, prominently marked H.H. on the side. Trying to approach the problem very diplomatically, Harry asked the student where he got those shoes. The student replied, "Man, I got these at the store." Harry replied, "You know, they look exactly like a pair I lost last month, and they have my initials on them, H.H." The kid said, "Oh no, those are my initials; those shoes belong to me!" The kid's name was Harold Horn. There was no way Harry could prove him wrong. This story offered entertainment in the faculty lounge for weeks, and Harry was chagrined to be outsmarted by a student.

Because of the ethnic makeup of the school, we had our share of minor racial problems to deal with but these were usually worked out successfully.

Mr. Eddie Washington, a talented artist and a black man who lived in the District of Columbia, formerly a teacher in an all-black school, was assigned to my school as art teacher and art department chairman. Staff, students and parents alike respected Eddie.

Eddie said that he showed artistic talent from the time he was a little boy growing up in the small town of Orange, Texas. As a teenager, he painted a portrait of one of the town's important men. The man was so impressed he offered to send Eddie to college to study art. Eddie Washington became one of the few young black men in his town to have that privilege. Later he acquired his master's degree in art. When I knew him, Eddie balanced three careers at the same time: he taught art in my school; he was an art dealer in Washington; and he ran an escort service – a legitimate one, providing models to gentlemen for companionship.

Eddie was just a likable guy. But he tended to be too easy on students and this could occasionally lead to discipline problems. He had one student in art class, a black girl, who had been transferred to us because of misbehavior in another junior high. LaVonda was upset about having to leave her regular school and thought if she made enough trouble at Gaithersburg Junior she could be sent back there. She deliberately set out to aggravate her teachers in art and math, Eddie Washington and Fred Smith.

Finally Mr. Washington got fed up with her misbehavior and disruption in the classroom. One day he marched LaVonda down to my office, and told me, "Dr. Busbice, something has to be done with LaVonda." LaVonda emphatically stated, "I get along fine with everybody except Mr. Washington. He picks on me, and it's not my fault!" Mr. Washington replied, "Oh no, I spoke to Mr. Smith, and he says you act the same way in his class." LaVonda replied, "Hmmmpphh, ain't no white m—f--- gonna teach *me* no math!" then looked my way for my reply.

I showed no expression and kept silent for a full minute, while she rolled her eyes back and forth between us, waiting for the eruption. Then I said calmly, "Well, LaVonda, then we're in a heap of trouble." She raised her eyebrows, "What do you mean?" I continued, "Because we don't have no *black* m—f—ers teaching math!" LaVonda was shocked, and Mr. Washington, who was fortunately seated near the door, literally rolled out of his seat and into the hall, where he could be heard roaring with laughter as he receded into the distance.

Gaithersburg Junior High was located on twenty acres on the outskirts of the city of Gaithersburg, and between the school and the town was a five–acre wooded lot. We had a student named Joe who was chronically absent, but he enjoyed just dropping in to socialize. He would often be seen around the school, but never came to class. His teachers pressured me to do something.

One day a teacher called in to the office that Joe was in the cafeteria chitchatting with his friends. As I approached down the long hallway, Joe ran out of the cafeteria into the woods, with me in my suit and tie running in hot pursuit. He got away. But not before yelling, "You're nothing but a bald-headed old son of a bitch!" punctuated by raucous laughter. I went back to the building and asked my secretary to call the police. While waiting for the police to come, Joe showed himself behind a tree occasionally to taunt me, with everyone in the cafeteria watching. If I moved in his direction, he ran and hid again. Soon two policemen arrived. They figured out a way to surround Joe, caught him, and put him in the police car. When they asked me in Joe's presence what he should be charged with, I said, "Well, he is a truant, and he has been dropping in and disturbing the environment in the school, and he called me a bald-headed old son of a bitch." And I added, "And when you write up this report, Officer, make sure you indicate that I object to that, because I'm not bald and I'm not old."

Not all my decisions were popular. One year the math department failed to recommend six good students for ninth grade geometry -- instead of algebra, the standard course for ninth grade math. Taking geometry in ninth grade put a student on the fast track for advanced high school math. Parents of the six appealed to me to get their kids into geometry class. I examined their cumulative records, which included standardized tests, grades, and extra-curricular activities. I decided that the six students should be given an opportunity to take a county-originated test to determine if they were eligible. The math teachers were upset with me for overriding their decision.

Three of the students passed and were placed in geometry class. Those three completed the fast track in mathematics. After high school, one of these three won an appointment to the Air Force Academy, and another to West Point. That geometry class had made the difference for them. Several years later in a grocery store, I ran into the mother of the young man who went to West Point. She couldn't thank me enough for making that decision that made his military career possible. The young lady who went to the Air Force Academy became my stepdaughter. Maureen is now an airline captain. Her mother thanks me nearly every day.

My best friend was Dr. Jerry Levine, an assistant principal at another middle school. Jerry had a wild sense of humor and was known to skirt the edges of protocol. He knew that my school had an agricultural program and a new pool, and one day he brought over a student who had been causing discipline problems. Jerry appeared in my office with this kid in tow with no pre-arrangement, and it was apparent by his statements that he had presented Gaithersburg Junior as a special alternative school for discipline problems.

He said, "Now Dr. Busbice, Johnny's not behaving in my school, and he's skipping school and causing problems, and I wanted to see if you would take him." I replied, "Tell me about this young man; if he qualifies, we'll consider it." Jerry said, "We'd need to work out a special program for him cleaning up after the rabbits and chickens, and working around the pool." Then he turned to Johnny and said, "Of course you have to get to school by four o'clock in the morning, on a special bus." I nodded, seeing where he was going. Jerry continued, "Dr. B., Could you describe a regular day here and what his special chores would be?" After I outlined a day filled with hours of sweaty dirty work cleaning the rabbit pens, the chicken houses, and laundering towels for the pool – but no swimming allowed for *him* – in addition to his regular classes, the boy decided he might be better off to shape up and stay in his home school. Jerry left with a contrite student, and neither of us had cracked a smile. But I sure did after they left. We were using unorthodox methods, but they worked.

My friend George, the principal of a junior high, also used unorthodox methods to get a positive result. George had a student who was known to be in the habit of stealing things. Several students reported to George that Bobby, a naïve seventh grader, was seen taking items from gym lockers. George needed proof to stop him, but the students had asked him not to use their names.

So George called Bobby into his office and said, "I know for a fact that you have been removing things from lockers, and you have been observed. I want you to tell me the truth: Did you take things from other students' lockers?" Bobby said, "Who me? I did not. I would never do such a thing." George asked, "Well, would you agree to submit to a truth detector test to prove it?" Bobby responded, "You don't have a truth detector." My friend replied, "Yes, I do, and I'll show you that it works." So George pulled out his blood pressure cuff from the desk drawer and placed it on Bobby's arm. George explained how it works: "I'm going to inflate this on your arm and it will cause this needle to move all the way to the right. Then I'll ask you a question, and if you're telling the truth, it will stay there. If you're not telling the truth, the needle will fall to the left."

So he demonstrated on Bobby, and sure enough the needle fell to the left. Bobby looked terrified, and said, "There's gotta be something wrong with that truth detector, because I didn't steal." George responded, "This detector is never wrong. But maybe I made a mistake. Let's try it again." Again the needle fell to the left. Within a minute or two Bobby was confessing. George had his culprit.

Due to our overcrowding, many students had to take gym at the same time. But these expanded classes always had extra teachers covering them.

One day in gym class a boy was showing his friends a forward roll starting from a flying leap. Coach Tom Sansom caught him, quickly stopped him with a warning, and lectured all the kids that they could be seriously injured if they didn't do the exercise properly.

A few days later when the coach was working with a different group in gym class, he saw the kids doing the forbidden exercise that same way. He firmly repeated his warning, and said if they were caught doing that one more time he would recommend that they be suspended.

One of the boys, Jim Harman, tried the dangerous exercise again while the coach's back was turned. This time the boy was severely injured. He realized that he was unable to move his arms and legs and asked someone to call the coach for help. The coach rode in the ambulance with Jim to the emergency room. The diagnosis was appalling: Jim had broken his neck and couldn't move anything from his neck down. He was a quadriplegic with little chance to recover. Everyone in the school was devastated. Coach Sansom visited the home to offer his regrets and to explain how it had happened. Ms Harman seemed to take it very well and said she did not blame the coaches or the school.

I conducted a complete investigation, independent of the one mounted by the Board of Education. I did this in the same way that I had investigated cases for the Air Force as inspector general. In the presence of my secretary Clara Knode, who took down the proceedings in shorthand, I interviewed all the students and the three gym teachers who were present, separately. I asked all of them identical prepared questions about the event, and any warnings that were given by the teacher. In a second session, each person -- teacher or student -- was given a copy of his interview. Mrs. Knode and I sat in my office and asked them to read the report she had typed up and to indicate any corrections, make any changes necessary, and add anything that had been omitted. When it was agreed that everything was correct I asked them to sign it. I also signed, and Mrs. Knode signed as a witness. Within a week the coaches, assistant principals, members of the board of education and I received letters that Ms. Harman intended to sue us all for negligence, in order to obtain compensation for her son's prolonged treatment. For some reason I was not personally named in the suit.

A law firm that specialized in accidents had taken the case. The suit alleged that there were too many students in the class, supervision was inadequate, and the facilities were below standard. The School Board offered to settle the suit for a million dollars, since that was the extent of their insurance coverage. I myself spoke to the lead lawyer for the plaintiff, who was Mrs. Harman's boyfriend, encouraging the family to take the million dollar settlement. But the law firm was holding out for three million. So the case went to court.

Coach Tom Sansom, who was a defendant, told me how some of the students got up on the stand and changed their stories about what happened. The lawyer for the board of education would then say, "Are you sure that's the way it happened? -- You signed a statement for Dr. Busbice that said something different. And now you want to change your statement?" Then the kid would reluctantly admit, "No, what I told Dr. Busbice and what I signed is the correct version. I just wanted to help out my friend." When the lawyer explained about perjury and the consequences, the witness, who was just a kid after all, had to agree that what he signed in my office was the actual fact. This kind of incident occurred two or three times during the trial.

The lawyers lost the case and did not get a penny for Jim Harman. Yes, the school system won, but it was a hollow victory, because young Harman is still trapped in his own body and has to live the rest of his life as a quadriplegic. Everyone in the school was deeply touched, especially the gym teachers.

The seriously inappropriate behavior of a science teacher by the name of John Resetar led to a landmark decision in Maryland.

Montgomery County Public Schools was downsizing the number of teachers because student enrollment was declining. A few teachers were being declared surplus as a result. Mr. Resetar became a surplus teacher and was assigned to GJHS without my knowledge, consent, or consideration. After reading his personnel file, I became very concerned about Mr. Resetar's ability to fit in. The file contained many incidents about his inability to get along with both staff and students.

In a conference I held with Mr. Resetar to welcome him to the school and discuss some of the incidents, he declared that he was usually the victim in the events noted. At the end I stated that I accepted him without reservation. I said if he couldn't make it at Gaithersburg Junior, he couldn't make it anywhere as a teacher. John assured me he would do his best.

During that school year Resetar displayed his explosive temper. He was the one who broke the glass countertop in the main office with his fist. He also brought a heavy chain with a lock on the end of it to school, which he stated he would use as a weapon against black students in case of harassment.

In June 1974, on the last day of school, a group of black students were outside his classroom on the sidewalk and making remarks to Resetar. One

170

kid called him "big head" – that upset and angered him. His response to that remark through an open window was, "Look at those jungle bunnies. Someone ought to feed them bananas."

Mr. Tootle, my assistant principal, was outside the window, and Lucille Goldsmith, and Jinny McCauley were in the room with Mr. Resetar, and all three heard him make the remark. When this incident was reported to me I set up a conference with the human relations specialist. Resetar did not deny the incident but claimed the stress of closing school and harassment from the black students caused him so much frustration he made the remark in the heat of the moment.

After the conference, the HR specialist and I were in agreement that Resetar should be dismissed from his teaching job. The superintendent of schools recommended to the board of education that he be fired for misconduct and insubordination.

This incident was only one of several involving Resetar and black students or other teachers. In the three years prior to coming to my school, infractions listed in his personnel file included using crudities in talking to a female librarian, saying the schools would be "better off without niggers and Jews", and having once told a black girl that she was a "dirty, filthy punk" and needed a bath. The superintendent said that in making his recommendation for dismissal he considered the cumulative effect of Resetar's behavior.

Resetar was not a member of the Montgomery County Education Association, so he joined the American Federation of Teachers so the AFT would help defend him at the hearing. The AFT had less than a hundred members as compared to MCEA with several thousand members.

Resetar's buddies from the AFT used threats, harassment and unprovable tactics attributed to some labor unions to intimidate the seven staff members who were to testify. Lucille Goldsmith received a phone call warning that her daughter, who performed at the Kennedy Center, would be killed on her way to work that night. The Goldsmith front door was taken off the hinges. Strange things began to happen at my house: a brake lining was cut; a bullet hole was found in my wife's car radiator; air was let out of the tires on our daughter's car. Many received late night hang-up telephone calls. All this time Mr. Resetar was living across the street from my house. We witnesses began to refer to our group among ourselves as the Baltimore Seven. The harassment continued for five years while hearings were held at the county, and state levels. The decision to dismiss Resetar was upheld each time.

A tenured teacher had never been fired in Maryland, so his next step was to file an appeal with the Maryland Court of Appeals. He lost his appeal; then took his case to the Supreme Court.

"The court refused to review the dismissal of a Montgomery County junior high school science teacher for making an allegedly racist remark to black students... The teacher, John Resetar, was fired from his job at Gaithersburg Junior High School because of the remark to black students..."

Soon after it was over, John Resetar sold his house and moved away and the harassment stopped.

One morning I picked up the newspaper and the headline jumped out at me: *Father Kills Son.* The story was about my friend, John Hebron, the building services manager in my school for seven years. He was a fine man, hardworking but easygoing. I knew he was a devoted husband and father, and that he often worked two jobs to get ahead and buy nice things for his family.

John was jailed on first-degree murder charges, with a very high bail. It took several weeks before his family could raise the money to release him. I sought him out to show support and to get the full story. He came to my house with his mother and several young nieces and nephews.

After hearing his description of the event, I firmly believed that John was innocent and was still the same trustworthy, admirable guy I knew. But many people, as well as the newspapers, assumed that he was guilty.

John gave me the background: His twenty-year-old son Jason, a young black man, had been dating a white girl who was only sixteen. Both sets of parents were trying to discourage this relationship. At one point, the girl had run away from home to be with Jason, but had returned.

One night the girl's father called John to say his daughter was missing and he believed she was at John's house. John denied this. The father angrily said he was bringing a friend and coming over to search John's house. John replied, "No, you're not coming into my house."

Feeling threatened and fearing the wrath of the girl's father, John felt that he should have protection. He happened to have a new shotgun in the basement. He brought it up and loaded it in the kitchen while he and his son Jason waited for the father to arrive. While Jason lay stretched out on a rug on the kitchen floor, they talked it over, and wondered if the man might have been bluffing.

John was unfamiliar with the gun and apparently forgot to put on the safety. When they saw through a window that the father was approaching, John said, "Here he comes. We'll meet him at the door." As he hastily

172

scrambled to his feet, Jason slipped on the throw rug. He jostled the gun with his head and caused it to discharge. Jason was killed instantly.

John called 911. The 911 tape was played at the trial. Crying, he repeated, "I just wanted to scare him." This was interpreted by the police to indicate guilt -- meaning he wanted to scare Jason. But it was the girl's father John wanted to scare.

I thought then, and still do, that John's being black was a key factor in the immediacy and harshness of the murder charge – first degree instead of second degree or manslaughter.

John was not allowed to attend his son's funeral, even with a police escort. My heart cried out for John when he told me this. I gave him a big hug and told him I would do everything I could to help him get good legal representation. Pat and I took John and his wife to dinner as a gesture of support and goodwill.

I set up a defense fund to help pay a good lawyer. Pat had established her own personnel company by this time, and she provided supplies, stationery, postage, telephone, copies and fax. I got some people involved in helping. We formed a committee and sent out letters to all the school system employees who knew John. His family provided us with a list of his friends and relatives. We were successful in raising $10,000 for John's defense.

When the trial date arrived, Pat took off work. Together with Jinny McCauley and her husband Joe, we occupied the first row in the spectator section every day of the trial.

When called to the stand as a character witness, I praised John as a reliable and dedicated employee. I had never known him to be intemperate or aggressive in any way. John and his pretty wife Joanne had been to our house for parties. I sold them their first house. Occasionally John would bring Jason to my office and I could tell their relationship was a good one. I told the jury I was convinced that John was incapable of a violent act. And John was so strong and muscular that if he had wanted to harm his son, he would not have needed a gun to do so.

There were no witnesses at all who could say a derogatory thing about John's character. After four days the defense rested. The defense lawyer's summation brought tears to everyone in the gallery. He recognized and was able to paint a true picture of John's qualities and good character.

The jury returned a verdict in only three hours. Pat and I had never left the courthouse, and we assembled in our customary first-row place with Joe and Jinny. When the verdict of not guilty was announced there was a great roar of approval in the courtroom. We couldn't contain ourselves -- Jinny and Joe, Pat and I leapt to our feet in a teary group hug.

In the courthouse lobby later, some jurors sought us out. They all stated they did not understand why the case ever came to trial; it was so clearly an accidental death. One juror said that the sight of us in the first row every day spoke eloquently of the kind of man who could inspire such loyalty.

Besides directing the educational activities in the school, principals sometimes deal with difficult parents. I received this letter from a parent in response to a health inventory form the school sent home, which was required by state law.

2-25-74

Principal------

May I introduce myself as the mother of a future pupil in your school. I am not hard to get along with as long as the faculty all behave properly. I tolerate no stuff, bunk or nonsense from anyone! You will NOTE I have enclosed more forms than are hereby requested ----please take note and heed-----best keep them on file for future reference.

At no time shall you ever discipline my child in any manner. You will notify me and you and I shall sit down with my child and discuss any problems ---should they occur. There will be no exception to this at anytime. My children are all taken at their word for they've been taught and avoid being punished so they are honest and straight forward and now learning to be outspoken. They do not hit first, they hit second. They don't cross my path twice. I seriously doubt you'll have any problems once you adjust to their upbringing. They do as I say.

Brace yourself, sir – there are two more coming after this one – one every year for the next three years.

Hopefully you and I shall get along quite well when you realize I don't tolerate bureaucratic garbage – period! – and I am to be advised of ANY and ALL problems that might arise. I am the parent and deal with my offspring. You are NOT paid to do anymore than give a good-rounded education and guidance to our future adults of the world Looking forward to a personal meeting with you PRIOR to my son's enrollment.   --------

-Mary

I retired in 1980 after thirty years in education, and eleven years as principal of Gaithersburg Junior High.

Twenty-five years later I received a letter from a fellow educator, now a high school guidance counselor, with whom I worked in the 1970s at Gaithersburg Junior.

Dear Dr. Busbice,

...I want you to know something. Over all the years I've been very fortunate to work for some excellent principals (only one dog in the lot)...

That's saying something! But you are the one that I measure them all against. Your professionalism, caring, good temper, and sense of humor. The ability to keep things in perspective, and greet the toughest situations with a smile (not to mention, put up with us boneheads.) Over the years I have found none your equal. I want you to know that, and that I think of you fondly, and more often than you'll ever know...

Curt_____

~19~

Calls to Duty

In Arlington National Cemetery, the Tomb of the Unknown Soldier was dedicated on Armistice Day 1923 to honor unidentified World War I soldiers who had fought and died in France. The Army brought one such soldier back to the United States and buried him on a hill overlooking the U.S. Capitol. Later, unknown soldiers from World War II, the Korean War and the Vietnam War were buried there. As a result, it was decided to change the name to the Tomb of the Unknowns, and in 1958 President Eisenhower presided over a ceremony for this event. The inscription on the tomb reads, "Here Rests In Honored Glory an American Soldier Known But to God."

As a captain in the D.C. Air National Guard, I was selected to join a ceremonial cordon for the president along Constitution Avenue on his way to the Tomb, and to be a member of the ceremonial formation at the cemetery.

While I was standing with my detachment lining Constitution Avenue waiting for the moment when we would snap to attention as the president passed, I had a flashback to my early teens. Our neighbor Nancy Fuller had proudly shown me a picture of her nephew, Hugh Poe. In the photo, Hugh was marching in his Navy dress blues alongside the caisson carrying the first Unknown Soldier. I can remember my awe when Nancy told me Hugh was in Washington. I had decided at that moment that nothing so grand and stirring could ever happen to me. But here I was, standing at the same place where he walked in that photo, at another ceremony honoring the Unknown Soldier.

The Tomb of the Unknowns is one of Washington's most popular tourist sites. It is guarded twenty-four hours a day, every day of the year, and in all weathers, by two Tomb Guards. The sentinels, all volunteers, are considered to be the best of the elite 3rd U.S. Infantry (The Old Guard), headquartered at Fort Myer, Virginia. Each soldier must be in excellent physical condition, possess an unblemished military record, and stand between five feet ten and six feet four.

Walking at a cadence of ninety steps per minute, the Tomb Guard marches twenty-one steps down the black mat behind the Tomb, turns, faces east for twenty-one seconds, turns and faces north for twenty-one seconds, then takes twenty-one steps down the mat and repeats the process.

After the turn, the sentinel executes a sharp "shoulder-arms" movement to place the weapon on the shoulder closest to the visitors, to signify that the sentinel stands between the Tomb and any possible threat. The number twenty-one was chosen to symbolize the highest military honor that can be bestowed – the twenty-one gun salute.

It should be noted that in 1998 DNA tests identified the Vietnam veteran as 1st Lt. Joseph Blassie, and at the request of his family he was disinterred and reburied in a family plot. His grave will remain empty.

On a very cold January 20, 1961, following a blizzard the night before, John F. Kennedy was sworn in as the thirty-fifth president of the United States. Inaugurations take place in front of the U.S. Capitol, flanked by the Senate office building and Library of Congress. The panoramic view from the inaugural platform is of the Mall, the Smithsonian buildings, and the Washington monument.

The D. C. Air National Guard was ordered to provide a marching group and organizing officers for the occasion. But because of the heavy snow, even some of the main roads were unplowed and only snow emergency routes were clear for traffic. I was forced to take a roundabout route to the D.C. Armory to pick up my assignment.

The inauguration parade committee needed an Air Force captain and an Army captain to report to the intersection of South Capitol Street and Independence Avenue. I was selected to represent the Air Force. I was stationed with my clipboard at the point of entry for marching groups, and I directed each marching unit, band, and float to enter the parade route at the proper time.

The snow had diminished to flurries, but it was bitterly cold and windy. I almost froze my ears off. Many parade marchers couldn't stand the hours waiting in the cold, and had to fall out of their marching units temporarily to get warm. But we military troops couldn't muffle up in warm clothes, beyond our regulation uniforms for the day. I was not supposed to leave my post, but I was forced by the freezing wind to take shelter periodically in the Senate Office Building for a few minutes to thaw out. My Army counterpart and I were perturbed to observe our supervising colonels cheerfully enjoying a thermos of hot coffee in a heated staff car while we shivered.

While I was out there freezing, I had time to wonder if my uncomfortable duty had anything to do with my rivalry with the chief warrant officer who was making the troop assignment decisions back at the cozy Armory. We were both vying for a slot for promotion to major.

In spite of the cold, probably to emphasize his youthful "vigah", Kennedy broke with tradition and wore only a suit – no overcoat and no hat. Nobody could tell that he was wearing long thermal underwear.

I was close enough to see and hear the swearing-in ceremony of both President Kennedy and Vice President Johnson. While Cardinal Cushing of Boston was giving the invocation and a short speech, a suspicious twirl of smoke began to rise around the podium. The colonel in charge barked orders for me to keep the parade crowd back. The fast-thinking Cardinal was alarmed and spoke longer than he had intended. He later said he stayed at the podium to shield the president with his body and take the impact of an explosion, if it came. But it soon was apparent that the smoke came from an electrical short and it was quickly corrected.

It was at this inaugural that Kennedy gave his famous speech urging Americans, "Ask not what your country can do for you – ask what you can do for your country." After his death, this phrase would be carved in marble on the walls of the Kennedy Center, a complex of theaters, concert and opera halls overlooking the Potomac River.

That night, several inaugural balls were held in the city. I was assigned to the ball at the D.C. Armory. My duties were to stand in the lobby to provide information and direct people to the seating area.

I noticed a group of twenty young officers milling around all decked out in their mess dress uniforms (military formal dress). I asked a young captain what his assignment was that evening. He said there were two busloads of Kennedy cousins attending the affair and most of them were unescorted young women. He and his friends were to be available to escort the ladies, and dance and entertain them during the ball. They seemed to really enjoy their assignment whereas I had a very boring time. My duty day was from six in the morning. until ten at night, so since there were no Kennedy cousins waiting to dance with me, I didn't stay until the ball was over.

Less than eight months after JFK took office, the Soviet Union unilaterally decided to build a ninety-six mile barbed wire barricade and concrete twelve foot wall to surround East Berlin, cutting the city in two. This was the Soviet reaction to the large numbers of East Berliners fleeing to live in the West. The wall was erected to prevent this, and it disrupted social, political, and family interaction in the city. (The wall was destroyed on November 9, 1989.) As a result of this insult, the United States Congress authorized the president to activate several Reserve and Air National Guard units to fortify our regular armed services in case the Soviets expanded their threat.

I was then a major in the D.C. Air National Guard, with duties as the wing base supply officer. Ours was one of those federalized units. We were notified in early October of the call-up. I had two weeks notice to take care of personal affairs before reporting for a year of active duty at Andrews AFB in October of 1961.

My family was in disarray at that time. Our daughter Martha was only six months old and Margaret was physically and emotionally too ill to take care of herself and the children. Our commander made it clear that no one was to be exempted, by Pentagon regulations. If anyone was exempted for any reason it would open up the floodgates and destroy the integrity of the unit. The military mission always comes first.

I made a hasty decision to rent our house in Rockville and Margaret's parents graciously offered to take in my family and look after them while I was in the service.

I had received my orders, but before I made it to Andrews, the phone rang one day at home. Some of my mischief-making buddies from the Guard were on the phone gleefully telling me the latest news. There was a lot of pressure on a chief mechanic at Andrews to get all the fighter planes on combat-ready status. They were all lined up on the flight line ramp for the final checklist. Entering one plane, he pressed a button and discharged a bullet that had been inadvertently left in the plane's gun chamber. Since the planes were all in a neat row, the bullet destroyed the nearest aircraft, sending it down in flames. It was a monumental gaffe, and no doubt there would be numerous investigations.

We all realized it was a very serious matter, but my buddies also thought it was humorous, and encouraged me to write a song about the event. I flippantly said, "If he gets two more he'll be the only noncom to become an ace."

When I arrived at Andrews, I was told the Deputy Base Commander wanted to see me in his office immediately. Col. Kester was seated behind his desk with big flags on either side, and a lot of military regalia on display. After I saluted and was seated, he said, "Major, I understand you've heard about the accident on the flight line. And I hear you're planning to write a song about it. I want you to know that would not be in the best interests of the Air National Guard." I assured the Colonel that I had no intentions of doing so, and was dismissed.

I moved into officers' quarters on the base at Andrews in order to be ready to ship overseas under secret orders to Frankfort, Germany. Of course I couldn't tell my family or anyone when or where the unit was going. But our deployment was cancelled at the last minute because the problem situation in Vietnam was growing. The Pentagon changed our status to hold tight and be "springloaded" to go either way, if needed. I spent most of that year on temporary duty (TDY) to California, Maine, Virginia, North Carolina, and South Carolina, chasing down supplies and equipment to bring our unit up to combat ready status.

The most interesting assignment I had was supply staff officer for "Exercise Quick Kick". I had to be cleared for Top Secret due to the nature and implication of the exercise. Our major objective was to prove that the AF Tactical Air Command, in a joint operation with Army troops, could set up and operate a bare base airfield using no buildings, just tents, and an above ground flexible fuel container. The fuel container was awesome, and constructed like a huge pneumatic mattress. Fuel would be flown in using KC-135 tankers who would unload their fuel into the giant flexible container; and the C-130s would refuel, load up the airborne troops, tanks and other combat equipment, take them to the practice drop zone near the Chesapeake Bay in East Virginia and deliver their goods. The first two or three drills were unsatisfactory but they finally got the hang of it. We teased the C-130 pilots about scattering the Army's equipment anywhere from Shaw to the Chesapeake Bay, but the teasing was all in good fun. The bare base we were using was North Field near Columbia, South Carolina, and it was a hot, dry summer with no air conditioning or other amenities. The army troops were roughing it living in tents on the bare base but Air Force troops were living on Shaw AFB at Sumter, South Carolina and going out to the bare base almost every day.

The operation command post headquarters was also on Shaw, and part of my job was to furnish office furniture and supplies for each office. Since we were temporary tenants on the base, the host base personnel were reluctant to share some things with us -- making it necessary to "midnight requisition" (scrounge) items we really needed. For example, office trash cans and ash trays were in short supply, so I had to be resourceful and liberate a few from those who had an abundance of them, without being conspicuous. I told my airmen to go into the command post headquarters and the airmen's club and announce that they had been detailed to empty all ashtrays and trashcans. My troops received a friendly greeting and a thank-you from the Shaw airmen, who then promptly returned to work. My instructions to my men were, take all ashtrays and trashcans outside, dump them, clean them out real good, keep a few for us and return the rest. It worked like a charm!

Major General Preston was our commander but we rarely came in contact with him except during briefings. He was all business and a hard taskmaster but everyone respected him. About halfway through the exercise we had a little party -- I had my guitar with me and played a few songs. Secretly, I had written a couple of songs about our plight out on North Field and one of them was entitled "Quick Kick Officers' Lament". Since General Preston was not in attendance at the party, I decided to sing it to the troops. It is sung to the tune of "Wabash Cannonball."

Quick Kick Officers' Lament
  By Wayne Busbice

We left Seymour Johnson about a week ago today
We landed at Shaw AFB and tried to get away
He said you'll paint the command post before you hit the hay
Major General Preston wanted it that-a-way

There's trash cans and field desks and ashtrays by the score
I scrounged all over this air base until my feet were sore
I tried to convince these people Quick Kick's here to stay
Because Major General Preston wanted it that-a-way

Well I got my field gear ready, personnel said "no TPA" [private autos]
And there'll be no per diem at North Field during your stay
There's a portable hydrant system and mess kits every day
Because Major General Preston wanted it that-a-way

Now there is Col. Hilpert and don't forget Rudell
And my old friend Col. Harris they all should go to ---Well
We all got out to North Field and ate some dust today
Major General Preston wanted it that-a-way

Those big C-130s how they glistened in the sun
They looked so very graceful when they made their run
But they scattered the Army's equipment from Shaw to the Chesapeake Bay
Major General Preston wanted it that-a-way???

There's a section across the street known as one-two-two-one [a beer-dispensing truck]
Where the Army, Navy, and Marine Corps really had their fun
But don't forget the Air Force, as "Quick Kick" had its day
Oh Major General Preston wanted it that-a-way!

The song was a big hit and the guys asked if I had another song about our unit. I sang "The Battle Of North Field", to the tune of "Red River Valley":

The Battle of North Field
*   By WayneBusbice*

To North Field they say you are going
You will miss your sweet wife and her smile
But out there they say the dust is blowing
It will occupy your time for a while

As you lay on your pneumatic mattress
And you gaze at the stars in the sky
19th Air Force says that they need us
But oh Lord, oh Lord, tell me why

On D + 4 I'll be leaving
To return to my home bye and bye
If I'm ever in another operation
Here's Quick Kick mud in your eye

I was unaware that the public information officer was recording our party shenanigans. The next day he played the songs for Major General Preston who really liked them. The general asked the public information officer to have me redo the songs since there was a lot of background party noise on the original. He wanted a copy for himself, as well as a copy filed in the 19th Air Force history file.

My good friend and co-worker, Maj. Bernie Ellis, was base equipment officer. We were having trouble acquiring equipment to meet the requirements for our anticipated deployment overseas. Bernie and I were sent TDY on a kind of a round robin to other bases with a printout of the items we needed.

When I was recalled to active duty in 1961, Ben Adelman released single recordings on the Empire label of my songs, "Back Home in the Air National Guard" backed with "I'll Be Back in a Year" – because the reactivation was to last a year. The record got good airplay in the Washington area and the Air National Guard troops often came up to me on base to say how much they liked it.

So Bernie and I stopped at every country music radio station we passed on our way to Myrtle Beach AFB in South Carolina, our sister base, and left records for the deejays to play. In Lumberton, North Carolina I was asked to hang around for an on-air interview in a few minutes.

Bernie and I had encountered a group of four or five scruffy guys on our way in, hanging around outside the radio station. They were loggers who had just come out of the woods to deliver a load of logs to the lumber mill. They introduced themselves as the Broad Slab Boys, and said they really were crazy about country music. They had been calling the station all day trying to get some of their favorite songs played, so would I please get the deejay to play something for them. When I passed on this request, the deejay said, "I'll play your record and dedicate it to them. Maybe that will please them". As we left these guys said that was a good record and thanked me for getting the Broad Slab Boys mentioned on the radio.

Bernie Ellis and I were prohibited from telling anyone, civilian or military, about our secret orders to acquire equipment, unless they had a security clearance. Even our wives and families were not to be told. We had orders and a specific date to deploy overseas before Christmas. We were scrambling around to make sure we had all the equipment and supplies that were needed to make the deployment.

The last stop on our trip was Langley AFB, and we were ushered in to see Col. Gomez, director of materiel, who controlled all logistics in Tactical Air Command. Our commanding officer Gen. Milliken had told us, "By the way gentlemen, when you see Col. Gomez, tell him I would very much like to have a credenza for my office. According to the table of allowances for generals, I am authorized to have a credenza."

Col. Gomez was very informal and did not possess a military air. He spoke matter-of-factly and made us feel relaxed, even though we were talking serious business with a bird colonel. After we finished going over our deployment needs with Col. Gomez, whom I would describe as a no-nonsense curmudgeon, we were still short a few items. At this point, we presented Gen. Milliken's request for his credenza including a quote from the reference in the appropriate table of organization. Col. Gomez just looked back and forth at us, then quietly and firmly in his heavy Hispanic accent said, "You got a *fokking peonsul*, I got a *fokking peonsul*, everybody has a *fokking peonsul*." Bernie and I were taken aback, exchanging glances thinking, "Where is he going with this?" Col. Gomez continued, "We want everybody to have a *fokking peonsul*. Now, we have some mechanics out on the flight line who don't have tools they need, we have people repairing equipment who don't have a *laith*. When all our mechanics have the tools they need and have a *laith* to do their work, then we get the general his credenza. Just tell him to be patient -- we haven't forgotten him -- as soon as we can get all these other things we need, we'll get him his credenza."

Bernie and I were quite amused at his comparison of the pencils, the credenza, and the lathe. When we returned to Andrews, Bernie and I gave our report to the general outlining the items we were able to obtain and he was pleased. We also reported on our unsuccessful attempt to obtain his credenza, albeit without the expletives.

I was released from active duty early in July 1962 in order to return to my job as a counselor at Eastern Junior High under a special authorization granted to educators.

On June 19, 1963, President Kennedy sent his promised civil rights legislation to Congress offering federal protection to African Americans seeking to vote, shop, eat in restaurants, and to be educated on equal terms. On July 2 at New York's Roosevelt Hotel a march organization was established by the "Big Six" civil rights leaders: A. Philip Randolph, Roy Wilkins, James Farmer, John Lewis, Whitney Young, Jr., and Rev. Martin Luther King. Baynard Ruskin was named chief coordinator and the march was scheduled for August 28, 1963.

Privately, President Kennedy tried to persuade the civil rights leaders to cancel the march. He told them, "We want success in Congress, not just a big show at the Capitol. Some of these people are looking for an excuse to be against us and I don't want to give them the opportunity to say, 'Yes, I'm for the bill, but I am damned if I will vote for it at the point of a gun.'" Failing to stop the march, JFK publicly embraced the event.

Fears of a possible riot were intense, and the Washington authorities and the march organizers were determined to ensure a peaceful day. D.C. police units had all their leaves canceled; neighboring suburban police forces were given special riot control training, and the D.C. Air National Guard was ordered out for special civil disturbance duty. The Justice Department and the Army coordinated preparations for emergency troop deployments, putting   an enormous number of paratroopers on alert just outside the city.

News reports indicated that FBI director J. Edgar Hoover was trying to scuttle the march. Hoover tried to persuade the president that King was being influenced by Communists and utilized wiretap information about King's sexual indiscretions and Ruskin's homosexual liaisons. These tactics did not persuade the president and the march was permitted to continue as scheduled.

Television news reports portrayed the marchers' convergence on Washington as a festive affair enlivened by freedom songs and the excitement of participating in an historic event. The marchers were to assemble around the Washington Monument and the Mall area. Estimates of the crowd size ranged from 200,000 to 500,000. It was believed to be the largest political demonstration ever seen in the country. It generated enormous press coverage.

The American Nazi party, commanded by George Lincoln Rockwell, was given a permit to assemble peacefully in a counter-demonstration, across the street on the Ellipse between the civil rights group and the White House. But they were not allowed to make any speeches.

When I reported for duty I was assigned twenty noncommissioned officers, issued a special police badge, a nightstick, empty canteen, and a lunch box filled with fried chicken, then loaded onto a bus with my men. We were driven to the Ellipse to stand guard between the marchers and about sixty American Nazi storm troopers, the only group protesting the march. In my opinion, the storm troopers looked like thugs. Besides my contingent, there were three other officers with twenty troops each. We alternated with the D.C. police – every other person – and were deployed in a straight line between the Ellipse (the rear lawn of the White House) and the Washington Monument.

We were told not to let the marchers or the storm troopers into each other's territory, in order to avoid a riot. Some of the marchers were curious about the Nazis and wanted to get closer to take pictures, which we could not allow. The storm troopers just milled around, not causing any trouble until about 10:30 a.m. when one of them began to make a hate speech with a bullhorn. Unknown to me, there were several plainclothes detectives and FBI agents nearby. They rushed the speaker and ordered him to stop, and he complied.

In the meantime, popular recording artists performed for the crowd on a stage that had been set up at the Washington Monument. Joan Baez opened the program with "Oh, Freedom" and also led the marchers in a rendition of "We Shall Overcome." Other performers included Josh White, the Albany Freedom Singers, Bob Dylan, and Peter, Paul and Mary who sang "Blowin' In the Wind". There were several warm up speeches to get the crowd in a good mood for the main speeches to be given at the Lincoln Memorial that afternoon. Roy Wilkins spotted Lena Horne in the crowd and asked her to come up to the mike and say a few words. Lena walked up to the mike, paused a moment as if she was gathering her thoughts, leaned in to the mike and yelled, "FREEDOM NOW!" and walked away. Roy seemed a little surprised, then he returned to the mike and said, "And she means every word of it," and the crowd just roared.

At my station on the Ellipse, at 11:30 a.m. an American Nazi Party lieutenant attempted to speak again and he was arrested and taken away. This action angered George Lincoln Rockwell. He ordered his storm troopers to form a single line, then marched them onto Constitution

Avenue, and withdrew over the 14th street bridge before he dismissed them. He later tried to sue the District of Columbia for denying him his right to free speech.

My men and I were no longer needed at the Ellipse so soon an Air Force bus came by and picked us up. It was about lunchtime so I ordered the men to eat their box lunch on the bus before we reported to the front of the Lincoln Memorial. A snow fence had been installed about 10 feet between the memorial and the crowd. Our instructions were to contain the marchers behind the snow fence and on the Mall, so no one could rush onto the Lincoln Memorial itself where the entertainment and speeches were to be presented. Just as we got positioned, a runner from headquarters came up and informed me that we were not to eat our box lunches because the food would not be safe after three hours without refrigeration. All I could say was, "Sorry --too late!" I did alert my troops and asked them to be sure to let me know if anyone began to feel ill. We all escaped illness, but some men in other squads were not so lucky.

The musical entertainment at the Lincoln Memorial was more or less the same as the morning groups at the Washington Monument. In addition, Charleston Heston, Marlon Brando, Sammy Davis, Jr., Ossie Davis, Sidney Poitier, Lena Horne, Diahann Carroll, Paul Newman and Harry Belafonte all made some appropriate remarks representing the arts contingent.

Whitney Young's speech focused on urban inequities and the conduct of future black marches but John Lewis gave a controversial speech calling the Kennedy civil rights bill "too little, too late". He stated, "We will march through the South, through the heart of Dixie, the way Sherman did; we will pursue our own scorched earth policy and burn Jim Crow to the ground nonviolently." Mahalia Jackson sang, "I've been 'Buked and I've Been Scorned," to warm up the crowd in anticipation for Martin Luther King's speech.

Rev. Martin Luther King gave the closing address with his "I Have A Dream" speech that became instantly famous and remains one of the great moments of modern oratory. He started his speech with the comment, "I am happy to join with you today in what will go down in history as the greatest demonstration for freedom in the history of our nation." He concluded his remarks:

"When we allow freedom to ring, when we let it ring from every village and every hamlet, from every state and every city, we will be able to speed that day when all God's children, black men and white men, Jews and Gentiles, Protestants and Catholics, will be able to join hands and

sing the words of the old Negro spiritual: Free at last! Free at last! Thank God Almighty, we are free at last!"

At that moment I felt honored to be present.

After Dr. Martin Luther King, Jr. finished his speech, we were dismissed and I had my troops help disperse the crowd and then fall out behind the Lincoln Memorial. Peter, Paul and Mary were still there enjoying refreshments and talking to a few fans. My troops and I had the opportunity to talk with them. They have always been my favorite folk singers.

Prior to this day, I was a little conflicted about Martin Luther King's movement because of the leaked reports shown in the media based on FBI files. Not to mention that I was a native of Dixie. The whole ambience of the day's activities impressed me. Many people had expected some rioting, but this was a peaceful demonstration by serious, dignified people who were worthy of respect. I didn't realize the full historical significance of the event, but it made a lasting impression. Being present that day altered my perceptions. This was the beginning of my conscious effort to lose all the remaining racist attitudes I possessed. Today, it is hard for me to imagine the repression this nation inflicted on a segment of its citizens just because of the color of their skin.

Demonstrations and protest marches against United States involvement in the very unpopular Vietnam War were common from the mid-1960s to the mid-1970s, especially on college campuses and in the nation's capital. Men avoided the draft by moving to Canada or requesting student deferments. Many of our citizens felt the war was a mistake.

During the many protests in D.C., my Guard unit was called up to protect the public during civil disturbances. We were specially sworn in as Special Capitol Police, and paired one-on-one with D.C. police officers to keep order. Protesters would organize, and descend on Washington to block traffic, conduct sit-ins, close bridges and disrupt the city with the aim of closing down the normal operations of the government. Many were arrested and thrown in jail. When the jails were filled to capacity, protesters were kept in sports arenas and meeting halls until parents and friends could bail them out. I observed a lot of drug use in these holding facilities, and sometimes the D.C. officers were quick to get involved. The protesters we encountered preferred dealing with the military. They did not expect any brutality from us. One young kid who was being manhandled ran to me repeatedly for help, declaring the police didn't have the right to search him. Three cops bundled him into the bathroom to deal with him privately, then let him go. Having no authority to intervene, I could only watch helplessly as he was roughly treated. Upon later reflection,

I suspected a deliberate setup by the protestor to undermine cooperation between military and police.

Later the courts often ruled that protestors were arrested illegally, based on their First Amendment rights. However, if they were involved in destroying or defacing property they would face some consequences. Peaceful protesters usually were released without having to pay fines.

I was assigned a squad of twenty troops. The airmen were issued a carbine rifle, and as the officer in charge I was issued a .38 caliber pistol and all of the ammunition for the squad, with orders not to issue the ammo to anyone unless in imminent danger. Luckily I was never required to issue ammo but occasionally some fellow officers were required to do so.

After school on a Friday, April 5, 1968, a group of faculty members and I were celebrating a long hard week by playing the guitar and singing hootenanny songs at a teacher's apartment in Bethesda, Maryland. My commander called home and reached my wife, tracked me down, and told me there was an emergency: that I should report to my post on Andrews Air Force Base in two hours with a full complement of uniforms, underwear, shaving gear, and anything else I would need for at least a week. He hurriedly explained, "Martin Luther King has just been assassinated in Memphis, and the blacks are rioting and burning down Washington."

I rushed home in about twenty minutes, picked up my required items, said goodbye to my family, and just made it in time to Andrews. When I reported to my duty station I learned the Guard had been federalized -- called to active duty in the regular service. We were shorthanded at this time because most of the Air National Guard units had been activated and were stationed in South Vietnam. George Huss, my counterpart officer, and I were given twenty troops each to command, and told to report to our headquarters at the D.C. Armory.

Upon arriving we were told to give each of our squads a call sign. I picked Hogan's Heroes for my squad, and Huss chose F Troop. We were in charge of protecting the D.C. Armory and its perimeter, D.C. General Hospital, and the Redskins football stadium. We posted our men inside and outside the buildings, with instructions to prevent anyone from approaching within fifty feet. We were to make sure no fires were set and no vandalism occurred. Around midnight Major Huss returned with his squad to the hangar at Andrews while my troops and I stayed on duty at the Armory. I was relieved by Huss the next morning and from that time on we shuttled back and forth to Andrews for meals, sleep and rest, twelve hours on and twelve off.

We shared the Armory with the Army Guard, sleeping on mattresses on the floor and eating C-rations. On our off hours, it appeared that the

Army guys were content to lie around and rest, but the Air Force guys were always looking for something to tinker with. In the dayroom, there was an old jukebox that hadn't worked for ten years, and our technicians thought they could fix it. In a couple of hours you could hear music all over the Armory. The Army men were impressed. They said, "Man, those Air Force guys are whizzes."

Angry people were burning down shops and buildings belonging to whites in the inner city. Some black business owners had their property burned down also if they didn't write in large letters "soul brother" or "soul sister" in prominent places on the outside of their buildings. The city was filled with smoke, and people were looting, and harassing pedestrians.

One of my sergeants on patrol at the hospital stopped a young man trying to bypass him and enter the hospital. The sergeant pointed his rifle at him, startled the kid, and he stumbled and fell. "Halt!" he said, "or I'll shoot." The kid looked up from the ground and replied with scorn, "You gonna shoot me with that, man? It's not even loaded." (The word had gotten around, true, that only officers had bullets.) But the sergeant answered, "You don't know that! You wanna try me?" The kid hesitated and then left.

The rioting, looting and harassment continued for two or three days with the Metropolitan Police handling the center of the disturbances; we were formed on the periphery. After things calmed down we were dispersed throughout the entire burned out area. It looked like a war zone; many businesses lost all of their assets and their buildings. Blacks had felt betrayed and this was one way they could express their anger about the mistreatment they experienced and the lack of progress in granting civil rights. I could understand where they were coming from, and at the same time I didn't feel this destruction was justified.

Our unit was kept on active duty for three weeks to ensure the protection of what was left of the inner city and the security of citizens living near that burned out area. This was as close as I ever got to a battle zone in all my years of military duty.

I was released from active duty on April 16, 1968 and reverted to my regular duties as supply staff officer. Soon thereafter, I was appointed Director of Logistics for all units of the DCANG located at Andrews AFB and in Washington, D.C.

In 1969, I was promoted to lieutenant colonel, and continued my position as Director of Logistics. In 1974 the commanding general, Major General Bryant, established a new position of Assistant Inspector General for all D.C. Army and Air National Guard units.

The commanding general asked my boss, Brigadier General McCall, to recommend three officers to fill this position, and his recommendations did not include me. So I was surprised when I was appointed. In my first interview with the commanding general, I told him I was curious why he chose me instead of one of the individuals recommended. He replied, "I reviewed the personnel records of all qualified officers and found your experience -- supply management staff officer and director of logistics -- combined with your educational level and civilian career experience, more suitable for the duties of the inspector general. I wanted someone who was easygoing and effective in working with people and your reports reflected that. Welcome aboard." I was to take on inspector general duties simultaneously with my duties as director of logistics.

During the six years I served in this capacity, only one case escalated to the Congressional level. A master sergeant felt he had unfairly been denied re-enlistment. He and two other noncommissioned officers had complained to Congresswoman Marjorie Holt of Maryland about the alleged mismanagement and poor leadership of the wing commander, Brigadier General Myles Kennedy.

I had previously investigated the issue and found no real substance to the sergeant's complaint. It had started when the master sergeant had a disagreement with a warrant officer -- over proper display of the flag, of all things -- and struck him in the chest. The wing commander asked me to investigate and recommend appropriate action. My recommendation was to court-martial the master sergeant and dismiss him from the service. Instead, the wing commander decided to deny him the right to re-enlist when his enlistment was up.

Congresswoman Holt, in turn, requested an inspector general investigation by the Pentagon. When the Pentagon inspector general team arrived at Andrews, I was called in to defend my report.

In preparation for a hearing before the Armed Forces Military Personnel subcommittee, I was temporarily assigned to the Pentagon. I developed a chronological history of the case and presented it to Mr. Kutche, Deputy Assistant Secretary of the Air Force in the presence of several other high-ranking officers.

I was given the assignment to coordinate the various chronologies to be used in the Congressional hearing. I worked at the Pentagon preparing my report and coordinating the content with Assistant Secretary of the Air Force Antonia Handler Chayes' office. On July 11, 1978, along with her staff, I accompanied Assistant Secretary Chayes to the committee hearing as her backup in case there were detailed questions that she couldn't answer. After the deliberation, the wing commander's decision to deny the master sergeant's re-enlistment was upheld.

I retired from the D.C. Air National Guard and the Air Force Reserve in the spring of 1980. I had served twenty-eight and a half years with the Air Force National Guard, and four years on active duty.

During my tours I had received several military ribbons to wear on my chest. The highest medal I received was presented to me upon retirement by none other than Assistant Secretary of the Air Force Chayes: the Air Force Commendation Medal for Meritorious Service as Director of Logistics and Inspector General. The next highest award I received was the Minuteman, a statue trophy, "for exemplary and meritorious service."

Lt Col Busbice receiving the Air Force Commendation Medal from Assistant Secretary of the Air Force Antonia Handler Chayes

I'll Be Back
  By Wayne Busbice
  Pub. Old Home Place Music

I'll be back in a year, little darlin'
Uncle Sam has called and I must go
I'll be back, don't you fear, little darlin'
You'll be proud of your serviceman I know.

Chorus:
I'll do my best each day for the good old USA
And we'll keep Old Glory waving high (hallelujah!)
I'll be back after peace has come to Berlin
Don't you worry, darlin', don't you cry.

How I long to be there at home with you, dear
This cold, cold war's a mighty sin
Each night I'll hold you in my dreams, dear
'Til I'm back within your arms again.

~20~

We Meet Halfway

That promise of happiness that Margaret and I had at our marriage began to darken within weeks of the wedding. While I was finding fulfillment in my teaching career and my music avocation, my marriage was disintegrating.

Margaret was mentally ill. Over the next ten years, Margaret's psychiatrists upgraded her diagnosis from manic depression to schizophrenia, and ultimately to paranoid schizophrenia with a revenge motive. She eventually refused all help and treatment – something I have been told is consistent with that disease. She was in a great deal of emotional pain almost all the time. She was unable to cope with a job, the household, friends or our children.

I became the mainstay parent for my children, taking over their entire care whenever I wasn't at work. My mother-in-law would sometimes come to stay to ensure their safety when Margaret was alone. We were very fortunate to have her help. Mrs. Woodward took over John's care from the time he was a few days old.

John was a beautiful blue-eyed, blond baby. He was a joy to me from the day he was born, and brought happiness and sunshine into my life in spite of the turmoil that existed in our home. John inspired me to write this song when he was five years old.

Be Careful of Your Father's Name
By Wayne Busbice
Pub. Old Home Place Music

Recitation:
In Proverbs 22:1 we read, "A good name is to be chosen rather than great riches."

You got it from your father, it was the best he had to give
And gladly he bestowed it, it's yours the while you live
You may lose the watch he gave you and another you may claim
But remember when you are tempted, to be careful of his name.

It was fair the day you got it, and a worthy name to wear
When he took it from his father, there was no dishonor there
Through the years he proudly bore it, to his father he was true
And that name was clean and spotless when he passed it on to you.

Chorus:
Be careful of your father's name, don't ever drag it into shame
It won't buy you wealth and fame;
It was his most worthy treasure,
So be careful of his name.

It is yours to wear forever, you should wear it while you live
If perhaps some distant morning to another boy to give
And you'll smile as did your father, smile above the baby there
If a good name and a clean name you are giving him to wear.

At an early age John became devoted to music. I taught him the basics of the guitar, and it wasn't long before he far exceeded my skill. He soon branched out to other instruments, and chose the bass as his favorite. By the time he was twelve, John was playing electric bass in a rock band with his friends at school. I began taking John with me when I played shows at places like the Montgomery County Fair or the school variety show, to back me up on bass.

There is a considerable difference in tempo and chord progression between country/bluegrass and rock music. Before a show John and I would rehearse an hour or two in his room. We jammed until he felt comfortable with the songs for that performance.

It was a father's dream come true. Our common interest in music has kept us close over the years. I reflect back and see how John's careers and hobbies in education, music, and military paralleled mine, and how mine paralleled my father's.

Our daughter Martha was born on May 4, 1961, and she was beautiful, and she became the apple of my eye. She and I were inseparable during her early years.

Martha developed a love for horses when she was hardly big enough to ride. She liked the game I played with her called Ride the Horsey when she was four. I would get down on the rug, put her on my back, and walk on all fours. She loved it when I bucked her off -- she would laugh and giggle profusely, but get right back on and say, "Do it again, Daddy, but no fair tickling."

My schedule allowed me to be home much more when Martha was small. When things got unsettled between her and her mother, it melted my heart when she would come running to me saying, "I want my daddy."

I wrote this song for Martha when she was a baby, but now I think it applies to all my daughters.

Live Your Life with Care (Advice to Daughters)
  By Wayne Busbice
  Pub. Old Home Place Music

You are always in my heart
And you know that I will always care
I hope someday you'll see just what you mean to me
So live your life with care.

Chorus:
Live your life with care
Though I can't always be there
Don't ever start to roam in this wicked world alone
Please live your life with care.

Someday you may meet a man
Who will love you and treat you fair
He'll want you to be sweet and heavenly
So live your life with care.

(Amazingly, in 2007 I am suddenly receiving royalties from this song being used on cell phone ringtones.)

Margaret gave birth to our third child in August 1962. Heidi was born prematurely, with severe brain dysfunction. Heidi passed away at six months; we were never able to bring her home from the hospital. John and Martha were never to see their sister alive. When they first saw Heidi laid out at the funeral home, Martha whispered, "Baby go night-night."

Margaret's illness worsened after that. Although we occupied the same house, she and I stopped living together as husband and wife in that year. Margaret often said that she would be better off divorced.

Ten years later I found joy in a totally unexpected quarter. While vacationing at a North Carolina beach, I had persistent visions of an employee, Patricia O'Connor, a mother of five children who worked as a library assistant in the school where I was principal. The vision appeared to me frequently and would not leave my consciousness, waking or sleeping. I was perplexed since the only time we had ever spoken to each other was for library business or to say good morning.

When school resumed in the fall I spoke to Pat on a personal basis for the first time. An irresistible force pulled us together, it seemed. Immediately we recognized that the attraction we shared was so compelling that we could not ignore it. Within five days from our first lunch together, we decided to marry. These were wild days. I felt like a giddy ninth-grader with a crush on the prettiest girl in school.

Maryland was founded as a Catholic colony in 1632. It was predominately a Catholic state 340 years later, and its divorce laws were very strict. A no-fault divorce could take five years if contested; a non-contested divorce took at least three years.

Margaret had decided to contest our divorce for, she said, moral reasons. As Pat and I were grappling with the problem of my divorce, Gov. Mandel of Maryland was having an affair with the wife of one of the state legislators, and the media discovered it. The governor was using a state trooper to surreptitiously drive him in an official state police car down Route 5 to Leonardtown for a tryst with his lover, Jean Dorsey. Of course, he denied all rumors regarding this matter. However, on the way back to Annapolis one evening, the car transporting the governor was in an accident. He was only slightly injured, but his secret was out. Many a resident could be heard joking that the name of Route 5 should be changed to "the road to Mandel's lay."

Gov. Mandel's wife kicked him out of the governor's mansion and refused to agree to a divorce. This meant that the governor couldn't get a no-fault divorce in his own state for five years. At the governor's behest, the legislature passed "Mandel's Law," changing the state divorce laws to require only a one year wait for an uncontested divorce and a three year wait for a contested no-fault divorce.

Gov. Mandel somehow met all of his wife's demands and she agreed to give him a divorce. On the day he signed Mandel's Law, he and Jean Dorsey had a public wedding. His woes were not over, however, as he was convicted of some financial irregularity and sent to prison. There he worked in the prison laundry while his lawyers appealed his case. Finally, just one week before his second term was up, he was exonerated and resumed his position as governor for the last few days.

Mandel's Law gave Pat and me some hope that I might be able to get my divorce earlier than expected. I was in my third year of separation by this time and we were eager to establish a functional life. The new divorce law gave me the opportunity to file for divorce earlier. But full court dockets and continuances intervened, so I did not get to court until just a few months before the five years were up.

To ease our frustration over my failure to get a court date to finalize my divorce so we could get married, Pat and I took special little trips (honeymoons) to help us keep our sanity.

Our friends the Summervilles offered us a weekend at their getaway country house in West Virginia. We drove through the mountains of western Maryland into West Virginia and through the little town of Red Horse, to our destination, an old farmhouse in Horseshoe Bend. On the way we stopped to see the Fairfax Stone, in a deserted field marking the headwaters of the Potomac. We managed to stand with one foot on each bank of the Potomac River, about two feet wide at that part – which meant we stood in two states at once. By legend, the Fairfax Stone was laid by George Washington in the 1750s to delineate the five million acres Lord Fairfax owned in the colony of Virginia.

We drove up to the old farmhouse with the house key in hand. We had been assured that the deadbolt was not on. We tried the key for twenty minutes before going around the house to check for other ways to get in. Pat noted that the screened back porch door was hooked from inside. I checked the windows and found one unlocked. I removed the screen and Pat slithered in through the narrow opening, landing in the bathtub.

Curious, we examined the front lock before bringing in our bags. It was indeed locked from the inside, by deadbolt. How had this happened?

We brought in the bags and explored our surroundings. The farmhouse was fairly isolated. Some other old farmsteads were within a quarter mile, and there were abandoned fields all around. The house itself had a tin roof, small downstairs rooms, and two attic bedrooms reached by a cramped, enclosed winding staircase. The only bathroom was the one we stumbled into, on the first floor. The kitchen, in the front of the house, overlooked an old cistern. We descended to the cellar to find rock walls and the floor cut by a large sluice – a large, open water channel leading from the outside cistern to handle overflow. There was a very complicated water system which required us to turn on the pump switch before using any water.

That night we sat out on the screen porch at twilight and I strummed my guitar. The song "Country Roads" was real popular then, and as I sang the sound must have echoed over the fields; for soon, to our surprise, we had a dozen neighbors drifting over to hear the music. They were very friendly and asked us if we were going to "Tralta" the next day. We soon figured out that Tralta was Terra Alta, a nearby hamlet, which conducted a weekly livestock auction. That served as local entertainment. We went, and enjoyed watching the auctioneer and the cattle buying and selling process.

In the middle of the night at the farmhouse I got up to go the bathroom and wended my way down the rickety stairs. The bathtub spigot was running full blast into the tub. Neither Pat nor I had been in the bathroom since bedtime, and neither of us had taken a bath. Coming back up the stairs to bed and puzzling about the running water, I felt a sudden icy chill, and hair stood on end all over my body.

During the day and even at night while we were in bed, we could hear water running in the basement sluice. Water was pouring in from the cistern, but no one had turned on a faucet! Pat and I, at separate times, would go to the bathroom and find water running in the sink. Once the nearby hand towel was draped over into the running water.

One afternoon we left the house for a walk. We argued briefly about locking the front door, but in the end, Pat left it unlocked. After our hour's walk we returned to find the lock firmly in place – but since we had the key, it was no problem to get in.

That night I had a vivid dream of a middle-aged woman with a limp. I can still see her in her old-fashioned yellow housedress. She said nothing, but her demeanor was disapproving. I had a very strong feeling she did not want us there in the house. In the dream she somehow conveyed that her name was Effie Mae Hardin. Effie Mae was as real to me as any flesh-and-blood person, and her image remains vivid in my memory.

All of this left us feeling spooked and fascinated, but not afraid. Much. On our last day, we visited local cemeteries looking for a Effie Mae's tombstone, but found nothing.

Thus ended our haunted weekend. Back home in Maryland, our friends the Summervilles claimed nothing similar had ever happened to them. In the end, we wondered if Effie Mae's sensibilities had been offended by the unmarried couple staying in her house.

Although this was an era when living together was beginning to be accepted, as a principal, and especially as Pat's children's principal, I felt it inappropriate to move into their house with her family. I lived separately from 1972 to 1977, bided my time, and saw Pat as much as possible. I took on the fatherhood of Pat's five children – Michael, Karen, Maureen, Kathleen and Veronica – whose own father receded further and further from their lives. We decided to stay in Pat's house after we married so we would not have to uproot the children.

Pat took me "home" to meet her family in Rochester, New York in the spring of 1973. On the drive, I discovered that upstate New York is a beautiful place, and any expectations I had of a similarity to New York City were soon quelled as we drove past the scenic Finger Lakes and through mountains, valleys, orchards and dairy farms.

I was anxious about meeting Pat's family since they were steeped in the Catholic religion and I was a Southern Baptist. Although they knew that we both had been in very bad marriages, I was concerned about being accepted because both religions frowned on divorce.

During that first visit I felt acceptance from Pat's mother, Dorothy, but her Uncle Gordon and Aunt Marian seemed very uncomfortable with me as a potential member of the family – even though Dorothy introduced me to them and added, "He's a doctor, you know." Pat's siblings, Michael, Kathie and Casey, seemed to understand and were very supportive.

Probably in an effort to make me feel at home, Pat's family took us out to Hillbilly Heaven -- a nightclub where country and western music was featured -- together with Casey's fiancé and Kathie's boyfriend. Someone whispered to the bandleader that there was a recording artist from the Washington area in our group. Before I knew it, they shoved a guitar in my hand and a mike in front of my mouth. I sang a few Hank William numbers and received enthusiastic applause and a call for encores. Dorothy was thrilled to have a "celebrity" nearly in the family, and the others were impressed and looked at me in a different light after that.

Pat and her siblings were – and are -- very close to their Uncle Gordon and Aunt Marian, and looked up to them as leaders of the family, as role models and as surrogate parents. Gordon and Marian had a Down's syndrome child, Sally, about ten.

On my second visit, Pat asked me to bring along my guitar. Marian was kind, but Gordon still kept his distance, clearly disapproving. The family gathered on the porch after dinner. As a principal familiar with special ed kids and their limitations, I was amazed that Sally had a lot of verve and was friendly and outgoing. When I began to sing she showed so much interest that I was very touched.

She edged closer and closer to me until she was hanging on my knee and looking right into my face, and soon I was singing directly to her. I played a few children's numbers especially for Sally. Everyone on the porch was visibly moved. Uncle Gordon observed this connection we made, and it melted his heart. I could tell by his behavior that I had now been accepted without reservation.

Each time I visited Rochester after that, I always had to perform a little concert for Sally. As she grew up, Sally went to live in a group house. We visited her there, and she took pride in introducing me to her friends. I performed a few numbers. I told Aunt Marian that if I had had more loyal fans like Sally, I could have been a great success as a performer. Sally and I really connected, and we remained good friends until she died, very young, in her early twenties.

The most appreciative audience I ever played for is the community of cloistered Dominican nuns in Elmira, New York, where Pat's Aunt Patricia (Sister Mary Michael) resided. Sister Mary Michael had a sharp mind and an elfin sense of humor, and was always elated to have a visit from family. Twice a year we drove the six hours from Maryland to see her. But it was clear on my first few visits to the convent that Pat's aunt, Sister Mary Michael, was cool to the idea of Pat marrying a second time. It must have been hard to reconcile her feelings for her beloved niece and namesake and her deeply held religious beliefs.

Pat suggested that the nuns might be interested in a little entertainment, and asked if it would be okay to bring my guitar and play a few tunes. Aunt Patricia seemed somewhat reluctant, so the first time I played she was the only audience. But Aunt Patricia enjoyed it so much she encouraged me to come back soon, and when we returned a few months later, all fifteen nuns were seated and waiting in their parlor. They even brought in aged Mother Blessed Sacrament in her wheelchair.

Soon they were all beaming, tapping sandaled feet and swaying as I sang gospel songs, old favorites, and love songs that I had written about meeting and falling in love with Patsy. Mother Superior, especially, was grinning from ear to ear. I actually think they liked the love songs best! Patsy blushed on cue when I sang directly to her, and the nuns loved it.

My Sweet Little Pretty Brown Eyes
By Wayne Busbice
Pub. Old Home Place Music

Chorus:
My sweet little pretty brown eyes
I love to see you smile
Your heart is so true, you know I love you
My sweet little pretty brown eyes.

We met a little late in life
They said it never could be
But our love was so strong it could never go wrong
And now you belong to me.

I waited a long, long time
To hold and claim you for mine
Now that I'm free, a blind man could see,
Patricia, you belong to me.

After that, my little concert became a tradition in the convent, and I had to play and sing at every visit. Sometimes one of the nuns --a Cajun from Louisiana; we had lots to talk about-- would bring out her guitar and play along. I was told by one of the nuns that Aunt Patricia treasured the tapes I had made for her, and sometimes invited individual nuns to her room to listen as a special treat.

Aunt Patricia died at the age of eighty in March 1995. After the funeral in the monastery church, the family was invited back inside the convent for refreshments. It was just a little awkward in that room, with the cloistered nuns standing enclosed by a half-wall, and the family on the other side. After a long pause, Pat asked the prioress if I could play. I got out my guitar, and the Cajun nun brought in hers. Immediately the mood lifted, and we had a good old hootenanny in Aunt Patricia's memory. At the end, all the family and the nuns were in tears, and we all sang together as I played.

Will the Circle Be Unbroken
Traditional

Will the circle be unbroken
Bye and bye Lord, bye and bye
There's a better home a-waiting
In the sky, Lord, in the sky
Yes I told that undertaker
Undertaker, please drive slow
For that lady you are hauling
Lord I hate to see her go.
Will the circle be unbroken,
Bye and bye Lord, bye and bye
There's a better home a-waiting
In the sky Lord, in the sky.

Pat's Uncle Gordon, Aunt Patricia's brother, gave me heartfelt thanks for playing and said it was the best thing we could have done to remember Patricia. Gordon is a stoic man, a tall and handsome Mohawk Indian, but when he shook my hand warmly I could see a tear in his eye.

At last my divorce was granted. Now we had to plan a wedding. Pat was an ex-Catholic and I was a non-practicing Southern Baptist. We had no close church connections at the time. My former Baptist minister declined to marry us. Pat didn't feel right about going to a Catholic church. We met a minister, a good friend of my cousin Bobby and his wife Nadine, at a party and asked him to marry us. Because his church was in another county, we held the ceremony at the home of our good friends, Jerry and Dusty Levine.

We fit well into the beginning of the ecumenical movement. We have often bragged that this former Catholic and this former Southern Baptist were married in a Jewish home, by a Presbyterian minister.

I barely made it on time to the wedding on May 1, 1977, and I was sunburned from a day outside at the early afternoon ceremony which opened the new aquatic center at Gaithersburg Junior High. Pat said the sunburn went well with my new navy blue suit.

Pat wore a long sleeved floor length dress in pale turquoise with turquoise jewelry I had given her. I carried her over the threshold into her own house, and into our new life.

We had no time and very little money for a proper honeymoon. Pat had asked around and her boss, the librarian at Montgomery Village Junior High, recommended Cacapon State Park in Berkeley Springs, West Virginia. It was affordable and close by, so we reserved a spot.

It was a pleasant surprise to find a private rustic cabin with fieldstone fireplace and front porch rockers awaiting us, in an isolated clearing on forested Cacapon mountain. We were charmed by the wildlife, especially the deer that came down to our stream to drink each evening. Entire tracts of the park were enveloped in blooming dogwoods. There could not have been a more romantic, appropriate place for a gal from New York and a boy from Louisiana to enjoy together.

Now the real challenge was to introduce my Yankee bride --and New Yorker at that! -- to my family. I was well aware that I was bringing a type of person into the family who might be considered questionable. Although I had left the Southern states and my Southern attitudes behind in 1953, I was not sure if my siblings had outgrown the many prejudices we grew up with.

My brother Temple and his wife Juanita held a reunion at their home in Dallas. My new wife was very interested in getting to know the people I'd told her so many funny stories about.

She wanted to know everything. I would just laugh and say, "Well, I think we should wait until you get to meet them and form your own conclusions." This annoyed her no end.

So she was full of curiosity and questions when we set out for Dallas. Pat enjoyed learning the attitudes of Southern women and comparing them to what was familiar to her. She later said she was relieved to find that her expectations of finding unsophisticated farmwives were shattered by these well-groomed and vibrant women – her sisters-in-law -- in diamonds and the latest fashions. All of my siblings were there, and several cousins.

Pat's anxieties were quieted because she made an instant hit with her charm and –yes, I'll say it – Yankee humor, spark, and personality.

It didn't take long for Pat to win them over with her charm and gregariousness. They were all so pleased that I had finally found someone exciting to love. My cousin Vivienne said, "I never told you, but I was so worried about your finding someone. Pat seems to be ideal for you."

A few of my family members had been skeptical about my marriage to a former Catholic and New Yorker. Many wanted to know how we were able to get to know each other, coming from opposite ends of the country. I would reply, "We just decided to meet halfway."

~21~

Packed House

Our greatest challenge as newlyweds was to integrate our two families of five O'Connor and two Busbice children, and make it work. It wasn't easy to take two dysfunctional families and meld them into one friendly, loving family, but we managed.

After attending Montgomery College for a year, my son John Busbice joined the D.C. Air National Guard in 1972 and went on active duty for a year at Chanute Air Force Base, in Illinois. (I had the privilege of swearing him into the service, an unusual and moving ceremony for a father.) After completing his Air Force training in electronics he returned to Andrews AFB, Maryland and was assigned to the F-105 autopilot shop as an electronics technician for the D.C. Air National Guard to complete his military obligation, serving weekends and two weeks in the summer as a ready reservist. After six years of reserve duty he had risen in rank to sergeant. Concurrently with his military position, John was employed as media technician at Wootton High School and worked there until retirement in his forties. He is married to Annette Coker and they live in Madison, Mississippi, where she is a paralegal in the law firm founded by her father, and John is the sound technician for Mississippi Public Television. He is an accomplished musician and plays electronic bass regularly in a classic rock band, Pieces of Time.

Martha Busbice graduated from Mary Washington College and National Security Agency Intelligence School; she has carved out a successful career in the State Department foreign service in embassies around the world, including Bahrain, Abu Dhabi, Islamabad, Kinshasa, Rangoon and Bangkok. She and her husband Jeff Chedister have two children, Zachery and Aimee, and we often joined them during their annual home leave at their beach house on the Outer Banks of North Carolina. Martha has finished her last overseas assignment and she is now the Air Combat Command Intelligence Squadron Senior Analyst at Langley AFB near Norfolk, Virginia. Martha enjoys horses so much that she and her husband have bought a 20-acre horse farm in North Carolina and started a business, Harvest Moon Farm, offering horse and carriage rides for weddings and special occasions.

Martha and best friend

Michael O'Connor attended Montgomery College and was a computer engineer for Tele-Systems International. He spent a lot of time in the Far East establishing military satellite communications systems for foreign governments. Michael recently suffered a stroke but is progressing fairly well and hopes to be back at work soon. Mike is very active in his church, and lives in Sterling, Virginia.

Karen O'Connor graduated from the University of Maryland with a BS in Finance. She and her husband, Steve Koback, own and operate a very successful lawn service in rural Howard County, Maryland. Karen is active in community organizations and very involved in her children's, Leigh and Tyler's, activities. She is an officer of the PTA, runs the county boys' basketball league program, serves as treasurer for the county baseball and basketball league, does the office work for the family business, and manages the horse facilities in an estate community comprising seven barns and thirty-four horses . Karen and Leigh each own a horse, which they keep at home, and they both love to ride.

Maureen O'Connor (now Kroeger) was in the second class of women allowed to attend the Air Force Academy in Colorado Springs. (Again, I had the privilege of swearing Maureen into the regular Air Force as a second lieutenant. For the ceremony I used the same lieutenant's bars I used when commissioned as a young officer.) Upon graduation in 1981 she attended pilot training and served eight years as aircraft commander of a KC-135. Maureen refueled jet aircraft, serving around the world in Alaska, England, Saudi Arabia, and the Straits of Gibraltar. After leaving the Air Force at the rank of captain, Maureen began flying for American Airlines and is now in the captain's seat. She and her sons Paul and Timmy live in Flower Mound, Texas, a suburb of Dallas.

Air Force Capt. Maureen O'Connor flies Wayne and
Pat to Alaska from , Texas, in her refueling tanker

Kathleen O'Connor was president of her high school orchestra and served as the drum major for the marching band. She graduated from Ohio State University and while there she played in the famous Ohio State marching band. She lived in Rockville, Maryland; Arlington, Virginia; Fort Collins, Colorado, and Wesley Chapel, Florida, doing office work and teaching Jazzercize. She married twice and was twice divorced, with no children. It broke our hearts when Kathy passed away in September, 2005. Kathy was known for her art, dancing, athletic ability, and her interest in spiritual development. We learned a lot from her.

Bonnie (Veronica) O'Connor graduated a year early from high school and enrolled in the University of South Florida in Tampa, majoring in the classics and philosophy. While working on her degree she began part time employment at Skipper's Smokehouse restaurant, shucking oysters. She used to philosophically state, "I shuck, therefore I am." She fell in love with the counterculture ambience and family atmosphere of Skipper's, and after her graduation cum laude, she stayed on as a full time employee, and is now the general manager. In 2002 Skipper's, a noted Tampa concert venue, was voted the number one blues club in the United States! All the employees got tee shirts saying, Best Waitress at the Best Blues Club, Best Bartender at the Best Blues Club, etc. Bonnie got a tee shirt that says,

Best Manager at the Best Blues Club, and made shirts for Pat and me that say, Best Manager's Dad…. and Best Manager's Mom at the Best Blues Club.

All seven of our children own their own homes. Pat and I are very pleased to have been able to bring them together as one family. It was very difficult emotionally as well as financially, since we had five teenagers for a while, and four kids in college at one time.

The O'Connor children's father opted out of their lives at an early age and refused to assist them in any way. Margaret, my children's mother, passed away in 1993 due to her many problems. So Pat and I enjoy parental responsibility for all the kids.

By 1987 all the children were living independently so we built our "dream house" on Banner Country Court in Woodfield, Maryland. We had three acres, a quarter-acre vegetable garden, and plenty of room to have big family parties as well as political and civic events that we all enjoyed until we moved to Florida in 1998.

John and Annette Busbice

Jeff and Martha Chedister, Zach and Aimee

Michael O'Connor   *Kathleen O'Connor*

Koback family: Tyler, Steve, Leigh, Karen O'Connor

Maureen O'Connor Kroeger

Tim and Paul Kroeger, budding musicians

Kathy O'Connor, Bonnie O'Connor, Karen O'Connor Koback

Pat and I hosted the first major gathering of my grandparents' descendants at our house in Gaithersburg, Maryland in 1980. My relatives came from Virginia, Louisiana, North Carolina, Texas, and Oregon.

My sister Helen Patterson, from Portland, Oregon, had a difficult time making the reunion that year. Mt. St. Helen's erupted and delayed her family's travel plans. Helen brought samples of the volcanic ash that covered cars, streets and lawns in Oregon and parts of surrounding states.

Helen and her husband Pat brought their four sons who were of an age with my teenage stepdaughters. The young people did a lot of partying on their own. With chagrin we learned early one morning that the kids had stayed up all night and my stepdaughter Karen was now "engaged" to one of her step-cousins. Fortunately the engagement didn't take – it lasted only for the weekend.

Most of the men in the family have a tendency to put on weight around the middle. My brother Connella established a reunion contest to line up the males and determine which one would receive the coveted "no-belly prize".

We had three days of visiting, and sharing photos and family news, and trips to the U.S. Capitol and the Smithsonian. The cap-off of the weekend was a family concert in our living room. With support from two guest musicians (including Lamarr Grier from Bill Monroe's band), we Busbices recreated the impromptu concerts we used to have in the cotton fields.

Billy regaled us with his deep bass voice in a scary version of "The Haunted House". I contributed guitar and lead vocal, while Buzz and Bobby and I gave renditions of the old songs we learned growing up. Buzz set the house rocking with his famous energetic mandolin, playing his old Starday Record hits. In his sweet tenor, Bobby offered a solo of "Rebel Soldier," about the Confederate soldier dying after battle in Yankee country, and begging the parson to assure him his "soul [would] pass through the Southland." LeMoyne and his wife Doris collaborated on duets with his fiddle and her guitar.

LeMoyne then soloed on the up-tempo classic "Orange Blossom Special" and the beautiful, melodic "Faded Love," popularized by Bob Wills. Buzz and Lamar Grier, a former banjo player in Bill Monroe's band, brought down the house with "Dueling Banjos" on banjo and mandolin. My son John submerged his rock tendencies and backed up each group with his steady electric bass. According to bluegrass concert tradition, we finished with two gospel songs, "Will the Circle Be Unbroken?" and "I Saw the Light"– as the whole house rocked with singing through tears.

Our living room was packed with about fifty people and overflowing into the dining room and hall. We had invited some neighbors for the concert, and Robert Busby and family from Charlottesville. Robert, a suspected cousin, and I had been corresponding regarding genealogy. He was blown away by the talent of the Busbice family and stated unequivocally that the performance of "Dueling Banjos" was the best he'd ever heard.

During this reunion we formalized the family reunion association, establishing a newsletter, and electing officers and family historian – me.

When I was sixteen, after a year living with Aunt Eva and Uncle Elton on Boeuf River, I had come back home for the summer to help with the cotton production. As I was plowing in the Old Flat, I unearthed a branding iron that my grandpa had devised and used to identify his cattle in the early 1900s.

The branding iron was a reverse B and an R attached, fused together to stand for Busby-Busbice-Rusheon, and I kept it for a long time in the barn as a memento. Branding irons went out of use prior to my generation because our jurisdiction passed a stock law that required farmers to keep their domestic animals fenced in so they would not graze on the field crops.

When we created our family association I fashioned a logo for it, using the branding iron as the focus. I added a circle around that, and wrote "Busby Busbice Rusheon" within the circle.

At this reunion as at all the others, the topic was always our Grandpa Rusheon. Had he really killed someone, and why? What kind of person was he? Who are we? It's clear when we get together that each of us had acquired hints and pieces of Grandpa's story, but no one was aware of the whole picture.

~22~

A Killing in Georgia

On July 22, 1896, my grandfather Oliver Allen Busby, Sr. awakened at five in the morning, dressed hastily, and slipped out the back door, careful not to awaken his wife and five children. My daddy, Oliver Allen Busby, Jr., was a young three-year-old sleeping among the other children.

As Oliver saddled his horse, he had many conflicting thoughts about his mission that morning. He was on his way to confront young Dr. MacArthur about some disagreement that had been festering in his gut.

On his way, Oliver passed the Burch cemetery where two of his children were buried. He decided to stop at the big iron gates to bow his head and say a small prayer for his sons who had passed away in their infancy. He was unsettled in his mind about what this day would bring.

It was about six o'clock when Oliver arrived at the Burch residence. He asked Mr. Burch if he could speak with his boarder, the young doctor. In Burch's presence, Oliver confronted W. MacArthur about the rumors he had been spreading among the neighbors. Dr. MacArthur apologized, and said it was meant to be a joke, and he would go explain to everyone that he had told. Oliver appeared satisfied and they shook hands. And after a short conversation among the three of them, Burch returned to his house. Oliver and Dr. MacArthur walked on down the lane, still talking together.

When Oliver left the scene, Dr. MacArthur was dead in the road, with bullets in his back.

Local newspapers gave contradictory reports about the killing:

THE TIMES --JOURNAL

Eastman, Dodge County, Georgia, Friday, July 24, 1896
Murder In Laurens.

Meager news comes to us of the killing of Dr. W. A. MacArthur by O. A. Busbee near Arthur, Laurens County, last Wednesday morning.

We can gather nothing authentic from the reports, but the details seem to be about as follows: Dr. MacArthur had told a joke on Mr. Busbee, which, it seems was somewhat of a reflection. Busby went over to see MacArthur about it Wednesday morning when proper apologies were made and accepted, and the two men started off down the road together, Doctor MacArthur leading his horse. Pretty soon pistol shots were heard in the direction they had taken, and when found Dr. MacArthur was lying in the road, dead, with four bullet holes in his back. It is said that this is the third man Busbee has killed, and it is said that there will be trouble arresting him.

THE MACON TELEGRAPH: FRIDAY MORNING, JULY 24, 1896
Killing of Dr. MacArthur.
Shot in the Back Three Times by Oliver Busbee,
In Laurens County
Dublin, July 23-(Special) Dr. W. A. MacArthur was shot yesterday morning about 6:00 a.m. by O. A. Busbee, near Arthur, Georgia, Laurens county.

No one was near the scene except the parties engaged. Evidence before the inquest disclosed the fact that it was premeditated murder, as Busbee had made threats against his victim.

Doctor MacArthur was shot in the back, in three places, one of the bullets passing through his heart.

Busbee called at Mr. MacArthur's home and the two walked quietly away together about 125 yds. from the doctor's house, where the shooting occurred.

The victim was buried at Burch cemetery, about 17 mi. from Cox, Georgia. The verdict of the coroner's jury was murder.

Busbee is at large, but the Sheriff and posse are in hot pursuit

Dr. MacArthur came to this county several months ago, and has successfully practiced his profession at Walker, Georgia. He was quite a clever gentleman, and was considered a peaceful citizen. And the people of that section are greatly aroused over his untimely death. His father lives in Macon and has been telegraphed for.

The scene of the murder is 20 miles below this place, and particulars are very meager at this writing.

ANOTHER ACCOUNT
Eastman, July 23 – (Special) – Dr. A. G. MacArthur was shot here and killed yesterday afternoon about 17 mi. from here in Laurens county by one Busbee. Dr. MacArthur was residing at Mr. John Burch's house. Busbee called him out to the gate and asked him to walk down the road with him, as he wanted to have a talk with him. When just a few hundred yards from the house, it is supposed, Busbee shot him in the back, and then shot him three times after he fell. Mr. Burch, on hearing the shots, hurried to the scene and found the doctor lying on his face, dead, with three bullets in his back, any one of which would have been fatal. It is impossible to obtain all of the particulars at this writing, and it is only a conjecture, as to the cause that led to the killing. Dr. MacArthur was one of the best

prominent men in this community, and was well and favorably known here, and is a relative of the late honorable Walter T. MacArthur.

A comparison of news articles published at the time reveals discrepancies. And the item reported in one article about Grandpa killing two other men was not true. The two other men had been killed by a man named Busbee, who was not Oliver Busby and appears not to be connected to him.

My grandfather Oliver was born about 1855 in Houston County, Georgia, near Busbyville. His parents were Allen Busby and Sarah Hayes Sangster. Before long the family moved to Laurens County, near Hawkinsville. Oliver was the twelfth child; he grew up with ten half-siblings, two full siblings, and five step-siblings, making a total of eighteen children in the family.

In his old age, Oliver's father Allen began to divide up his large farm, with a considerable amount of acreage going to Oliver. Allen Busby died in the summer in 1878 at the age of eighty. By this time, however, Oliver was farming with an uncle in Dooly County, Georgia. He decided not to return home to Laurens County. It was not that he admired his uncle that much, but rather that he had his eye on a pretty little redheaded girl, Mary Frances Byrd. Mary Frances was about to become sixteen, marrying age in those days. Oliver was ten years older, but the age difference didn't seem to be a problem.

Mary Frances's mother, Martha Thompson Sangster, had been married to Oliver's half brother, Durham Sangster, who died in the Civil War. Martha and Durham had produced two sons, Benjamin F. and Will, and a daughter, Matty.

A year later Martha married an older gentleman named Byrd, and they had one child, Mary Frances, born in 1865. Mr. Byrd died when she was an infant. Oliver Busby was half-uncle to the Sangster children, but no relation to Mary Frances.

Martha Sangster Byrd was very concerned about her daughter's plan to marry Oliver. She consulted her former mother-in-law, Sarah Sangster Busby, who was Oliver's mother, about the issue. Oliver's mother advised, "If I were you, I would let this one pass." Nevertheless, Oliver and Mary Frances were married in 1882.

Martha had now married a third time, to Mr. Dickson, and she moved to his big farm. She appointed Will Sangster, Mary Frances' half-brother, to manage the 400-acre farm where the Sangster family resided, along with Oliver and Mary Frances. She planned to divide the farm equally among her four children, hoping this would keep all her children nearby.

The Sangster children were resentful of Oliver and they were opposed to sharing the farm equally with Mary Frances. After some negotiation it was decided that they would agree to give Mary Frances her share of the farm if Oliver could prove himself as a successful farmer. They agreed upon a two-year trial period for this.

Oliver was confident of success and welcomed the challenge. He had bragged about his farming ability, creating more resistance and animosity among the Sangsters. Will Sangster pleaded with his mother to back down from her plan to divide the property equally. Martha said she couldn't change her mind, so Will tore up the legal papers.

Martha had new papers drawn up and called a family meeting where she insisted that her daughter Mary Frances receive a full share of the property. And she pointed out that Oliver had been her brother-in-law when she was married to Durham Sangster, so in essence he was family, too. Her other children reluctantly agreed.

In the late fall of 1889 the meeting to sign the documents was held in the farmhouse living room in front of the huge fireplace. Will had brooded a lot about this issue, and he seated himself at the edge of the gathering. Possibly he feared losing his position as farm manager.

Each person signed the papers as they were handed around, but when they came to Will, who was last, he tossed them into the fireplace. At this insult, Oliver drew his revolver and shot Will in the arm.

The family declined to report the incident to the sheriff, but urged Oliver and Mary Frances to move away. It was now impossible for Oliver and Will to live on the same farm.

On November 7, 1889, Oliver bought 202 acres of land near Hawkinsville, in Laurens County, for six hundred dollars from a Mr. Clark. Clark had purchased it from a state official, Hon. Walter MacArthur. Mr. Clark had made a gentleman's agreement with Mr. MacArthur that he would not sell it to a neighbor, Mr. B.D. White. The very next day after Oliver Busby purchased this piece of property, he sold it to B.D. White for the same price, thereby keeping Mr. Clark's word and integrity intact.

Possibly this action set up an adversarial relationship between Oliver Busby and the MacArthur family. Other rumors hint that the feud which developed involved romantic entanglements. Possibly Dr. MacArthur had been involved with Mae Belle, oldest Busby daughter. Or Oliver and the doctor were sharing the favors of a lady of the neighborhood. Or the doctor had knowledge of an illegitimate child that he attributed to Oliver.

In any case, in 1896, Dr. MacArthur began to denounce Oliver Busby throughout the community. Stories passed down in the family imply that the doctor indicated that my grandpa was not scrupulous about land deals and marriage vows.

Just nine days before he killed the doctor, Oliver "sold" all of his land to his wife. Did he take this action because he planned to kill the doctor and wanted to make sure his family had some security? Or was he afraid he would not come out alive when he confronted Dr. MacArthur?

No one but my grandpa really knows what happened at the scene. His explanation that has been passed down to friends and family is self-serving, and may be examined with skepticism.

Oliver declared that as they walked, he had reached down to untangle the reins of his horse from its hooves, and MacArthur struck him on the back of the head and knocked him down. In reaction, Oliver said he drew his revolver and opened fire as he was falling. If true, does this explain how the doctor was shot in the back, three times?

Busby family 1896, taken soon after the killing. Oliver Allen and Mary Frances with Seaborn, Oates, Emery, and Elton; Mae Belle standing

Oliver was generally well regarded in his home community. In the early 1890s Oliver Busby had served as deputy sheriff of Dodge County. Local law officers in nearby Laurens County sent for Sheriff Busby to help them subdue a violent man who had killed his neighbor and was holed up in a vacant house with a shotgun. He had vowed to kill anyone who tried to capture him. Oliver rode in with his gun. He devised a plan to sneak up to the side of the house while the gunman was distracted by others. Oliver reached the outside of the window, slammed open the shutter, and sprayed bullets through the house. The fugitive was shaken by the attack, and he surrendered. This episode enhanced Oliver's fame in the area as a tough lawman and not somebody to tangle with. Decades later, a lifelong resident would tell my Aunt Eva that Oliver was extremely fierce and nervy, with a reputation in several counties as a very capable law officer.

Oliver's allies believed that Oliver had acted in self-defense in the MacArthur affair while people allied to the MacArthur family insisted that he was a killer. Oliver made it clear that he would not be taken alive. He declined to surrender to the law, and continued to farm on his property for two and a half years without being arrested. The county sheriff arrived on the farm at least once a month to serve an arrest warrant, but Oliver, who possibly had prior knowledge of the visits, could not be found.

Oliver had constructed a false floor under the corncrib. When he suspected the sheriff was coming, Oliver crawled under the barn and onto planks lowered from above. The help of friends was then required to raise the cutout plank floor into position under the corncrib, so Oliver was invisible both from inside and under the barn.

In 1898, the MacArthur family became impatient and hired Pinkerton detectives to find Oliver and arrest him. The Pinkertons were a private company who had instilled professionalism into law enforcement. Their motto was "We never sleep." They were so effective as a crime fighting organization that the FBI would be modeled on their methods in the twentieth century.

The Pinkerton agent began surveillance by just showing up in the field where Oliver was working. He stood motionless and silent in the field, close enough to be visible but out of gunshot range. Oliver would make no gesture or acknowledgment of the detective's presence. Oliver went back to work, and later he would notice the detective watching from the woods, or elsewhere on the farm. "The Pinks", as they were known, played this cat and mouse game for several months without confrontation.

Friends were told not to drop in unexpectedly. Oliver placed a curfew on his family. No one was allowed outside after dark. One evening as the family was having supper, a loud knock was heard at the front door. In one sweeping action, Oliver grabbed his rifle and knocked the oil lamp off the table with the gun barrel. He yelled to the family to get on the floor and stay there. Oliver fled out the back door to the house of a loyal friend, Joe Wright. No one ever determined who knocked on Grandpa's door that fateful night. If it was the Pinkerton agent, he did not follow through on his capture attempt.

Oliver never returned to his dwelling. Joe Wright made all arrangements for them to escape from Georgia together. Grandpa Oliver reasoned that his presence in the home put his wife and children at risk. Soon, Oliver's wife and family left the home too, and moved in with Mary Frances's half sister and her husband.

Grandpa Oliver and Joe Wright fled to Mississippi, where Oliver could take refuge with some Busby cousins. Together they developed a plan to establish a new life. Grandpa assumed the name Allen (his middle name) B. (for Busby) Rusheon, and he and Joe Wright moved on to Bassfield, Mississippi, in early 1899. Grandpa and Joe Wright both became very friendly with a young widow there.

In Bassfield Oliver a.k.a. Allen Rusheon entered into a sharecropping agreement with a Mr. Hawkins, a local farmer. Verbal agreements were the norm. But at the end of the crop year, Grandpa had produced so much more cotton than the other tenant farmers that Mr. Hawkins was reluctant to divide the profits according to plan. Oliver made it very clear in no uncertain terms that Hawkins should live up to his word or it could be injurious to his health; and Mr. Hawkins wisely agreed to abide by the original terms of the agreement.

Now Allen B. Rusheon and Joe Wright continued westward to northeastern Louisiana. Grandpa was about forty-four at this time. The Georgia census records from 1860 to 1880 indicate that Oliver was born about 1855. But in his new location in Louisiana, Allen told the census taker that he was born in 1850 -- perhaps to avoid detection.

Grandpa purchased 200 acres from Dan Frantom near the small town of Eros. The farm, in a remote area served only by wagon and buggy trails, straddled Ouachita and Jackson parishes. This would be convenient in case the sheriff of either parish came looking for him; he could step over the line to another jurisdiction while remaining on his own property.

Neighbors were told that Allen B. Rusheon was a widower from Mississippi, who was sweet on a widow there. But his cousin in Georgia, a Mr. Busbice, had recently died and left a widow with six children, and Allen planned to marry her.

The ever-loyal Joe Wright returned to the Georgia farm to guide Mary Frances and the six Busby children -- Seaborn, Elton, my father, Emery, Pauline, and Eva Mae Belle -- to their new home. Secretly, they boarded a train bound for Louisiana. In the middle of the night, Joe Wright and Mary Frances called the children together as they crossed the Mississippi River to notify them they had a new name, Busbice, to use from that moment on. And that their mother's new husband, Allen B. Rusheon, wanted to be addressed as Cousin Allen.

One or two older children were sworn to secrecy, and the younger children were not told that Cousin Allen was really their father. He continued to be called Cousin Allen by all the Busbice children during his life.

The family was reunited on Christmas Day in 1899, and shortly thereafter, on December 30, 1899, Oliver and Mary Frances were remarried, using their new identities as Allen B. Rusheon and Mary Frances Busbice.

In the years that followed, five more children were born. Of course, they were named Rusheon: Joe Wright (after Grandpa's good friend Joe Wright), L. B., Alden, T. O., and Violet. This gave the family eleven children, of whom six were named Busbice and five were Rusheons.

To protect their father, the younger children were allowed to think that they were indeed half-brothers and sisters. Mr. Rusheon's fugitive status required that the family secret be maintained at all costs, and children were not informed of the truth until they reached maturity. Mae Belle remembered the entire incident. She was sent to Dixon, Tennessee, to school to study for a teaching career.

Standing in rear: Elton and Seaborn. Mae Belle in center, flanked by Joe Wright and Mary Frances Busby. Children in front: Oates, Emery, Pauline

After the flight to Louisiana, my father's name -- which had been Oliver Allen Busby, Jr. -- became Oliver Allen Busbice, Jr. But this would not do because it was feared that the name might attract attention and lead to Grandpa. Therefore, my father's name was changed to Oates Allen Busbice.

Joe Wright returned to Mississippi, where he married the attractive widow and raised a large family.

As they grew older, Daddy and his brothers and sisters lost much respect for their violent father. My daddy Oates decided that he didn't like sharing his father's name, Allen. So he changed his name from Oates Allen to Oates Oliver Busbice, "Double O."

Grandpa Allen continued his violent ways. It is said that he carried a pistol until the day he died, twenty-five years after the death of Dr. MacArthur. Grandpa never faced charges for the killing.

~23~

A Portrait of My Grandfather

My grandfather Oliver Allen Busby Sr. (Allen B. Rusheon) spent twenty-five years of his life covering up his past, and I spent twenty-five uncovering his story.

As a young teen, I had been incredulous to learn there had been killings on both sides of my family. It took years for this information to sink in. My parents had always avoided discussing the family scandal, so it was easy to live in a fog of denial. I was unable to reconcile the murder of my maternal grandfather and the violent past of my paternal grandfather with the kind and mild-mannered relatives I knew.

As the years went by, gradually more details, some conflicting, were revealed by cousins, aunts and uncles. The taboo that surrounded any discussion of these topics only increased my curiosity and my desire to find out about what my ancestors were like. These questions remained in the back of my mind throughout my life, and I became determined to learn as much as I could about the family secrets.

By now we all accepted that there had been a killing, that Rusheon was really Busby, and that there was an untold story in Georgia just waiting to be discovered. Over the years I collected all the stories I could from my family to shed light on our roots.

Uncle Emery liked to sit on his back porch and tell stories. One day Bobby and Billy and I were telling him about a boy we knew who resented his stepfather for being harsh and unfair. Uncle Emery remembered being disciplined by Grandpa Rusheon, his stepfather. Emery said when the spanking ended he turned, looked him right in the eye, and said, "You can't do that to me – you're not my daddy." Grandpa Rusheon didn't say a word, but picked him up again and spanked him harder. Emery told us, "I knew right then, he was my daddy."

Aunt Eva knew my Grandpa Rusheon well. Uncle Elton had built their first house on Grandpa's farm for his young family. She told me she got along well with her father-in-law, but he was abusive to his sons. Aunt Eva told me a story about my grandpa beating Elton, who was then a young man, with a razor strap. Elton was left bloody, and so injured that he ran away for a few years.

In 1947, Billy said, he lived with Uncle Emery and Aunt Ivie for a year, to help Uncle Emery with the farm work after his heart attack. During that time Joe Wright came from Mississippi to visit. Uncle Emery and Joe Wright settled with their coffee on the back porch overlooking the barn. It was only natural for their talk to veer to the killing incident in Georgia. Billy, still a teenager, didn't ask questions but he listened carefully. By this time we were all curious to get the name of the man Grandpa killed, and the reason. Since Joe Wright was involved in bringing the family to Louisiana, Billy thought he was going to learn something he could share with his brothers and sisters. He didn't learn many details, but he deduced that Joe Wright had no first-hand knowledge about the incident.

Bobby, Donald, Vivienne, Lannie Mack, Lancelot, Ivie and Emery

Cousin Donald, who had volunteered for the Navy right out of high school, returned from the war in the late 1940s. Uncle Emery asked him to stay on the farm and work with him as a partner, and Donald was willing to try it out.

One day they sat down to rest in mid-afternoon under the big pine tree near our pond. Without preamble, Uncle Emery told Donald all about the trouble Grandpa got into in Georgia, how our name was changed, and how this created legal problems for all the Busbice children in Emery's generation. Donald tried to share this startling information with his brother Bobby when he returned from college for the summer, but Bobby was suspicious and refused to believe it.

From the stories I realized that Grandpa was a violent man, and could indeed have killed someone; and that there were people named Busby in the

225

South who were related to us. And that he was my real grandfather, not my step-grandfather. And that I was living with a made-up name.

One summer while I was in Denver Colorado, I called Uncle T.O. Rusheon's widow Edith to see if she knew anything more about Grandpa's experiences in Georgia. I mostly wanted to know who he had killed, and why. I asked her if T.O. ever discussed the family history with her. Edith said when she asked T.O. about his family, he chuckled and said only, "Lightning struck our family tree." She never asked again.

Over the years there were a few missed opportunities to learn more about our extended family. We just didn't know enough at that time to be curious and follow the clues that presented themselves. My cousin Thad sheepishly tells of a missed chance to make family connections. Thad had just received his doctorate in plant genetics in 1968, and was teaching agriculture at North Carolina State in Raleigh. To get acquainted, his wife June attended a Newcomers' meeting in Raleigh, where a lady named Busby came up to welcome her and said, "I'm sure we're related." June said, "No, I don't think so; our name is Busbice." The woman replied, " Please have your husband contact me. I know the background and history of your family, and I'm sure we're related." Thad never followed up with the woman.

Buzz related that one day during his TV show, a tall gentlemen came to the studio. He introduced himself as Congressman Jeff Busby, a former congressman from Mississippi. He told Buzz he was a faithful viewer of the show. And he had come to see him because he knew they were related.

Buzz was puzzled and said, "Busby is my stage name. My real name is Busbice. So how could that be?" With a grin, Congressman Busby replied, "Yes, I know the story. Here's my number; give me a call and we can discuss this."

Buzz was polite but brushed it off. He was unaware or uninterested in the questions about our family history. He figured the congressman was just another fan.

When Buzz told me about this later I said, "I've been trying to find somebody who knew about this change of our name; you should follow up." But Buzz never did.

As I began to fill in the portrait of my grandfather, I recalled the stories I had heard as a boy at family reunions, the stories of his days in Louisiana as Allen B. Rusheon.

Allen Rusheon was a strong man, six foot two and muscular. He had the reputation of being the best farmer and the hardest field worker around our neck of the woods. And he demanded the same of his sons. His policy was, women were expected to do garden work but not allowed to work in the fields.

Although he was feared for his harshness and strict authoritarian discipline, everybody both inside and outside the family respected Grandpa Rusheon for his work ethic. He was also known to be scrupulously honest in business dealings.

Grandpa went to great lengths to find the right church for his family to attend. As a child, he had been raised in the Primitive Baptist church – a very conservative group sometimes referred to as hardshell Baptists. There were no Primitive Baptist churches in our part of Louisiana. So every Sunday Allen loaded up all the women and young children in a two-seat buggy to visit various churches, while the boys rode horseback alongside.

Grandma Mary Frances was a Methodist, and her church, Frantom Chapel, was less than a mile away. But Allen didn't approve of their doctrine. For a while they all attended Oak Grove Baptist, five miles away, but he didn't approve of that church, either. Next they drove ten miles, to Walnut Grove Baptist, but he found something to disapprove of there. Salem Baptist church was next, seven miles from the farm. It was not exactly right, but it was more conservative than the others, although they did allow musical instruments – unlike the Primitive Baptists. So he decided to stay.

A hundred years ago, boys collected cigarette butts, peeled them, and saved up the tobacco until they got enough to roll their own. One of the teenage boys, possibly Elton, was sneaking some smokes in the barn and accidentally set the corn shucks afire. Soon the entire barn was ablaze.

Emery climbed up on the roof and began pulling the pine shingles off to prevent the fire from spreading. Dry pine shingles were like a tinderbox and once they caught, the fire would expand quickly. Emery was in a panic and working fast, when the extreme heat caused him to faint. He fell from the top of the barn, hit the ground, and was knocked out. This distracted the family from the fire, and before they realized it, it was out of control. Grandma and one of the girls took Emery in a buggy to a tenant house a half-mile away, where he lay unconscious for three days.

Although Grandpa and the older children tried to fight the fire with buckets of well water, the barn was too close to the house, and the house burnt to ashes as well.

With a family of eleven children to care for, Grandpa Allen had to decide whether to rebuild or to buy another house. It so happened that Mr. Phillips was interested in selling his farm next door, which consisted of 160 acres and a good house. The Rusheon family bought it, increasing their total acreage to 360. They must have slept more securely knowing the barns were now 200 yards from the house.

During the process of selling Grandpa his new house and land, the Phillips family was living their own drama. A weird thing occurred. Houses were usually built on the top of a hill to take advantage of the cool breezes. Doors and windows had to be kept open to cool the house. Window screens were not generally in use.

One day as Mr. and Mrs. Zack Phillips and their son, Ab, were sitting in the living room, a dove flew in, made three circles near the ceiling, and then exited the front door. The dove then flew northeast in a straight line until it disappeared.

Since birds don't normally enter a house, and doves do not fly in straight lines, people believed this was an omen of impending death. Within a year all three of the family members died of unknown diseases, and were buried in Antioch Methodist Church's graveyard, which was located in the direction the dove flew.

Grandpa and Grandma Rusheon had to finalize the purchase of the Phillips property with the heirs.

Whether it was due to the incident of the house burning down or for some other reason, when he was in his late teens Elton was a frequent target of Allen's rages. One day, Grandpa Allen gave the day's assignment for plowing the fields to Elton and Seaborn. At the end of the day, he measured the acreage plowed by each son, and Elton was found wanting.

Grandpa flew into a rage in spite of Elton's protest that he had been using the slowest mule. He beat Elton brutally with a razor strap across the back, until he bled. Elton left immediately and went to Eros. Grandma, very upset, asked the preacher to find him and beg him to come home. The minister found him, but after Elton showed the preacher his bleeding back, the good man gave him five dollars and told him, "I don't blame you. Keep on going, and God bless you." Elton stayed for a few years in Mississippi with Joe Wright before returning to Louisiana to settle down.

In spite of this harsh treatment, Elton and all his brothers grew to be very calm, gentle and kind men.

In gossip at the syrup mill with the local farmers, the name of Sam Crowell came up regarding his courtship of some young ladies. Grandpa remarked that he didn't understand why the ladies would be interested in Sam, since it was well known that he was illegitimate. Word got back to Sam, and he came to the syrup mill to confront Allen. Soon they were fighting, and Sam, younger and stronger, was getting the best of it.

In their struggle, both men fell into the fire pit under the cooking pan. Uncle Seaborn, by now a strapping young man, grabbed them both and shamed them into stopping the fight. But Grandpa couldn't let it pass.

That evening he went home, got his gun, and announced to his wife that he was going to go kill Sam. Mary Frances followed him on foot for two miles, entreating and begging, and reminding him what had happened the last time he killed someone. To her relief, he finally turned back before committing the deed.

Allen Rusheon was prone to "spells". In his violent mood, his oldest daughter, Eva Mae Belle, was the only one who could handle him. He would ask her to lock him up in the smoke house until the fit passed, because he was known to have a very volatile temper and was afraid he would lash out and possibly harm his children. The family attributed these spells to heart trouble.

Some have speculated that Grandpa was afraid he might die and have to face an accounting in the afterlife for killing Dr. MacArthur in 1896. Close friends in the community, not knowing of his history, were puzzled about this quirk in his behavior. But Allen was not the only man who asked to be locked in his smokehouse.

Luther Kilpatrick told this story about Jack Clark, a man who lived in Okaloosa. Clark had killed a Mr. Bailey because Bailey, a married man, was having an affair with Clark's oldest daughter. Mr. Bailey was working in the field one day and stopped to drink water from a glass jug. A shot rang out and smashed the jug in his upraised hands. Before he could react, another shot killed him. Luther said that Jack Clark periodically asked someone to lock him in the smokehouse because he had violent and guilty fits regarding his evil deed.

Hosea Russell, Grandpa (Busby) Rusheon, and Uncle Emery with prized foxhounds, 1918

229

When Elton was a young man living at home, he loved to go fox hunting. One Saturday night, Elton, Emery and a few neighbors went hunting with five or six foxhounds. A widow called Old Lady Lewis lived about a quarter of a mile from the Rusheon home and the foxhunters with their leashed dogs had to pass by her house both coming and going. Old Lady Lewis owned a very vicious bulldog that invariably attacked any dog that came by, unless she was there to call him off. Uncle Elton got tired of having his foxhounds injured every time they passed Old Lady Lewis' house at night. When returning home this particular Saturday night, he told all the other hunters to go ahead, and he would follow with the dogs. He had an idea to break the bulldog of this bad habit.

When the bulldog attacked, Elton tried to fend him off, but the dog would not respond. So Elton took his .22 pistol and shot the bulldog "graveyard dead". All the dogs were madly barking and snarling. Then he saw a match struck in an upstairs window as someone tried to light a lamp to see the cause of the commotion. Elton turned his pistol, and shot at the rooftop of the house. The match was immediately extinguished and no one came out.

The next day Miz Lewis came by to complain to Grandpa about one of his boys, and said she suspected it was Seaborn who killed her dog. Grandpa replied he knew nothing about it. Miz Lewis was so angry she drove her buggy the twenty-five miles to Jonesboro to file a complaint with the sheriff. When Seaborn was served with court papers, he assured his father that he couldn't have done it; he had been visiting his sister Mae Belle in Winn Parish that weekend. Grandpa told him, "Don't worry about it; just go to court."

Miz Lewis told her story on the witness stand and said that Seaborn had killed her dog. When asked if she had actually seen the person, she answered, "No, it was too dark, but I knowed it was Seaborn. That's like something he would do." Seaborn took the stand and explained that he was not even in Jackson parish on the night in question. Seaborn had brought along several people who verified his statement, so the judge threw out the case. Until the day she died, Miz Lewis believed that "Seaborn done it," and got away with it.

There was no leash law in those days, but the code of the hills was quite well known. Vicious dogs should be kept chained or enclosed. It was well understood that anyone, either walking or riding horseback, who was attacked or threatened by a bad dog had a right to kill the animal.

All my uncles and aunts became emotional when they talked about their brother Alden Rusheon, who died at age fifteen. I can remember the love in their voices and the tears in their eyes as they reminisced.

Near the end of 1919, Alden fell ill with a bad cold that settled in his lungs. He was able to enjoy Christmas, when he received a new pocket watch. But the cold worsened for months, until he could hardly breathe and was in constant pain. Dr. Phillips came by and diagnosed Alden with rheumatic fever, but in spite of all care, he slipped away. They say that for the last two weeks Grandma held him in her arms night and day to help him breathe.

Alden died at the farm in early February, 1920, while my parents Oates and Fay were away living in Shawnee, Oklahoma. They could not attend the funeral because Momma had the flu. My father received the following letter from his brother L.B. Rusheon:

Dearest brother,

Our darling brother was laid down to sleep in the Salem Grave Yard yesterday. He died Saturday night…He died praying. His mind was perfect until death struck him. He looked at his watch to see what time it was as death struck him. All the children were at home except you. Maebelle fainted three times. He called on Mamma to help him as long as she could help and when she failed, called on God. I wish you could have heard his little prayer. It beat everything you have ever heard. I believe if we live right we will see him another day to come.

We laid him in a stone coffin, a black suit, white tie, white stockings, and white shirt. He looked as natural as I ever saw him, and he had a death smile on his face. We persuaded Mamma and Pappa to go home with Maebelle. It looked like it would kill both of them too.

Jim Spillers preached the funeral, and he did fine. How is Fay with the flu?…I am in Eros at Finley's store. That's why I am writing so sorry. The people have been mighty good to us since he was sick.

Hoping to see you soon, I am as ever,

Your loving brother, L.B. Rusheon

After I reached my teens, I was helping Luther Kilpatrick chop cotton one afternoon and I asked him to tell me about my Grandpa Rusheon.

Luther told me that when he was a teenager, his father sent him to chop cotton for Grandpa in exchange for some work the Busbice boys had done on the Kilpatrick farm. Mr. Kilpatrick told Luther, "I don't want to hear any complaints about your work. Be sure you do your share for Cap Rusheon, and don't disgrace our family—or you'll have to answer to me!" In those days fathers used a peach tree switch or razor strap to discipline their sons until they reached the age of twenty-one and adulthood.

Grandpa, Luther and several Busbice boys were toiling away under the sun in the field we called Old Flat. Grandpa took the lead right away and set a fast pace. Luther said he tried as hard as he could, but still fell behind.

Ol' Cap Rusheon, as Luther called him, would yell out to chastise the boys: "Seaborn, you're not keeping up! Elton, you're falling behind. Oates, what's the matter with you today? – you sick?" His voice went through the field like electricity. That spurred everyone to work harder.

Luther toiled as fast as he could, but he could not close the gap between him and Grandpa. "I'm gonna get a whipping for sure when I get home if I don't catch up," he thought. Finally, feeling like a failure, he sat down and cried.

Ol' Cap Allen Rusheon asked him what was the matter. Luther replied, "I just can't keep up with you. My father will probably give me a whipping." Grandpa said, "That's all right. I don't expect anybody to keep up with me. I'll tell your father you worked hard and did fine."

This story was the first time I remember hearing something good about my grandpa. Luther said it was true that Ol' Cap Rusheon had shown many times that he could do more work in a day than any man in the community. He and Grandpa were close and supportive friends from that time on.

Luther Kilpatrick grew up to marry and have five sons and a daughter. His daughter passed away when she was five years old. Luther and the family were devastated, not only because of the loss but because they had no money to give her a proper burial.

Grandpa went over to offer his condolences, and learned of the family's financial predicament. He reached in his pocket and gave Luther a twenty dollar bill. Luther protested, "I can't pay you back." But Grandpa said it was a gift, he did not expect repayment, bringing tears to Luther's eyes. In those days and in that place, currency was so rare, it was called "actual cash money".

Luther Kilpatrick was one of the few personal friends of my grandpa, Ol' Cap Rusheon.

Grandpa Rusheon had a deep-down love and affection for his family, although it rarely surfaced. One of his last acts was an expression of love for his children.

Uncle Emery was the first of the children to be married. Early in their marriage, Emery and his wife Aunt Ivie lived in "the house that Elton built," on the same farm, but a little more than a mile from my grandparents. Elton had planned to live there, but because of his ongoing feud with his father, he left to manage Aunt Belle's plantation. Within three years Emery and Ivie had two small boys, Lancelot and Lannie Mack, the first grandchildren to be born.

One day Uncle Emery looked out his window to see his father walking toward his house leading a cow. Without preamble, Grandpa said, "You know, I won't be around very long. And when I go, you won't inherit as much land as the Rusheon children, and I can't do anything about that. So I want to give you this cow to help even things out."

Emery was grateful, because he had a young family to support, and the cow was worth more than the land he would not be inheriting.

Within a year or two, baby Lannie Mack came down with "summer complaint", a common diarrhea that can be life-threatening. Grandpa went to see him and held the baby. Little Lannie Mack recovered, but Grandpa caught the disease and it killed him in September 1921.

His children seemed afraid of Grandpa even after death. He had extracted a vow from them that they would keep his secrets forever.

I never made such a vow. Grandpa died eight years before I was born. In order to get to know him, I had to uncover his secrets.

My Search for Identity through Genealogy

My fascination with the stories of my grandfathers led me inevitably to the study of genealogy.

I began by systematically talking to everyone living in the older generation. My Aunt Ivie, then in her seventies, still would not speak of Grandpa's past, but suggested I talk to Cousin Austine, a member of my grandmother's branch of the family which had lost touch with our branch. I traveled to Orlando, Florida to see her, and then to Georgia to retrace the family's steps and see the area where they lived in Houston and Dooly Counties.

Austine had a delightful sprightly manner, and she was full of useful information and stories about the 1890s that she didn't hesitate to share. Her information, gleaned from her own family stories, provided some good leads but was not completely accurate, as I learned when I began to collect official documents and contemporaneous newspaper articles.

It was 1992 before Cousin Hollace and I discovered the news clippings of the killing and learned the name of the victim, a Dr. W. Arthur MacArthur. This breakthrough came from our sending requests for information on the murder to public libraries in Houston, Bibb, Crawford, Peach, and Dooly counties, in Georgia.

Pat and I took a research trip to Georgia. We visited the South Carolina Archives in Columbia, libraries, courthouses in Dooly County, Houston County, Macon, and churches and graveyards in Unadilla, Salem, and Byromville. Armed with very limited information to begin with, we gradually uncovered newspaper stories, census records, deeds, land lottery records, wills, church minutes, an obituary, and nuggets of information.

I learned to search under a variety of names for my ancestors. Because people of earlier centuries -- including court clerks -- were often uneducated and spelling was not standardized, the family name could be found spelled Busby, Busbee, Buzbee, Buzbie, Busbay, Buzbay, or Buzby. In one land transaction my great-grandfather's name was spelled five different ways in one paragraph. Of course the Busbice name itself didn't occur until 1899, when my grandfather changed his identity and those of his wife and children.

Genealogy is like detective work; a clue leads to another clue that leads to more information and it just keeps unfolding. I was hooked, and

I continued to look for the names and life stories of previous ancestors, all unknown to me. I had my share of blind alleys. There were plenty of unconfirmed family legends, but no bibles, letters, or other resources I could refer to. It was all uncharted territory.

Our friend Sondra Gregory introduced us to the National Archives in Washington, D.C. I was thrilled to find my great-grandfather Allen Busby in the federal census. This was my first official verification of his existence. Allen Busby was born in South Carolina in 1798.

I found that an interesting and exciting aspect of tracing my roots was locating prominent people in my family. I had heard rumors from these internet cousins and others about a possible connection to the former governor of Georgia, George Busbee. Pat suggested that we just email him and ask. To my surprise, Gov. Busbee replied and offered to send me twenty pages of his lineage that had been prepared by the Church of Jesus Christ of Latter Day Saints, but some portions were unverified. From a church record I had found about an ancestor's division of property in Georgia, I was able to clear up and confirm Gov. Busbee's line, adding two more generations and linking him to my family. My great-grandfather, Allen Busby, was a brother to his ancestor James Busbee, making Gov. Busbee my third cousin.

Pat and I visited China in 2000 and upon our return I had an email from Governor Busbee:

Thanks for sending the web page for William Reese.

Seems like you have become a world traveler. China is an interesting country, and the changes there since 1978 have been astounding.

In 1979, the year after our normalization, I had a call from the President saying that Vice-Premier Deng Ziaoping would be visiting the U.S. and...would like to visit Atlanta and see the results of the "modernization effort" in the Southeast. Deng also wanted to meet with the 17 Governors on the trade committee of the NGA. Mary Beth and I hosted a State Dinner at the Governor's mansion and then a luncheon for Deng to meet the Governors.

The next year Vice-Premier Deng invited us to lead a delegation of CEO's to China. After meeting with him in the Great Hall of the People, we were guests at a banquet, and then had a great tour of China. I have made many trips since and seen the changes.

Gov. George Busbee's wife Mary Beth, from Ruston, Louisiana, happens to be a good friend of my cousin, Juanita Busbice. They used to tease each other that they must be cousins even though their last names were spelled differently. Juanita was very pleased when I determined that they *are* actually cousins.

When tracing ancestors of my grandmother Mary Frances Byrd (wife of Oliver Allen Busby), I learned that I was related to the Murrays and Thompsons from central Georgia. Through my genealogy lists, I found a living cousin on this line, Laverne Brown, from Perry, Georgia. Pat and I visited Laverne and she off-handedly remarked, "You know, of course, that we are cousin to Rosalynn Carter." But she didn't know the actual connection.

I spent a lot of time researching President Carter's genealogy hoping to figure out how we were connected. Out of frustration, Pat again said, "Well, let's just email her!" We contacted her through her website and received a reply from her administrative assistant outlining her lineage, but it was limited. I put out a query on the Thompson and Murray internet lists and a cousin from each line responded, sending me documents on the Murray-Thompson connection. I was able to combine all three documents to determine that Rosalynn and I are indeed distant cousins. Our common ancestor is James Murray who emigrated from Scotland.

My research success led Pat to investigate her own genealogy. Pat became proficient on computers in the 1990s just as an information explosion occurred on the internet that has continued to this day. We each established a computer database to manage our growing files. Thousands of genealogy websites and databases were developed. With the development of search engines such as Google, millions of resources are out there. We found that resources still need to be checked, and most websites led us to sources of paper records, which still had to be ordered by mail, or searched on site.

Pat searched diligently for three years using computer and library resources before she discovered she descended from the famous Mather family. Her ancestor Timothy Mather was the brother of Increase Mather and the uncle of Cotton Mather. Researching this line through colonial times led her to two direct ancestors who were on the Mayflower, Edward Fuller and William Brewster. This was a key factor in getting her back to the European ancestors, some of whom were royal, like William the Conqueror and Charlemagne. This is not as remarkable as it seems, since it has been estimated that millions of living people descend from Charlemagne.

Pat's excitement about her finds was contagious, and soon I registered on internet lists used by genealogy researchers to share information. For the first time I realized I could get real answers. Within a year I had correspondents all over the U.S., plus Australia, England, France and Japan, who were researching the Busby name, focusing on the states of

Georgia and South Carolina and the various counties my ancestors had lived in.

The genealogy community online has a tradition of freely sharing and performing "random acts of genealogical kindness." I put out a query on one of these lists and a stranger, Gaila Merrington from Australia, who turned out to be a cousin, responded with information about my great-great-grandparents. Sandra Riner from Tennessee is another newfound cousin who shared a lot of data with me. I met a new Connella cousin online, Marion Oberhauser, and visited her in Mississippi. It was occurrences like these that helped me break through to more and more interesting material on my ancestors. I now belong to a regular network of cousins and fellow researchers for each of my family names: Busby, Noble, Connella and McQueen, Thompson and Murray.

After compiling all the information I could glean from legal documents, land records, wills, censuses, and researchers on genealogy internet lists, I became very interested in verifying the extent of my relationship with the other Busbys with whom I was corresponding. I learned that recent scientific advances made DNA technology a helpful tool in providing relationships to assist us in the search for ancestors.

Gaila Merrington encouraged Pat and me to coordinate a Busby Y-DNA surname project online. It was necessary to work only with the male line because the most reliable and informative test is based on Y chromosome DNA. The Y chromosome from the father is passed from generation to generation only through the male line. Y chromosomes mutate very slowly over time, at a fairly predictable rate, allowing identification through DNA of specific individuals as belonging to the same line of descent.

The Busby Y-DNA project has 21 participants. Through testing, we have been able to align these men within three distinct groups: Group I has twelve participants who are closely related. Group II has five men, and Group III has two. I am closely related to all members in Group I. I am not related to members of Groups II and III. This means all the members of Group I have a common ancestor. The lab results indicate there is a fifty percent chance our Most Recent Common Ancestor (MRCA) is no further than seven generations back. And there is a ninety percent chance that our MRCA is no more than sixteen generations back.

Benjamin Buzbee, Sr., born in 1699, is my oldest known male Busby ancestor. Based on timelines, it appears Benjamin Buzbee, Sr. and William Busby, both early American settlers in the 1600s, were brothers or father and son. Several members in Group I descend from one or both of these men.

During my DNA search for cousins, I discovered that our surname participants matched up with some members in three other surname groups: Johnson, Carter, and McGraw. There are only three possible explanations for this: adoption, name change, or "false paternity." In the Johnson case, we discovered an unofficial adoption that occurred during the Civil War. I have been unable to determine the reason for the others.

A man named Busby from England contacted me and asked how he could verify the long-held belief in his family that his great-grandmother had borne a child by a man outside the family. I suggested DNA tests for him, and for a cousin descended from that line. The test results proved that he and the cousin were not related in the male line.

In another surprise, we Busby/Busbice men matched up with a large number of genetic cousins by the name of Ivey, that we didn't know existed. According to the DNA results, I am as closely related to them as to my own first cousin, Roger Busbice. The Ivey migration pattern – Virginia, North Carolina, South Carolina, Georgia -- matched the Busby pattern for both place and time. We have been unable to discover a common ancestor for Iveys and Busbys. The president of the DNA testing laboratory is intrigued by this connection and suggests there could have been a name change or an adoption – official or unofficial -- going back to Europe. But it seems clear to me that one of the Busby men went out a-wandering one evening.

BUSBY Y-DNA SURNAME PROJECT

Group I

Name	Oldest Known Ancestor
Bobby D. Buzbee	William Busby c 1700-?
Charles C. Busby	Jefferson Davis Busby
Charles L. Busbice	Benjamin Buzbee 1699-1815
Farrell T. Busbee	Miles Tillman Busbee 1805-1875
Howard R. Busby	Benjamin Buzbee 1699-1815
John M. Busby	Benjamin Buzbee 1699-1815
M.L. Busby	Zachariah Busby 1765-1870
Roger Busbice	Benjamin Buzbee 1699-1815
T.F. Busby	?
Vohn Busby	Seaborn Buzbee 1815-1873
Wayne Busbice	Benjamin Buzbee 1699-1815
Bobby Don Johnson (adopted, DNA of Busby)	?

Group II

Name	Oldest Known Ancestor
Bret Busby	Michael Horton Busby 1803-?
Dan Eugene Busby	Micajah Busby 1780-1855
J.C. Busby	John A. Busby 1870-?
John Walter Busby	John William Busby 1558-?
Julius Busbee	Elisha Busbee 1765-1840

Group III

Name	Oldest Known Ancestor
E.L. Busby	William Jasper Busby 1859-1932
Edward G. Busby	Jeremiah Busby

Men in Other Surname Projects Who Match Wayne Busbice's DNA

Name	Oldest Known Ancestor
S. Carter	S. Carter Isaac 1813-?
B. McGraw	Andrew Jackson McGraw
James D. Ivy	Zachariah Ivy
George P. Ivy	Anthony Ivy
Jerry E. Ivey	Charles Wesley Ivey
Grant Lloyd Ivie	James Russell Ivie
Lawrence Ivey	Jarrett J. Ivey
Jerry R. Ivey	James A. Ivey
Donald E. Ivie, Sr.	Curtis Ivie
Jerry Lee Ivey	James Ivey
James C. Ivey	James Ivey

~25~

Striking a Lighter Note

My retirement gave me time to again embrace my lifelong interest -- part of my soul – music.

For fifteen years, I booked the acts and was a featured performer in the Montgomery County Fair's country music show, which starred headliners from the Grand Ole Opry.

In Gaithersburg, Maryland, our county fair was a real family experience. It was bigger than the Maryland State Fair, and had the reputation of being the biggest county fair east of the Mississippi. Farm families came in trailers, and camped out with their animals for the entire week. We had crowds strolling the midway, enjoying ice cream and cotton candy, riding the Ferris wheel and the Tilt-a-Whirl; and little kids swarming the petting zoo. In between display buildings, the 4-H teens washed and groomed their show animals: dairy and beef cattle, swine, horses, sheep, goats, poultry, rabbits. Schoolchildren and adults alike entered their paintings, quilts, photographs, and pickles, hoping for a prize. There was a midway and entertainment. But the real reason for the Fair was to promote agricultural education, and to provide a competitive outlet for the 4-H clubs, Future Farmers of America, and school programs. Typically on Saturday, the night of the show, there'd be a tractor pull, a cattle auction, a pig race, and cattle judging by local students.

I looked forward to playing the live shows, because I got so much pleasure out of it. That is not to say I didn't have stage fright beforehand, and for the first few minutes of each performance. But after I went onstage, marched up to the microphone, and belted out a couple of numbers, the stage fright just melted away, especially if the audience was enjoying the performance. A positive response from the audience was energizing, and made me want to do everything I could to please the people. I will admit, I usually had Buzz and other professional musicians backing me up, and that made a world of difference in giving me confidence.

I can remember only one occasion when I was embarrassed onstage, when playing at the Ouachita Valley Jamboree in West Monroe, Louisiana. I was on the road visiting radio stations from Maryland to Louisiana, and dropping off my first record, "Goin' Back to Dixie." The deejay at KUZN liked my record very much and invited me to sing a few songs onstage that night at the Jamboree. I had my guitar with me. He assured me that the staff musicians at the show would back me up, and that they were good. Wrong!

I did very well on my numbers, but I had selected Jimmy Davis' "Suppertime" for my signoff gospel song. Everything was going fine until I got to the recitation segment, and the musicians seemed to get lost -- the music just faded away. I guess they had never played for a recitation before. The audience seemed displeased, so I just stopped.

I turned around to the musicians to see what the problem was. Then Jack Hollingsworth, who was a great rhythm guitarist and married to my cousin Lois, popped up from backstage and said, "Let's start over, Wayne. I'll back you." He did, and I finished my part of the show fairly decently. I was very embarrassed, but it was a good lesson. I never performed again without knowing the quality of my backup musicians.

Backstage at the Fair: Dudley Connell, Ernest Tubb, Wayne, Eddie Stubbs

The *Montgomery Journal* wrote about my performances at the Fair.

MONTGOMERY JOURNAL - 1977
Leading a Double Life
Principal is Country Music Star at Night
By Stewart Straus

Sitting in the high-backed chair behind his desk at the principal's office in Gaithersburg Junior High School, Wayne E. Busbice has the calm, quiet manner of an efficient administrator.

His sports jacket and tie make Busbice look like any other professional. By day.

But Busbice is leading a double life. By night, he's Red McCoy, country music star dressed in a black sequined suit, cowboy hat and boots.

There's a guitar in his hands and a microphone in front of him. He's belting out the Wabash Cannonball to an appreciative crowd and they can't get enough of him.

There is a big name singer from Nashville, Tennessee, at the top of the bill, and Busbice chats comfortably with him between numbers. They're both pros...

Picking and strumming his acoustic guitar while singing one of his country gospel songs, Busbice's earthy voice is marked with an authentic twang. His brow is furrowed and his eyes are fixed on some point on the ceiling while he intones the words he wrote: "Heaven is my home...There's a ship a-coming to take God's children home."

...Jerry Gray... characterizes Busbice's music as traditional country in the style of Bill Monroe, the acknowledged father of bluegrass music. But adds that Busbice is not an imitator. "Wayne is a guy of genuine accomplishment." Said Gray. "He's keeping alive the roots of modern music."...

Despite the many original tunes to his credit, Busbice says he cannot write music. "I just make up songs," he said. " I sit with my guitar and strum and hum."

I retired from Gaithersburg Junior High in 1980, wanting to spend more time with music. *Goldmine Magazine*, a collector and promoter of country and rockabilly records, had somehow obtained copies of some of my early efforts as a recording artist and asked if it could re-release "Goin' Back To Dixie". It was released in England and it made the rockabilly charts over there.

Not long into retirement, I decided to establish my own record company as a hobby. The *Gaithersburg Gazette* asked if it could do a story on my music activities. Of course, who wouldn't want free publicity?

THE GAITHERSBURG GAZETTE, April 2, 1981

Retired Educator Creates Recording Studio
by Kathy Panagos

For the past 30 years, Wayne E. Busbice has dedicated his knowledge, strength, and time to the Montgomery County Public Schools system. He was a teacher and principal at Gaithersburg Junior High School. He recently retired from that life and is channeling his energy and efforts into his longtime intrigue and avocation, music. He has established WEBCO, a recording studio, in Gaithersburg...

"Doctor B," as he is called in the education field, has also recorded his music. He says, "from the late 50's to 60's I made several singles and three albums...

Because of Buzz's early success and fame, when I started my record company I turned to him in order to get immediate recognition; and to try to recapture some of that success for him, since he had basically hit the skids.

Buzz was considered the father of Washington D.C. bluegrass and many people wanted him to play at clubs and shows, and to resume recording. I had talked with some of Buzz's former recording companies -- they said they would love to have him again but he was not reliable, and would probably start a project and not complete it. As a result, I decided to produce an album showcasing Buzz.

BLUEPRINT - 1981
WASHINGTON'S BLUEGRASS NEWSPAPER
Webco Brings Back Buzz Busby
By Robert Kyle

He taught bluegrass pioneer Buzz Busby how to play mandolin and guitar. Under the name "Red McCoy" he recorded country and rockabilly music in the '50s. He spent 32 years in the military, retiring last year as a Lt. Col. In the DC Air National Guard. He has earned a bachelor's degree from the University of Southwestern Louisiana, a master's degree from the University of Maryland and his doctorate from The American University... This year he has launched his own record label, recording studio and music publishing house.

Who is this with such a varied and colorful background?

Wayne E. Busbice, older brother of bluegrass great, Buzz Busby...

While Buzz recorded many albums in the early days, a new release by him is a rarity today. But thanks to his brother Wayne and his new record label, WEBCO, there is a fresh album entitled, "Buzz Busby, A Pioneer of Traditional Bluegrass."

The album contains a combination of remakes and new material, and also features a back-up band of the area's best: Lamar Grier, banjo; Eddie

Stubbs, fiddle; Dudley Connell, guitar and vocals; Doug Ward, bass; and Herbert Currie and Wayne Busbice, vocals.

I produced the album using well-known bluegrass artists as a studio band. I wrote two of the songs, and sang lead on several cuts. Because Buzz had not recorded in several years, he had faded out of the musical picture – I wasn't sure if people still remembered him. But it was apparent his playing was just as good as ever. The album was well-received in the regional market, but I didn't have the money to do a lot of marketing and distribution. I sent copies to promoters and to radio stations for airplay.

Blueprint, the bluegrass newspaper, had some nice things to say in their review:

Wayne Busbice...chose to feature Buzz on the debut disc not only because they are brothers, but because Buzz is indeed a pioneer who's kept a pretty low profile in recent years and is still capable of making good bluegrass.

...Buzz's brother, Wayne, contributed a pair of originals: "Lost Without You", an uptempo traditional tune, and "Heaven Is My Home", an excellent gospel song with nice four-part work. It, too, is one of the album's best, and other musicians in search of a fresh and spirited gospel number should find it a real prize.

I hadn't intended to do commercial work, but this album was so successful I changed my concept to commercial recording. To control the quality of the sound, I had used a small professional studio for half of WEBCO's first album, and a larger one for the other half. After the songs were mixed down and mastered, we – Buzz, Eddie Stubbs, Dudley Connell and I - couldn't tell any difference in the quality of the finished product. The fact that there was no difference in sound quality between the small studio and the large studio gave me the idea to set up my own studio in the basement of my home.

My son John and I went to a music store that sold professional recording equipment. We selected professional recording equipment and special microphones that were top-notch and highly recommended in a major studio. We bought a full eight track recorder, soundboard, two-track mixdown recorder, and speakers. We had plenty of room in the studio since bluegrass musicians primarily used acoustic instruments, which didn't take as much space as amplified instruments for a rock band.

I researched the literature on how the inside of a studio should be constructed. I learned that the walls in the recording room should not make a square box, or a lot of feedback would result. The walls had to be different lengths, and the control room had to be separate and closed off from the musicians. Acoustical treatment included carpet on the floor and a false ceiling with four inches of foam placed between the ceiling and the hardwood floor above. I built a sound-proof booth for the vocalist, to prevent sound leakage from the instruments. This made it possible for the sound engineer to raise and lower the volume of the vocalist during mix-down without changing the sound level of the instrumentation. This could produce a better separation of sound.

I was very fortunate to have two technical experts, Nick Mitsilias and my son John, to help me run a fledgling recording studio. They both taught me how to be a sound engineer, and we rotated the duties.

There are tricks that can be used to enhance a recording session. When one of the musicians in the session made a mistake, the group was always instructed to keep on playing, so as not to break the rhythm of the others. Mistakes were corrected by overdubbing later, since each instrument, as well as the vocalist, was recording on a separate track. The technician worked individually with the erring musician by recording over the mistake, or on a vacant track, by transferring the corrected track to the original track. To free up a track for an additional instrument, or add more vocals, the rhythm section could all be transferred to one track.

Wayne at a performance with son John

When we record in a studio, vocalists normally do not play while they sing. However, in bluegrass about half of the musicians also sing. While recording I put in a "scratch" (temporary) track so I had the timing; then in the mixing I would erase the track by recording over it with my own voice singing – this is referred to as dubbing. In this way I was able to concentrate on the vocal track by putting it in later. But it can be a problem because some musicians, especially country and bluegrass, can't sing unless they're playing an instrument in order to keep the beat. Most bluegrass musicians can't read music: John was the only one of our Busby Brothers group -- John, Buzz, Bobby, and me -- who could read music.

Buzz liked to play everything fast. In one of our recording sessions, he included a couple of mandolin instrumental solos. Buzz played so fast that two or three of the musicians -- well-known, schooled, professional bluegrass musicians -- said, "I can't keep up -- I just can't play that fast."

So I had to get new sidemen for guitar, fiddle and banjo who could keep up with Buzz with their instruments on these cuts. Buzz was picking so fast that the sound seemed like one long continuous note – like Bbbrrrrrrrrrrr on the album.

After producing two fairly successful LPs featuring Buzz, I was introduced to the old Broadway and vaudeville star, Brooke Johns, who lived in nearby Olney, Maryland. Brooke was eighty-seven when I met him and had retired to his million-dollar farm and adjacent country club.

Brooke had as much energy at eighty-seven as a man in his thirties. He was a great guy to spend an afternoon with. His personality drew me in, his energy was magnetic, and his memory was faultless. Once he got started with his stories, hours flew by. Brooke regaled Pat and me with many interesting stories about his career on Broadway, where he was a protégé of Flo Ziegfeld in the Ziegfeld Follies. He had been a stunningly handsome young man, by the standards of the 1920s. Ads of the time call Brooke "six-foot-four and oh so different!" *Variety*, the theater trade paper, profiled him.

Brooke knew everybody. As a child in Washington, he had played with President Teddy Roosevelt's daughter Alice. He was proud of his relationship with many of the top stars of the 1920s through 1940s, including Al Jolson, Eddy Cantor, Jimmy Durante, Buddy Ebsen, George Burns, Will Rogers, Sophie Tucker, and Gloria Swanson. Brooke played leading man opposite Gloria Swanson in two silent movies. He was a song-and-dance man in many stage musicals.

Brooke was fond of saying that when he was in London, he played at the Palace Theater and also at *the* Palace. Edward, Prince of Wales (who was to become King Edward VIII until his abdication), invited Brooke over to jam. The prince got out his own drum set and played along – amateurishly, as Brooke told it.

Brooke said, "The Prince was nuts about American jazz music. He was a drummer; had twelve or fifteen beautiful drums. He would have parties five nights a week with my piano player, and myself, and maybe four or five couples. He was atrocious. My piano player loved his brandy, and I'm a bum banjo player -- we never finished together. We were the lousiest trio you can ever imagine…

"Edward used to drum loud as hell. One night…I heard the most excruciating noise over my shoulder. He had a tomato can with gravel in it, and a broom handle, shaking it over his shoulder. It was awful: sounded like a bum differential on a Model T Ford. When we got through with the number, the prince said, 'Brooke, how do you like that instrument?' I must admit I was two-faced. I said it was wonderful. Edward smiled and said, 'A buddy over in the Montmartre district made it for me.'"

I was elated to be the successor to Flo Ziegfeld in managing Brooke, and working with him on our first album together, where he played banjo and sang songs of the Roaring Twenties. I gathered a piano player and a trumpet player to back him up; my son John played bass and I was on guitar.

Side one was recorded live in my studio in Gaithersburg; but side two consisted of re-recorded old 78rpm records released in London sixty years earlier, and never before heard in the United States. We electronically transferred them to a master tape, preserving the primitive early sound but eliminating much of the static. Brooke explained that when he was recording in England in the 1920s, he had no microphones. Megaphones were used for amplification. He was instructed to face the wall and sing into the wall. The sound that bounced back is what was recorded.

Cuddle Up
    By Brooke Johns
    Pub. Old Home Place Music

Said he to she, Honey can you see that great big foreign chair?
Said she to he, It's all right with me, but please don't muss my hair.
Said him to her, Would you prefer to see a movie show?
Said her to him, Oh no! All right, said he, Let's go!

Cuddle up, cuddle up, cuddle up, cuddle up, treat your papa nice
Cuddle up, cuddle up, cuddle up, cuddle up, show me paradise
I've got a fever you alone can cure
I don't want to eat, don't want to sleep, just want to love my sweetie

Cuddle up, cuddle up, cuddle up, cuddle up, I'll be satisfied
I want a hug, I want a squeeze, want a lot more besides
It's time to broadcast a tip or two from station Y-O-U

So, cuddle up, cuddle up, cuddle up, cuddle up
And let your conscience be my guide.

248

Pat wrote the liner notes for Brooke's album:

...Today, the famous pep and personality are intact. In this album Brooke shows the style that endeared him to generations: warm, personal, humorous, self-deprecating, but with a showmanship that years have not dimmed.

Brooke Johns' music takes the listener back to the quiet drawing rooms and ornate vaudeville halls of the 20s, before OPEC, nuclear proliferation, and traffic congestion. This album is sure to refresh the spirit for a little while.

After the album was released, I was surprised that it stirred up so much interest -- Brooke got many calls and letters from geriatric fans who remembered him from the old days.

MONTGOMERY JOURNAL

Album Makers

WEBCO rediscovers old stars, records unknowns big firms ignore

By Rhonda Strickland

How did a small local company like WEBCO come to record and produce Brooke Johns, sparking a rediscovery of this once-famous star in the 1920s? Like WEBCO itself, a small family operation, the Brooke Johns albums grew out of family and friend connections and a love of traditional American music...

Dr. Busbice's dedication to digging up unknown local talent and rediscovering former celebrities has resulted in a wide variety of excellently produced albums covering everything from bluegrass to barbershop quartets to colonial American music.

Brooke's wife Hazel and his children told me that working on my albums revived Brooke's interest in entertaining and prolonged his life. He considered me one of his best friends. Brooke continued to perform and speak at schools, clubs, and private parties up until a year before he died at age ninety-two.

The WEBCO Brooke Johns albums were "Brooke Johns: Treasures of Broadway, Then and Now," and "Return of the Roaring Twenties."

While doing the Brooke Johns album I got to meet Taffy Nivert, the songwriter who wrote "Country Roads," John Denver's biggest hit. One of the musicians brought Taffy along to meet Brooke. In my studio, I had a chance to ask her how she came about writing "Country Roads". She was inspired by Clopper Road in nearby Gaithersburg, which Pat and I had often traveled. Clopper Road is now covered with strip malls and suburban sprawl. But in Taffy's childhood it was a long, scenic country road to her uncle's farm in Boyds, Maryland.

Taffy thought the song had potential, but "Clopper Road" didn't sound too romantic. She called it "Country Roads" and inserted the lines about West Virginia to make it sound more rural. Taffy took the song down to Constitution Hall in Washington where John Denver was playing, and she had an opportunity to sing it to him backstage. John Denver said he would record the song if she gave him one-third of the royalty rights. And the rest is history.

While Taffy was in the studio Brooke asked her to join him on a couple of songs. Taffy harmonized with Brooke on "Bye Bye Blackbird" and "April Showers."

BUSBY BROTHERS

Busby Brothers on the cover of "Louisiana Grass":
Wayne, Buzz, Bobby, and John

Looking around for another project, I decided to ask Buzz, Bobby, and John to join me in making a Busby Brothers album. The *Washington Post* gave it a pretty good review.

WASHINGTON POST 1986
Busby Brothers' Timeless Tune
By Mike Joyce

"LOUISIANA GRASS" *marks the first time the Busby Brothers have recorded an album since the '50s, and to hear them sing and play it, bluegrass hasn't changed all that much. The fans of traditional acoustic music, especially older listeners who might recall Buzz Busby's pioneering days on Washington television in the '50s when bluegrass was just a seedling here, should regard this as good news indeed.*

The album celebrates the group's early influences, neatly gathering up several country and bluegrass standards the Busbys sang while growing up in Louisiana: Jimmie Davis' "Let's Be Sweethearts Again," as well as a couple of newer pieces by Wayne that possess a similarly timeless country flavor.

As always, it's Buzz's tremolo-humming mandolin style that stands out most, but the singing is heartfelt, the playing surefooted and songs almost always worth hearing again.

The Busby Brothers gained in popularity and we played several clubs and festivals. We knew we'd reached the top, for Washington, when we were invited to the Birchmere, a bluegrass venue that showcased national artists like Johnny Cash, the Country Gentlemen, Seldom Scene, Jimmy Martin, and Mac Wiseman.

Each year the Folklore Society of Greater Washington sponsored a multicultural Folk Festival for all ages at Glen Echo, an old-fashioned amusement park on the banks of the Potomac. The Busby Brothers usually got top billing in the music portion. Washington radio station WAMU, whose extremely popular bluegrass deejay personality was my friend Jerry Gray, provided emcees. Our performing stage was right on the midway between the carousel, the cotton candy stand, and the yak yurt.

When the Busby Brothers were announced, we bounded onto the stage energetically and launched right into an up-tempo intro: "Come along, everybody come along – Come while the moon is shining bright. We're gonna have a wonderful time at Glen Echo Park tonight." The crowd loved it when banjo, fiddle and mandolin each took a musical break.

To keep the tempo going, we jumped right into another fast song like "Salty Dog" before the applause could die down. Next would be something like Buzz's highly popular "Just Me and the Jukebox," and then we'd slide into an instrumental like "Mandolin Twist." It went on like that for several songs with no letup, until the audience was breathless. Our trademark was high energy, tight playing, and smooth professionalism.

In addition to vocals, my job was bantering with Bobby at the mike, where we served as co-announcers. We knew each other so well, there was never a lull in the comments and the jokes we told on each other, and the audience could detect the spark and the humor in our warm relationship. Our final song for the gig would always be a gospel number, like "Will the Circle Be Unbroken," or "I Saw the Light," or my own song, "Heaven Is My Home." As soon as they recognized the strains of the old gospel songs, you could see heads nodding in the audience. Old folks, young couples, and families with children on dads' shoulders clapped and swayed to the beat.

WASHINGTON POST
The Brothers Who Planted Washington Bluegrass
The Busbys, Stars of A Then-Now Style
By Mike Joyce

Between them, mandolinist Buzz and guitarist Wayne Busby have been playing bluegrass for longer than Bill Monroe himself, and just as Monroe deserves credit for creating the style, the Busbys deserve credit for helping popularize it in the Washington area.

Buzz, 53... well remembers the chilly reception bluegrass received here in the '50s. But if his television show "Hayloft Hoedown," which made its debut on WRC-TV in 1954 didn't cure the problem entirely, he says, it certainly helped...

Wayne, 57, who followed his brother to Washington in 1953, agrees that "Hayloft Hoedown" made a big difference locally, but adds that radio stations were also instrumental in getting listeners attuned to Monroe's music even though bluegrass wasn't the main staple...

Ironically, it was Wayne, the school principal, who met and encouraged a fellow bluegrass enthusiast, fiddler Eddie Stubbs of the highly acclaimed Johnson Mountain Boys. At the time, Stubbs was a seventh-grader at Gaithersburg Junior High. He impressed his classmates so much that his music teacher introduced him to Wayne, knowing of his background in bluegrass. Eventually, the three formed a group, performing at various functions throughout Montgomery County.

"It's been phenomenal," says Wayne, looking back on the rise of the Johnson Mountain Boys. "It didn't take them but a very few months to gain national and even international recognition in the bluegrass field once they finally got together."

Wayne wasn't the only Busby to witness the promise of a rising star. Shortly after leaving "Hayloft Hoedown," Buzz landed a job with the "Louisiana Hayride" show in Shreveport, where he shared the stage with a number of bluegrass and country stars and every now and then, a rockabilly upstart like Elvis Presley.

In 1987 I produced an album that generated a lot of interest in my WEBCO record label and gave it professional status -- "Tennessee 1949".

In addition to Bill Emerson and Pete Goble, other bluegrass notables appearing on this album included Larry Stephenson, Bryan Smith, Joe Meadows, Mike Auldridge, Jeff Tuttle, and Jimmy Gaudreau. I had a lot of fun and considered myself working "in tall cotton" with such fine talent.

I was gratified but not surprised that this album made Number One Bluegrass Album in the U.S. for 1987, as selected by music industry reviewers.

Bluegrass Unlimited magazine is the most prestigious publication covering the bluegrass industry. The May 1987 issue highlighted "Tennessee 1949" based on these criteria: solid performance, great picking, fine lead singing, strong blended harmonies, clear recording, a well-balanced mix, and interesting material.

This album was an opportunity for the songwriting team of Pete Goble and Leroy Drumm to showcase their composing talent, and the first time for Pete to record some of his own songs. It was also notable because it marked a return to bluegrass by Bill Emerson on banjo, after fifteen years as the chief musician for the Navy's popular band, Country Current.

During the 1980s the popularity of the Johnson Mountain Boys soared. This quintet included three of my former students at Gaithersburg Junior: Eddie Stubbs on fiddle, Dudley Connell on guitar, and Larry Robbins, bass. They joined in vocals with Richard Underwood, banjo, and David McLaughlin, mandolin. The Johnson Mountain Boys played at fairs, festivals, and clubs, and were called to perform at the White House. They traveled to Africa as official United States goodwill ambassadors, appeared on the Grand Ole Opry, and made several records on the Rounder label, the premier bluegrass record producer.

My WEBCO label continued to grow and win several minor awards in the independent bluegrass record industry, and we were rated third by 1989. Bluegrass, as a roots type of music, was not making much of a profit at this time but I was enjoying the activity and the recognition, as well as other aspects of the business, including the perks of success. But since CD technology was overtaking albums in the marketplace, staying competitive would have required re-tooling my studio.

Instead, I decided to follow my longtime interest in politics and run for office. I asked Bill Emerson, if he would take over my label. I would keep the master tapes I had produced and continue ownership of Old Home Place Music publishing company and receive royalties from the 200-plus songs in my catalog. Bill brought his son, John, into the business with him and they produced some top bluegrass hits for several years, changing the name to WEBCO Records of Virginia. In 1990, Pinecastle Records of Orlando, Florida, bought WEBCO Records of Virginia and some of my early master tapes. Pinecastle has since re-released some of my old masters on CDs.

Selling WEBCO freed up my time to once again follow in my father's footsteps -- this time into politics. Singing, playing and songwriting professionally gradually faded into the past for me. But I had had the strong satisfaction of fostering the spread and appreciation of bluegrass music, and the thrill of performing on the same stage with some of the great names: Tex Ritter, Charlie Louvin, Kitty Wells, Johnny Wright, Ernest Tubb, Johnson Mountain Boys, Don Reno, the Seldom Scene, the Country Gentlemen, Bill Harrell, Red Sovine, Little Jimmy Dickens, Bill Emerson, George Morgan, Jean Shepard, Carl and Pearl Butler, Larry Stephenson, Riders in the Sky, the Carter Family, Charlie Walker, Jerry Gray, Pete Goble, and of course Buzz Busby and the Bayou Boys.

When I Reach My Journey's End
By Wayne Busbice
Pub. Old Home Place Music

A long, long time ago, my life was in a whirl
Engaged in sinful things of this old wicked world
But I prayed to God above to save and cleanse my soul
He taught me how to live, now heaven is my goal.

Chorus:

When I reach my journey's end, my Jesus will be waitin'
To claim my soul for Him and keep away ol' Satan
Jesus died on the cross to save us from our sins
I know I'll go to heaven, when I reach my journey's end.

Now listen all you sinners if you want to hear
How life can be eternal, with nothing left to fear
Just place your trust in Him, read your bible every day
Be sure to love your neighbor, and don't forget to pray.

~26~

When Politics Is a Pleasure

I had been interested in politics all my life from early days in Eros, where Daddy was so admired for his work in politics.

Montgomery County abuts Washington, D.C. and contains many municipalities including Potomac, Bethesda, Chevy Chase, Silver Spring, Rockville and Gaithersburg. Since population and wealth were clustered near the D.C. line, the lower county received a disproportionate distribution of government goodies like libraries, new schools, parks, swimming pools, and other public amenities. What's more, the political election districts had been gerrymandered to make the votes of residents in the upper county even less effective. As principal, and as a homeowner in the upcounty, as we called it, I had observed this firsthand.

Thinking I could make a difference, I made a decision to try for a seat in the Maryland House of Delegates. I began visiting many Democratic Party activists, and was encouraged to run. With this positive response from the political elite in our district, I established a campaign committee that included some influential people: Anne Swain, a member of the State Democratic Central Committee; Dr. Jerry Levine, my longtime friend and a former assistant principal; Hon. Elizabeth Tolbert, mayor of Barnesville, Maryland; Colonel Wayne Brown, former deputy chief of police; Sandy Saidman, an accountant, as my treasurer; and several other Democratic leaders in our district.

Being a newcomer to politics, I knew nothing about establishing and running a campaign. With the advice of my campaign staff I approached many elected officials to get acquainted with them and to ask for their support. After receiving encouragement from the sheriff, the state's attorney, a newspaper columnist who was the son of a former governor, and several county commissioners, I felt comfortable, and confident that I could mount a viable campaign.

Anne Swain ordered "Busbice for Delegate" tee shirts and boaters (straw hats) for all of the volunteer workers. Mayor Tolbert and others made sure I was invited to all functions where candidates could get exposure. All Democratic candidates for all offices invited one another to their political functions, so there were several things to do each week. I attended picnics, old time days, and the Maryland state jousting contest. I made appearances at local community fairs. We staffed a booth to meet people and promote my campaign at the Montgomery County Fair where 100,000 people came during Fair Week. I rode in parades for Fourth of July, Gaithersburg Days, and

256

Labor Day. I rode in classic convertibles and handed out candy and pencils to kids, and brochures, jar grippers and nail files to adults. All the paraphernalia had my name and logo on them. We had car-top signs for the cars of all key workers.

Campaign chair Anne Swain, Barnesville Mayor Lib Tolbert,
Pat and Wayne at Civil War battle re-enactment

Armed with a list of registered Democrats, Jerry Levine and I went door to door to hundreds of homes. We handed out literature and answered questions on the spot, one to one.

The most important, but also least-liked, process was fundraising. My campaign finance committee sent out flyers and announcements suggesting contributions. Some campaign workers and friends hosted neighborhood coffees and "meet the candidate" evenings. We mounted a phone bank in the evenings to ask for money and votes. Pat contributed her office suite and several phones for this purpose, and provided copier, fax, and office supplies. She arranged a private phone number for my campaign which was answered by the secretary at her office with, "Wayne Busbice for delegate!"

We set up political rallies featuring live country music, so people could get to know me better.

THE DAMASCUS COURIER-GAZETTE - August 8, 1990
Busbice Rally Draws Large Turnout in Damascus
Candidate Delights Crowd by Playing Guitar

257

About 150 supporters turned out on July 22 for Wayne Busbice, Democratic candidate for state delegate in District 15, at the American Legion Hall in Damascus. The hall was packed with friends, politicians, a former Washington Redskin star and Prairie Rose country and western band.

Ray Schoenke, former Redskin football player and current Laytonsville civic activist and business owner, introduced Busbice to the crowd, after which U.S. Rep. Beverly Byron (Dist. 6) spoke in his support. Busbice then delighted everyone by singing and playing his guitar along with the band...

The crowd included civic and Democratic party leaders from Barnesville, Beallsville, Clarksburg, Damascus, Darnestown, Gaithersburg, Germantown, Laytonsville and Montgomery Village. Rep Beverly Byron mentioned above had taken the Congressional seat of her husband, Goodloe Byron, upon his death a few years earlier. When he was in office, Rep. Goodloe Byron had appointed our daughter Maureen O'Connor to the Air Force Academy.

All told, our fundraising efforts brought in about thirty thousand dollars, including cash and contributions in kind.

Pat, granddaughter Leigh (standing), Wayne and supporters

Sister Mary Michael (Aunt Patricia) supporting
Wayne's candidacy in the convent

Briefly, my message consisted of three points. I wanted to, above all, work with honesty and integrity for the people of my district. Secondly, I wanted to address the funding inequities that the state government promoted. And lastly, I felt it was important for a resident of the upper county to give a voice in government to the approximately 200,000 people who lived there.

On the stump I touted myself as a consensus builder using the example of my role in the establishment of the Gaithersburg aquatic center that required the coordination of the school system, city government and the local parent-teachers association. I made it clear that I would work for more state funding to improve public transportation, roads, and school construction. I advocated victims' rights, innovative criminal justice programs, affordable housing, and the preservation of open space and farmland.

My candidacy was endorsed by several newspapers, as well as Americans for Democratic Action, Montgomery County Retired Teachers Association, Montgomery Village Citizens' Coalition, and Maryland State Troopers' Association.

Then came primary election day, and my campaign workers and I were present at every polling place working hard trying to glean votes up to the last minute, but to no avail. The top Democratic three vote getters were to face the top three Republican candidates in the election. There were nine Democratic candidates, and I was the only upcounty candidate. I came in fifth in the field of nine. I did win in the upcounty precincts where I was well known, but fell short down-county where the highest concentration of voters lived.

WESTERN MONTGOMERY BULLETIN
SAMPLE BALLOT IS CALLED "DIRTY TRICK"

A sample campaign ballot for the primaries, circulated just before the primary and reportedly prepared by Democratic Delegate Gene Counihan and others angered many Democrats and may have been illegal, according to some of the angry delegates...

The incumbent delegate had 15,000 flyers distributed on election eve displaying a picture of himself and two other candidates with the governor and implying an endorsement of their slate by him. The flyer, printed to resemble a ballot, erroneously gave the impression that it was authorized by the Party. It was suspected that the governor, William Donald Schaefer, had paid for the brochure. If true, this was probably illegal, and the first time a governor had interfered in a local election. The ballot was called a fraud by some Democrats.

According to several political analysts, the "fraud ballot" altered the results of the primary. Two of the three candidates pictured on the flyer won the primary. Since the fake ballot was mailed three days before primary election day, there was no way anyone could take action to correct the damage.

The excitement of my campaign for office and the political connections I made encouraged me to stay involved.

Pat was elected president of the Northern Montgomery Women's Democratic Club. As a result, together we were in charge of the two most influential Democratic political organizations in our district.

I was elected chairman of the District 15 Democratic Caucus, and I also served as precinct chairman, was appointed to three county committees advising the County Council and the County Executive, and became active in the Damascus Chamber of Commerce, where I established a farmer's market.

In 1991 I was appointed to the Committee on Committees by Neal Potter, Montgomery County Executive. A Committee on Committees was constituted every ten years in Montgomery County to evaluate all aspects of the county committee system.

People snickered at the name of our committee and the bureaucracy that created it. Our first recommendation was that the name of the Committee on Committees be changed to Committee Evaluation and Review Board.

There was no process in place for us to follow. Everything had to be created from scratch. I was elected chairman, and I developed a comprehensive methodology, creating forms and setting up data teams of two people each to attend meetings, interview, and collect data on each of sixty-one committees. After that we met frequently and distilled the reports into a set of findings, conclusions, and recommendations. This task took eighteen months. Eventually we presented our report to the County Exec and the Montgomery County Council for approval.

In the 1992 and 1996 presidential elections I was appointed the coordinator for the Clinton/Gore campaign in my election District 12. I got my marching orders from the Democratic Central Committee of Montgomery County. I had three precincts to manage in my district for the campaign, and I was also area precinct coordinator for the entire upper county containing thirty precincts.

I attended nearly every political meeting that occurred in the county to stay abreast of the issues and plan strategies for the campaign. Part of my job was to make appearances at all community functions like rallies, forums, meet-the-candidate nights, and town hall meetings, where all Democratic candidates for national office -- President, Vice-President, and Congress -- would either attend or send a surrogate to be recognized and possibly speak a few words. I recruited workers and educated them about the issues, put up signs, distributed literature, supervised workers who went door-to-door for the candidates, managed a phone bank (Pat donated the ten phones at her office again), and scheduled workers to run the Democratic booth at the Montgomery County fair for a full week, where issues could be debated. I went to some thirty coffees and meetings in private homes. We showed videos about the candidates to the political elite.

On election day, I made two or three rounds of my thirty precincts in my new little white Saturn – getting lots of compliments – taking vote tallies throughout the day, and passing the information to the Central Committee.

Democrats won in District 12, and of course Clinton and Gore took the election. This effort cost me many late nights and a lot of hard work, but brought great satisfaction because I felt I was having an impact on the values and direction of the country.

Oath of Office Reception
Representative Beverly Byron
January 3, 1991
Washington D.C.

In 1992 and 1994, Pat and I played an active role in helping Democratic candidates get elected. We held a political rally for U.S. Senator Barbara Mikulski in our home with over a hundred friends and neighbors, including many of Maryland's political movers and shakers.

Having never met the senator before, we were amused when her assistant appeared carrying a stool Barbara used for all her speeches. Barbara is probably about four feet, nine inches on her tiptoes, and she needed the stool to see and be seen over the heads of the crowd. Otherwise, she'd be in the forest looking at the tree trunks. I stood on her stool myself when I introduced her to the audience.

Though diminutive, Sen. Milulski won over everyone with her firm and confident manner. Barbara is known as a feisty political fighter from inner Baltimore. She is folksy, humorous, and down-to-earth. But there is an unmistakable thread through her persona of dedication and seriousness of purpose.

Sen. Mikulski was re-elected and is still serving her Maryland constituents well in the Senate.

Mark Shriver is the nephew of President John F. Kennedy, and the son of Sargent Shriver and Eunice Kennedy. Many in our district feared that Mark's participation in our district campaign would bring a circus-like atmosphere to the election process. There were many Kennedy supporters in our area as well as Kennedy opponents among Republicans and Democrats alike.

I met with Mark and his campaign staff so we could work out a plan to get him elected to the Maryland statehouse. (This was a position his great-grandfather Shriver had also held.) Mark asked me to brief him on the situation in our local district, and advise him and his campaign of the caveats and the strategy to be employed in our district. I told him that while many citizens were delighted to have him as a candidate, some were upset about it. I also suggested that he make every effort to meet with the elite and get to know them. I advised him not to use his middle name, Kennedy, on his campaign literature so people would not think he was trading on his name to get elected.

Mark was a very likable, personable individual and he worked hard to win votes. Mark's sister Maria Shriver and brother-in-law Arnold Schwarzenegger made some campaign appearances with him. After he won the primary, he invited me to serve on his steering committee.

Mark's parents, Sargent and Eunice, had a big rally at their estate to promote Mark. We were invited to their home a few times to send out the invitations and to help organize events for his campaign.

The Shriver home was a compound in Potomac, Maryland surrounded by a berm to keep out the curious. A walk through the house with Eunice was revealing. The grand piano was covered with dozens of family photos of John F. Kennedy. Pat was especially impressed by Eunice's collection of madonna and child art, from medieval to modern. To Pat, Eunice explained one very large and garish painting of mother and child that dominated the living room wall with, "Oh, Arnold gave me that. I admired the one he gave to Maria, so he gave me one, too."

Sargent Shriver, Mark's father, came from a founding Maryland family. He had run for vice president with George McGovern in the 1960s, and established the Peace Corps under President Kennedy. Eunice Kennedy Shriver had been very close to her brother, John F. Kennedy. For Eunice, founder of the Special Olympics, I took on the job of manning the Special Olympics table to solicit donations from people at Mark's political events.

Mark won the election with little or no difficulty. I was proud to be involved in getting him elected, since he proved to be a good representative for his constituents and the whole state. One of Mark's outstanding contributions in Maryland was the crafting of his law on "deadbeat dads," which gained national attention. It closed the loopholes that enabled divorced fathers to avoid paying child support, and brought relief to thousands of single mothers. Mark served two terms very well but lost in his bid in 2000 for a seat in the United States Congress.

Doug Duncan, mayor of Rockville, and I met at many political events during campaigns. In Maryland, the county is the political unit of government, and Doug asked me to serve on his steering committee when he ran for Montgomery county executive. This position is like mayor, but encompasses the entire county, with approximately 900,000 people.

Pat donated a couple of desks and chairs, a microwave, and a complete telephone system. I chauffeured Doug to political functions in the campaign staff car and assisted him in passing out literature at supermarkets and Metro stations. Together, we went door to door to talk to voters. I walked in holiday parades with Doug in towns and cities and, while he was riding and waving to the crowds, I passed out his brochures to people lining the parade route.

Doug won his election and served three terms as county executive.

Doug Duncan, along with county Police Chief Moose, gained national prominence in 2003 from the TV coverage of the search for the two snipers terrorizing the Washington area. The entire country watched with horrified fascination as innocent people were gunned down at schools, stores, and gas stations. Doug is the kind of person who can remain calm in stressful situations. Chief Moose also gave a great deal of reassurance to the community by his sincere demeanor and his strong commitment to public safety. Because of all the publicity, late one night a truck driver recognized the snipers' car at an obscure highway rest stop thirty miles north of Montgomery County.

Parris Glendenning had been a professor of government and politics at the University of Maryland; then he was elected as the county executive of our neighboring county, Prince George's. When he decided to run for governor of Maryland, I was selected to help in the campaign as someone who knew the political ropes in upper Montgomery County. Pat and I hosted a dinner at our house to introduce Parris to eighty local people.

After the election, I was appointed to the governor's rapid response team. Our team prepared probable questions and suitable responses to them, for occasions when Parris was interviewed on radio or television. One of us would stand by during the program, watching the television interview at home. When someone from the public called in a controversial, tough question, the person on duty would call in immediately with an easy clarifying statement or a "softball" question on the same issue, to enable the governor to clarify his first statement.

In his campaign for governor, Parris' running mate was Kathleen Kennedy Townsend, who was running for lieutenant governor. Kathleen Kennedy Townsend and Mark Shriver were first cousins but Mark told me he hardly knew her. Because of my background as an agriculture teacher and my connection with farmers through the county fair, I was assigned to escort Kathleen through the upcounty to introduce her to rural voters. I took Kathleen and her entourage around to dairy farms, swine and beef cattle operations, orchards, plant nurseries, and farms raising corn, grain, alfalfa hay, and truck crops. Kathleen is the oldest daughter of Robert Kennedy and it was evident she was trying to use the Kennedy name to her advantage. She always introduced herself with her full name: Kathleen Kennedy Townsend. It worked on some voters, but I saw others turn up their noses in response.

Because of our campaign work for President Clinton, a small group of Montgomery County Democrats was invited to come to the Old Executive Office Building, a nineteenth century architectural masterpiece next to the White House containing executive staff offices. For a week, we worked as volunteers in the mailroom, opening and sorting the president's mail according to issue, so appropriate replies could be sent.

People across the nation were writing to the new president. Some letters were requests for assistance, and they were heartbreaking: people were facing eviction and bankruptcy; had been fired; had lost their insurance; had medical conditions they couldn't afford to have treated, or other misfortunes. The writers felt the federal government should provide a safety net for people who, through no fault of their own, had come upon hard times. These letters went into a separate box for a more personal response.

Many letters expressed the writers' opinions on the new health plan being developed by Hillary Clinton. Some criticized what they believed was the president's lack of support for the military, complaining about the "don't ask, don't tell" policy regarding gays in the military, or cuts in the Pentagon budget. And some resented that Clinton was able to avoid military service, and believed that should have disqualified him from being Commander-in-Chief. There was considerable hate mail. Any real threats

-- and we read a few -- were brought to the attention of a presidential staff person, who stayed nearby.

We felt extremely proud and privileged to be involved behind the scenes in the new administration. Our reward was a private meeting with Socks, the First Cat. It was what we in Eros would call a dubious honor. I'm not a cat lover, and am allergic to them. Behind closed doors, Socks was carried in by an aide and allowed to prowl over the tables and be petted for a time.

A special private tour of the working areas of the White House, rarely seen by tourists, was arranged for us. It included the areas where the day-to-day work is done by the president and his staff. On a day when the president was traveling, our small group entered by the private Rose Garden entrance to the White House. We were escorted through the Cabinet Conference Room, the Oval Office and the adjoining staff offices, and were allowed to linger awhile in the nearly subterranean Press Briefing Room.

This room had been built in the basement as a private pool for Franklin Roosevelt, before being converted into a surprisingly small facility for national press conferences, televised to the world. On television, the room seemed much larger and more impressive. It appeared to be about the size of a regular classroom. It contained only a dais and podium backed by a hanging curtain with the presidential seal, regular chairs for the reporters, and no other furnishings. It was much plainer than I expected. I clowned around standing behind the podium, and gave a little talk to "mah fellah Amuricans" in the Lyndon Johnson style.

The Oval Office was also smaller than I expected, but very impressive. The furnishings were lavish, centered by a brilliant blue carpet depicting the Seal of the United States surrounded by golden stars. Flags flanked the large presidential desk, and priceless works of art hung on the walls. The Oval Office was vacant that day, and we were allowed time to browse and take in the enormous historical significance of this special place. Thoughts of the many history-making decisions made in that room that impacted the entire world ran through my mind.   This memorable tour took place in 1993.

At Christmastime of the following year, I was among a group of local Democratic officials invited to the White House to see the holiday decorations. We were to arrive early, before the daily crowds of the general public were allowed to enter.

It was on this private tour that I was first suspected of sabotage. As our group of devoted Democrats entered the White House security gates, I set off the alarm, to my surprise. I was immediately pulled aside by a plainclothes agent and checked over very thoroughly. Since there seemed to be no visible reason that my shoes or clothing would set off the alarm, I was hastily escorted into a tiny closet-sized room with the Secret Service operative. His first action was to broadcast "Code Red! Code Red!" on his walkie-talkie. And he explained the situation to someone on the other end. During the entire process, the agent was in frequent contact through his walkie-talkie with, apparently, a White House supervisor. After I took off my shoes and socks and stripped to the waist, he swept my body with sensing wands. The agent was visibly frustrated because he could not determine the reason the alarm had activated. He began questioning me about my identity, where I lived, why I was there, my social security number, my mother's maiden name, military experience, and my doctors' names. As we talked, the supervisor was checking my answers, I assumed on a database, on the other end.

Then while I put my clothes on, the agent was silent and thoughtful, gazing into space. Meanwhile I was thinking, "Oh my gosh, I'm on my way to Leavenworth." After what seemed like an eternity, he asked, "Have you had a stress test lately?" I said, "Yes, about two weeks ago." I didn't know the doctor's phone number and the guard had to make a couple of calls to find it. Then he called my cardiologist for verification. The recent test probably left a residue of thallium, a radioactive metal, in my body. The Secret Service agent apologized and thanked me for cooperating. He made sure I was escorted back to continue the tour with my group of friends, who took great glee in the fact that I had been swept away by the Secret Service which was protecting the White House from a harmless former principal and Air Force colonel.

I was meeting many people of all kinds through my political connections in the Washington area. A lady named Ruthann Aron was a prominent political activist and real estate millionaire, well known in Montgomery County for her aggressive attitude, burning ambition, and her work on the real estate commission. Ruthann's residence and her political base were in upscale Potomac, Maryland.

When she decided to run for United States Senate, Ruthann needed some upcounty connections. She approached me while we were in line waiting for the Fourth of July parade to start. I was in the contingent marching with Doug Duncan that day. Ruthann asked if I would be willing to work on her campaign in the upcounty, because of my strong support there. I had to decline her offer because as a Democratic precinct official and chairman of the legislative caucus, I didn't feel I could campaign for a Republican.

It wasn't long before we were reading about Ruthann Aron in the *Washington Post* – but the story was not about her campaign. Ruthann hit the front pages when she was arrested leaving the Courtyard Marriott in disguise – a long wig, sunglasses and a raincoat. She had tried to solicit a Potomac landfill owner, also prominent in the news for his regulatory problems with the county, as a hit man. The victims were to be Ruthann's husband and a lawyer who had opposed her in a previous real estate case. In the hotel lobby she had given money for the murder to an undercover cop.

(This hotel, near Pat's office, was also near county office buildings, and is a common meeting place for political chitchat. Pat and I lunched there frequently, and I met with many candidates and officials in the restaurant.)

During the investigation into the murder for hire, it was revealed that Ruthann had previously poisoned her husband's chili in an unsuccessful do-it-yourself attempt to kill him at home.

Ruthann, who had campaigned on a law-and-order platform claiming to be tough on crime, pleaded insanity and childhood abuse as mitigating circumstances at her trial. After one mistrial she was convicted of soliciting murder, and ultimately served three years in jail. She was allowed to remain in the county jail instead of being sent to prison. Later she was released on home detention. Because of the delicious spectacle of a millionaire senatorial candidate being prosecuted for murder, this case was profiled by Dominick Dunne in his television series, "Power, Privilege and Justice".

In the 1960s, Senator Eugene McCarthy was the first anti-Vietnam maverick – that is, he was the first senator to speak out against the terrible toll the war took on our troops, and to advocate United States withdrawal. His opposition to the war galvanized and legitimized the antiwar movement, which had previously been fragmented and ascribed to communists, hippies, and fringe elements. This played a significant role in eroding support for President Lyndon Johnson, and kept him from seeking a second term. McCarthy ran for president in 1968, 1972, 1976, 1988, and 1992.

While I was having lunch in the National Press Club restaurant in Washington, the club manager, realizing by our conversation that we were a group of Democrats, asked if we would like to have Eugene McCarthy join us for lunch. "Of course!" we all said in unison. When he escorted the senator to our table, the manager introduced us by saying, "Senator, I thought you'd like to meet twelve of the twenty votes you received in your last election." The senator enjoyed this as much as we did.

McCarthy was charming and personable, and I took an instant liking to him. He sat right down and began entertaining us with political jokes. At one point he reached inside his coat pocket, pulled out one of his favorite poems, and read it to us. He enjoyed writing poetry in his spare time and was an accomplished poet.

The *Washington Post* once quoted Senator McCarthy, "Being in politics is like being a football coach. You have to be smart enough to understand the game, and dumb enough to think it's important."

In 1992 I applied for a position as a contract employee with the Department of Labor Academy, which was staffed by a private contractor. The jobsite was right across the street from the Senate Office Building in Washington. I was hired because of my doctorate in educational administration, counseling and psychology, my experience as a school counselor, and my ten years working in Pat's company, Careers III, as a job counselor and placement director.

For the regular Department of Labor employees, my job counseling consisted of advising individuals on how they could advance to a higher position, or change career paths within the government. I gave them a series of vocational and career tests to identify their aptitudes and interests.

I sometimes traveled to Department of Labor field offices in Ohio, Virginia, and West Virginia to present seminars for employees in the morning, and counsel individually with them in the afternoon.

From Careers III, and the DOL job, I learned some fundamentals of promoting a candidate to personnel: give sound bites – small bits of information, not a whole lot at a time; less is better; quantify and qualify to get the attention of personnel supervisors. For instance, instead of saying, "I answered the phones and directed calls to the proper person," say, "I answered phones for twenty people and handled 200 calls per day."

We ran seminars for employees and provided individual counseling for their job searches. One person that I worked with was very impressive and was recognized by many supervisors as a good employee. The reason Tom came to me was, he had submitted his application (Standard Form 171) for a new position several times and it was always rejected. Together we determined that he was omitting a youthful brush with the law. I pointed out that there is a section on the form to explain such circumstances, and I recommended truthfulness. This was especially important because the regulations required personnel to reject -- without comment – a 171 form that contains a discrepancy. I saw Tom eight or ten times for counseling and we got his SF171 in top shape. After my help, he got a promotion and a raise, and progressed in his career path.

Secretary of Labor Robert Reich, then newly appointed by Clinton, wanted to demonstrate to DOL employees how the internal system worked, and how they could advance if they worked hard and applied themselves. He selected Tom to use as an example of a success story: Tom accompanied Secretary Reich to many meetings with groups of employees, to explain how to use the resources available to them for career advancement.

Each time there is a change of administration in Washington, there's a whole horde of people who lose their jobs in the changeover: political appointees of the previous president or assistants to legislators who have lost the election. After George H. W. Bush left office and the Clinton administration took over, as a career counselor at the Department of Labor Academy it became one of my duties to help Republican political appointees seek employment elsewhere in the government. As a good Democrat, the irony of being assigned to help Republicans get jobs was not lost on me.

From 1993 to 1997, I was chairman of the Montgomery County Retired Teachers' Association legislative committee. The MCRTA represents 4000 retired teachers. I organized meetings for our members to meet our state representatives and senators in Annapolis. I was also a member of the legislative committee for the larger Maryland Retired Teachers Association. For both of these organizations, I made many trips to Annapolis to speak before committees and to lobby the legislature for better compensation and health benefits for retired teachers.

At one state committee meeting on a teacher retirement issue, the chairman of the committee complimented the teachers for being very active. He said, "I have received over a hundred calls on this issue and I give them an A for effort." When comments were solicited from the Montgomery County delegation, I rose and said, "Mr. Chairman, did you say you received more than a hundred calls and you gave them a grade of A? Well, I'm disappointed. You only received a hundred calls regarding this issue, and you should have received more than a thousand. I give them a C!" The audience just roared. After that I became familiar to the legislators.

In 1998 the Montgomery County Council established a new Office of the Inspector General for the purpose of making county government more efficient. In view of my background as an inspector general in the Air Force, I was selected for the committee to recommend qualified candidates to the council. We reviewed resumes of 64 applicants from all over the nation, then narrowed it down through the interviewing process to recommend three candidates to the County Council for final consideration.

~27~

"Let's Grow Old Together"

On the coldest day of 1996 I suffered a heart attack with cardiac arrest. I was fortunate to make it to the hospital in time, since the first two ambulances couldn't make it up our long, icy driveway and finally had to drive over my neighbor's land to reach my front door. I was doubly fortunate that I could be revived after my heart stopped, and then successfully came through quadruple bypass surgery. At first I spent a lot of time trying to figure out why God spared my life. But I gave up figuring, and decided God's plan for me was to spend my time enjoying my wife, seven children and six grandchildren. My youngest grandchild, Aimee, was born on the day I came home from the hospital.

With my renewed, fresh appreciation for life and family, I was eager to see my brothers, sisters and cousins at the next Busby/Busbice/Rusheon reunion.

LeMoyne left, his wife Doris right, Wayne on guitar,
Buzz on mandolin

More than 100 people attended the July, 1996 reunion in Dallas, the year I was president of the association. By this time more families from the younger generation were attending, and the affair had outgrown being held in a home. My niece, Tracey Busbice Harris, had arranged for our entire group to be bused to the Ft. Worth stockyards, a country and western show at Billy Bob's, and a dinner at a Tex-Mex restaurant where we were serenaded by a mariachi band.

We noted the passage of three milestones at this Dallas reunion.

The reunion featured entertainment – both music and skits – as well as visiting among three generations of relatives, some met for the first time. I was still recovering from my heart attack and quadruple bypass surgery the previous February, and I was concerned that I wouldn't be strong enough to run the meetings and perform. When I got onstage with my guitar, backed by Buzz, John, and LeMoyne and his wife Doris, it was very emotional for me to discover I could still sing, play, and entertain. My family in the audience was teary, and all seemed to appreciate what an accomplishment this was for me.

This was the first reunion Buzz had attended since 1988, and everyone was eager to hear him recreate his famous high lonesome tenor sound. Amazingly, in spite of his Parkinson's he was able to play the mandolin, and we all wanted to hear him do "Just Me and the Jukebox." This event was Buzz's last performance for the family.

My niece Kate appeared as Kate at this reunion -- her first in nearly twenty years. She had not felt accepted by some in the family.

Kate was born Charles Busbice, son of LeMoyne and Doris. Charles soon discovered he was meant to be a girl and behaved like one. Her parents discouraged this and made every effort to have her gender clarified through misguided medical intervention. After a tortuous adolescence, including hormonal treatment, suicide attempts, and hospitalizations, at the age of twenty Charles decided to declare her womanhood and took the legal name of Katherine Connella, honoring my mother's family. Kate looks a great deal like my mother did in her youth.

In her twenties, Kate learned from doctors that the reason for her gender confusion was probably the absorption during gestation of her unborn twin. This occurrence is sometimes given as an explanation of gender anomalies.

Pat and I had always supported Kate, but much of our family was mystified, and unsure what to think. Kate and her parents were vilified by some members of their church in Texas, who considered Kate to be a homosexual, and headed for hell. But Kate had the strength to follow her feelings about who she is, and the determination to live the way her mind and heart led her to. We admired her for this, and loved her for her intelligence, her dramatic flair, and her buoyant personality.

Kate had been living in Hollywood. She had some success in cabaret and even acted in a few independent films, making a lot of contacts in the filmmaking community.

Pat strongly encouraged her to attend the reunion and make her debut as Katherine before the family. So Kate and her cousin Tracey charmed the audience with a duet of the rockabilly song "Rock and Roll Atom," a bouncy novelty song I wrote in 1961, and recorded by MVM Record Company in New York. For accompaniment, they placed my old LP record as backup.

Rock 'n' Roll Atom
*   By Wayne Busbice & Don Higgs*
Pub. Old Home Place Music

Well, the teacher says we oughta know
All about the atom from a-head to toe,
Now let us think, what can we say,
About the tiny little atom that we know today.

We know it's round and full of space,
With electrons a-swingin' around the nucle-ace,
Electrons swingin' around the nucle-ace.

If we could see the atom, boy that's fun
Protons a-dancin' with the neu-hoo-tron.
Frisky little electrons swingin' in space –
Ya gotta have a proton in the nucle-ace.

You be my electron every day
And I'll be your proton, what do you say?
We'll all get out on that hardwood floor
And dance all night, then dance some more

Come on baby, listen to me –
That rock 'n' roll atom's gettin' through to me.
That rock 'n' roll atom's gettin' through to me.

That rock 'n' roll atom's goin' round
It's spreadin' knowledge all over town
So it makes no difference where you shake or stroll
You can learn about the atom as you rock 'n' roll.

Now instead of Cupid shootin' his darts
He shoots a rock 'n' roll atom right through your heart,
Rock 'n' roll atom right through your heart!

(In the 21st century, my song "Rock 'n' Roll Atom" was included in a group of 100 "atomic" songs to be offered on the internet as Conelrad Atomic Platters, "cold war music from the golden age of homeland security". Conelrad was the acronym for a government method of broadcasting to the U.S. public during the cold war in case of attack.)

The *piece de resistance* of the show was Kate's skit and soft-shoe, spoofing members of the family with a riff on Peggy Lee's rendition of "Is That All There Is?" She managed to skewer many of us with her re-written lyrics. Although weak from laughter, the audience rose to its feet with applause. Kate had managed her debut beautifully.

Pat and Kate reconnected that weekend and have stayed close. Kate has appeared on national television and has written a book about her experiences as a transgendered person. Ten years later, the critically acclaimed film "Transamerica" would be inspired by her story.

After I recovered from my heart attack and surgery, I became very sensitive to cold weather. I announced to Pat that I did not intend to spend another winter in Maryland.

We sold our dream house in Gaithersburg and spent the winter of 1997 in Florida, looking at houses. That winter was very lonely in our little apartment, as we felt adrift from all that was familiar. We filled our time checking out dozens of developments, rejecting each one for some reason or another. While driving from gated community to gated community looking for houses, we passed along a beautiful stretch of highway bordered by open fields, which were occupied by the unique scrawny Florida cattle and goats, dotted with ponds, and shaded by immense stately live oaks. I commented, "*This* is what we need – a goated community, not a gated community." This became our password for the environment we were seeking. That month we found, and bought, our new house.

Although the house was purchased in January, it had yet to be built. We spent a long eight months living in our isolated log cabin in the Blue Ridge near Paw Paw, West Virginia.

Log cabin on the Cacapon

The Cacapon River at the end of our property was clean, clear, and scenic. From our canoe we could see huge carp lazing in the deep pools. A fisherman passed our porch one day with a three-foot carp in his cooler. He proudly stopped to show it to us; and when I asked if it was good to eat, he explained his recipe for carp: "First you clean him, put him on a plank with salt and pepper and seasoning, and bake him in the oven until done. Then you remove it from the oven, throw the fish away and eat the plank."

For all its beauty and appeal, our little neighborhood in the mountains in Paw Paw was very rural, and too sparsely populated to offer much in the way of activities or friends.

We were so desperate for companionship that year that we attended the local church in nearby Largent, West Virginia, a tiny frame building over a hundred years old, with, literally, three members. Generally on Sunday service there were six to twelve people in the pews, largely Washington transplants like us. A circuit-riding preacher, Elder Payne, usually showed up.

Enon Primitive Baptist church was a foot-washing congregation, although we never saw any. The notable characteristics of the church were the prohibition of any musical instruments, a stricture against women leading the prayers or songs, and the unique pronouncements of Elder Payne. Elder Payne was quick to say he "didn't have no education", and "never planned a sermon", but he "spoke to the Lord and the Lord spoke to [his] heart."

Privately, we are still quoting his sermon on creationism. Elder Payne orated: "Now I don't have much book learning. I never went to college, like some of you. But I know this: I'm not descended from no monkey. I know this because the Bible says God created us in his own image. That means God looks like us, and we look like him. Do you think Jesus was related to some monkey? I know I'm not related to no monkey, because I don't look like no monkey, and I don't pray to no monkey." Here, he paused for applause.

For all our humor about this church, we did enjoy the fellowship of the residents of the local hollows.

In the fall of 1998 we moved into our new house in Florida, located on a small pond containing "our own" alligator. Pat immediately named him Beauregard, and along with dozens of exotic birds, he provides endless hours of entertaining viewing for us and our guests.

Sadly, two members of the Busby Brothers left this world in the first decade of the new century. Bobby died at age 75 in Lanham, Maryland. A news article in the Washington Post February 25, 2005 remembered him:

Born on a family farm near Eros, La., Mr. Busbice grew up picking cotton, tending chickens, cows and pigs and singing at barn dances with his cousins. He graduated from the University of Louisiana at Lafayette and earned a master's degree in science from the University of Maryland in agricultural education in the early 1950s...

Mr. Busbice, who retired 20 years ago, joined his cousins in recent years as a tenor vocalist in a well-known bluegrass group, the Busby Brothers, and played at several local events including the Washington Folk Festival. His singing was featured on two Webco Music bluegrass albums that received national airplay...

Survivors include his wife of 50 years, Nadine Clendining Busbice... two daughters, Lisa Boss..., Lori Fullmer..., and a son Robert Wendell; a sister, a brother, and four grandchildren.

BOB BUSBY
WEBCO RECORDING ARTIST
FOR INFORMATION & BOOKINGS
CALL 301-253-5962

Cousin Bobby Busbice

My brother Buzz passed away on January 5, 2003 in Ellicott City, Maryland. Stories about his contribution to bluegrass music were published in the Washington Post, Baltimore Sun, The New York Times, Bluegrass Unlimited, posted on the internet, and appeared in many other newspapers. There was no question that he earned the title of the Father of Bluegrass Music in Washington D.C. Many of the musicians who got their start with Buzz attended; some of them became bluegrass luminaries in their own right.

Ira Gitlin, a reporter who covered the funeral for Bluegrass Unlimited, wrote,

In the 1950s Buzz was the most visible and influential figure in Washington, D.C.'s emerging bluegrass scene...A generation of young musicians...would carry on the work that Buzz started.

In the front row sat Buzz's son Tim, his grandson Kolaan, and his brother Wayne Busbice, a musician and founder of WEBCO Records... During the service the Patuxent Partners performed... Wayne Busbice's 'Heaven is My Home' and Hank Williams' 'I Saw The Light'. The slippery tremolos and syncopated double stops in Tom Mindte's mandolin work paid tribute to Buzz's distinctive style. The service proper was conducted by pastor and amateur musician Brian Mindte... Pastor Mindte suggested that we can view death as a reunion with God, and tied this in to the theme of homecoming that shows up in many of Buzz's songs...Despite the cold Charlie Waller took out his Martin and sang, "Lord, I am Ready to Go Home". Everyone joined in on the choruses, and uncannily, moments after the last note had been played, the sun broke through the clouds...

In the *Washington Post* Richard Harrington wrote,

When Buzz Busby died last Sunday at 69 after a long illness, his place in bluegrass history was secure only within small circles of genre historians and regional bluegrass musicians who remembered his soaring high tenor, mastery of the mandolin and crucial impact on Washington music.

'If anybody deserved the title of father of Washington bluegrass, it would be Buzz Busby,' says Eddie Stubbs, voice of the Grand Ole Opry and a former member of the acclaimed Johnson Mountain Boys, who was tutored by and played briefly with Busby a quarter-century ago.

Joey Kent of the Louisiana Hayride invited me to come to Shreveport to attend a bluegrass festival on March 22-23 at the Municipal Auditorium, the original home of the Louisiana Hayride. Eddie Stubbs, my former student and longtime friend, was co-hosting the main show with Hayride announcers Frank Page and Norm Bale. Jimmy Martin was headlining the show and was to be inducted into the Louisiana Hayride Hall of Fame, along with Buzz and Mac Wiseman. Buzz played with both their bands early in his career. The Hall of Fame is a portrait gallery located in an inner hallway of the auditorium and is maintained as a part of the Cradle of the Stars Museum.

I took Marilyn and LeMoyne, and their spouses Steve and Doris, to be present onstage when I accepted the portrait from Eddie in honor of Buzz. (I learned later that James O'Gwynn, who was also inducted that night, is a distant cousin and a Busby descendant.) Eddie Stubbs said some kind words about how Buzz and I had influenced both his career and his life. I felt honored and proud for Buzz as he finally received the recognition he deserved for his contribution to the music he loved so much.

Heaven Is My Home
  By Wayne Busbice
  Pub. Old Home Place Music

Chorus:
There's a ship a-comin', o'er the dashing foam
There's a ship a-comin' to take God's children home.
The pilot is my Jesus, with Him you can't go wrong
He will sail us all to heaven, and heaven is my home.

I can see the mast now rising, it reminds me of the cross
Where our precious Savior died, to save the world from lost
This ship won't drop anchor 'til we reach the sea of love
The angels will deliver us to that home above.

Have you received your ticket for the voyage 'cross the sea?
Jesus said I'll pay the fare if you place your trust in me
If you give your life to Jesus He will bear you o'er the deep
Forever you'll be happy and your soul He'll always keep.

~28~

Near the End of the Road

We Busbices have a saying in my generation: "Since we didn't know where we came from, we weren't able to start out at the scratch line like most people -- we had to take a running start just to get up to the scratch line". I write this memoir so my six grandchildren can have a good understanding about their origin and begin their lives at the starting line.

I descend from generations of southern farmers: a few plantation owners and slaveholders, and some subsistence farmers -- all hardworking and close to the land. Being born into a family of nine siblings and growing up in the Great Depression during the 1930s and early 1940s gave me a traditional southern identity. Having no electricity, telephone, running water, radio or television deprived me of knowing about the lifestyles of others, or the wider world, except through hearsay. Nothing seemed to change much during my early years and if it did, it changed very slowly.

Since my birth in 1929, more progress has been made in communication, transportation, agriculture, electronics and just about every field of human endeavor than in all the previous years. The world that this rural American boy once lived in doesn't exist any more. Everything is completely different from what it was then. However the attitudes and principles I acquired as a youth still have meaning for me. Every choice I've made along life's way has been to honor personal relationships. My walk through history has taken many twists and turns, some predictable and some unpredictable, filled with many challenges. I'm convinced that the road I've traveled helped me realize that the most important relationship in life is family. Becoming rich with material things of this world was never a high priority of mine. In my view, service to others is its own reward. It is fitting that my journey of seventy-plus years has finally brought me great understanding of family

Meeting my wife Pat was the great watershed of my life. The years I lived before then seem like an existence unfulfilled. From the beginning of our relationship in 1972, Pat and I have shared a love and intimacy so rare that we wonder about a karmic influence – surely there was another force that brought us together, against all odds. Looking back, the years seem like one continual honeymoon. Even though we're well into our senior years now, we can't remember ever having as much time as we would like just to be together. Whether this marriage was made in Maryland or made in heaven, it's been a wonderful ride and we haven't run out of gas yet.

On May 1, 2007, we invited a few close friends to celebrate a renewal of vows on our thirtieth anniversary. Bonnie, "matron of dishonor" as she terms it, read some passages from Kalil Ghibran; my cousin Donald stood up for me; and Rev. Warren Clark blessed our marriage. With a backdrop of white flowers and our small pond, we sat on stools before our guests while I played guitar and sang to my bride.

Have I Told You Lately That I Love You
By Gene Autry and S. Wiseman
Pub. by BMI

Have I told you lately that I love you
Could I tell you once again somehow?
Have I told you with all my heart and soul how I adore you
Well, Darlin' I'm telling you now.

Chorus:
This world would end if ever I should lose you
I'm no good without you, anyhow.
Have I told you lately that I love you
Well, Patsy, I'm telling you now.

Pat and Wayne enjoying retirement

Let's Grow Old Together
   By Wayne Busbice and Connella Busbice
   Pub. Old Home Place Music

Chorus:
Let's grow old together
Just as long as we're contented let us try
We can live day-by-day dreaming dreams of yesterday
That's the way we'll pass the time away.

We can go to church each week
And learn to turn the other cheek
Even though people say we will part someday
Through God we can find a better way.

If we pray to God each night
I know he will make our burdens light
Then instead of our dreams we can have everything
And our children will make our glad hearts sing.

APPENDIX I

THE TREE I GREW ON

Ancestry Chart of Wayne E. Busbice

```
                    ┌ 6-Benjamin Buzbee Sr. (1699-1815)
              ┌ 5-William Reese Buzbee (1775-1844)
              └ 6-Susannah (        -        )
        ┌ 4-Allen Busby (1798-1878)
        │     └ 5-First Spouse Unk. (       -       )
    ┌ 3-Oliver Allen Busby Rusheon (1855-1921)
    │         ┌ 5-James Hays (      -      )
    │   └ 4-Sarah Hays (1817-1880)
    │         └ 5-Elizabeth Hays (      -      )
  ┌ 2-Oates Oliver Busby (1893-1943)
  │     ┌ 4-Unknown Byrd (1800-1866)
  │   └ 3-Mary Frances Byrd (1865-1929)
  │                 ┌ 7-William Thompson Sr. (1749-1816)
  │             ┌ 6-Daniel Thompson (1778-1863)
  │             │   └ 7-Charity Murray (1752-1826)
  │         ┌ 5-James P. Jarvis Thompson (1804-        )
  │         │   └ 6-Sarah Sally Murray (1787-1859)
  │       └ 4-Martha Thompson (1835-1916)
  │           └ 5-Mary A. Gross (1808-        )
1-Wayne Evon Busbice (1929-    )
  │           ┌ 5-McKeelie Connelley (1775-        )
  │       ┌ 4-Levin McKeelie Conley (1800-1871)
  │   ┌ 3-Charles Allison Connella (1854-1915)
  │   │       ┌ 5-Daniel McQueen (      -      )
  │   │   └ 4-Sarah (Susan) Anne McQueen (1815-1876)
  └ 2-Talitha Fay Connella (1894-1956)
        │       ┌ 5-James Nobles (      -1835)
        │   ┌ 4-Morris Nobles (1831-1863)
        │   │   └ 5-Martha Harris (      -1835)
        └ 3-Sarah Anne Noble (1861-1910)
            └ 4-Lucinda F. Birdwell (1832-        )
```

284

Paternal Lineage of Wayne E. Busbice

1

Otis Oliver Busbice Jr. (1921-1948)
Connella Allison Busbice (1922-1998)
Helen Fay Busbice (1924-   )
Charles LeMoyne Busbice (1926-2004)
Temple Allen Busbice (1928-1983)
Wayne Evon Busbice
    b. 28 Mar 1929, Chatham, LA
    d.
Billy Alston Busbice (1931-1999)
Bernarr Graham Busbice (1933-2003)
Marilyn Kay Busbice (1935-   )

2

Eva Mae Belle Busby (1883-1951)
Eddie O. Busby (1886-1887)
Seaborn Louis Busby (1888-1956)
Walter Busby (1890-1894)
Elton Basil Busby (1892-1967)
Oates Oliver Busby (Father)
    b. 21 May 1893, Laurens co. Georgia
    m. 17 Sep 1919, W. Monroe, LA
    d. 15 Jul 1943, Monroe, Ouachita LA
Emery Fulton Busby (1896-1971)
Pauline Lucy Busby (1897-1971)
Joe Wright Rusheon (1900-1945)
L.B. Rusheon (1903-1945)
Alden Rusheon (1905-1920)
T.O. Rusheon (1907-1954)
Violet M. I. Rusheon (1911-1961)

Talitha Fay Connella (Mother)
    b. 11 Nov 1894, W. Monroe, LA
    d. 12 Nov 1956, Monroe, LA

3

William Burnett Busby (1848-   )
Oliver Allen Busby Rusheon (Grandfather)
    b. 20 Dec 1855, Pulaski Co. GA
    m. 1882, Dooly County, Vienna, GA
    d. 1 Sep 1921, Eros, LA
Lucy Busby

Mary Frances Byrd (Grandmother)
    b. 25 Sep 1865, Dooly Co., GA
    d. 9 May 1929, Lula La

4

Allen Busby (Great Grandfather)
    b. 15 Oct 1798, South Carolina
    m. 17 Aug 1846, Perry, Houston GA
    d. 3 Aug 1878, Pulaski Co. GA
James W. Busbee (Abt 1800-Abt 1847)
Inman Busby

Sarah Hays (Great Grandmother)
    b. 1817, South Carolina
    d. After 1880, Pulaski Co. GA ?

Paternal Lineage of Wayne E. Busbice

5

Zachariah Buzbee (Abt 1768-   )
William Reese Buzbee (2nd Great Grandfather)
    b. Abt 1775, SC
    m.
    d. Abt 1844, GA
Benjamin Buzbee Jr.
Jeremiah Buzbee
Miles Buzbee

First Spouse Unk. (2nd Great Grandmother)
    b.
    d.

6

Benjamin Buzbee Sr. (3rd Great Grandfather)
    b. 1699, MD
    m.
    d. 1815, Edgefield Co., SC

Susannah (3rd Great Grandmother)
    b. Unk
    d. Unk

Maternal Lineage of Wayne E. Busbice

1

Belle Lucille Connella (1881-1944)
Alice Elmo Connella (1882-1884)
Laura E. Connella (1884-1936)
Charles James Connella (Abt 1885-1887)
Alison Jones Connella (1886-1887)
Jetta L. Connella (1888-1926)
Lillian Connella (1890-1890)
Zona M. Connella (1892-Cir 1976)
Talitha Fay Connella
    b. 11 Nov 1894, W. Monroe, LA
    d. 12 Nov 1956, Monroe, LA
Charles A. Connella Jr. (1897-1959)
Heloise Connella (1900-Cir 1992)

2

Henrietta Rebecca Connella (-1852)
James Wright Connella (-1845)
Joanne Connella (1844-1923)
John Levin Knox Connella (1840-   )
Lovett Duncan Connella
Luther Rice Connella
Martha Jane Connella
Rufus Russell Connella
Thomas B. Connella
Laury V. Connella (Abt 1845-   )
Marcella Connella (Abt 1852-   )
Margaret J. Connella (Abt 1853-   )
Charles Allison Connella (Father)
    b. 8 Aug 1854, Connella Plantation, Ouachita Parish, LA
    m. 10 May 1880, Ouachita Parish, LA
    d. 14 Aug 1915, West Monroe, LA
William Webster Connella (Aft 1854-   )

Sarah Anne Noble (Mother)
    b. 12 Dec 1861, Abbeville, Henry, AL
    d. 11 Jun 1910, W. Monroe, LA

3

Levin McKeelle Conley (Grandfather)
    b. 20 Feb 1800, Chester, PA
    m. 25 Jul 1837, Montgomery Co. AL
    d. 7 Nov 1871, W. Monroe, LA
Alexander Argo Connelley

Sarah (Susan) Anne McQueen (Grandmother)
    b. 23 Sep 1815, Abbeville, Montgomery AL
    d. 13 Sep 1876, W. Monroe, LA

4

McKeelle Connelley (Great Grandfather)
    b. Abt 1775, Poss. PA
    m.
    d.

APPENDIX II

BUSBICE MUSICOLOGY

WAYNE BUSBICE/RED McCOY/WAYNE BUSBY
DISCOGRAPHY

Label and Number	Title	Date
Ott H-101 (45rpm)	Going Back to Dixie I'll Love You Forever	1958
Ott H-202 (45 rpm)	Tomorrow I May Be Gone What Will Your Heart Say	1958
Empire 45-506 (45 rpm)	Goin' Back to Dixie Just for Me	1960
Empire EP45-510 (with Buzz Busby)	Life Your Life with Care I Just Couldn't Tell You Goodbye First Battle of Bull Run I Carry a Torch	1961
Olympic 45-004	Going Back to Dixie	1975
Olympic, Flame 001, Collector CLCD, MVM	Rock 'n' Roll Atom	1959
Empire 45-513	Back Home in the Air National Guard I'll Be Back	1961
Almanac 45-808 (as Red McCoy)	3.000 Miles Lonesome What's the Use	1962
MVM 181 (as Red McCoy)	Hootenanny: Rainbow Joe Going Back to Dixie	1964

WAYNE BUSBICE/RED McCOY/WAYNE BUSBY
DISCOGRAPHY

MVM LP (as Red McCoy)	Country and Gospel	1962
Sutton 308-LP	Country and Gospel Songs	1963
Sutton 335-LP	Memories of Jim Reeves	1964
WEBCO 0101-LP (with Buzz Busby)	Traditional Bluegrass	1981
WEBCO 0117-LP (Busby Brothers)	Louisiana Grass	1986
WEBCO 0125-LP (Busby Brothers)	Stained Glass Bluegrass	1987

Published Songs Written
by
Wayne Busbice
All songs published by Broadcast Music, Inc. (BMI)

Song Title	Publisher	Date Registered
Back Home in the Ang	OHPM	5/26/2006
Be Careful of Your Father's Name	OHPM	5/26/2006
Calling Me	OHPM	7/10/1987
Darling Do	OHPM	5/26/2006
Do You Know Who Loves You	OHPM	5/26/2006
First Battle of Bull Run	OHPM	5/26/2006
God Called Jim Reeves Away	OHPM	5/26/2006
Going Back to Dixie	Cedar Music	9/30/1959
Headin' Back to Dixie	OHPM	12/26/1985
Heaven is My Home	OHPM	12/1/1980
He'll Be Walking By Your Side	OHPM	7/10/1987
I Carry A Torch	OHPM	5/26/2006
I Heard My Savior Calling	OHPM	5/26/2006
I Just Couldn't Tell you Goodbye	OHPM	5/26/2006
I Want to See Mother Again	OHPM	5/26/2006
I'll Be Back After Peace has Come to Berlin	OHPM	5/26/2006
I'll Love You Forever	Jiffy Pub. Co.	1957
I'll Share It With You	OHPM	5/26/2006
Just For Me	OHPM	5/26/2006
Let Jesus Come Into Your Heart	OHPM	5/26/2006
Let's Grow Old Together	OHPM	5/26/2006
Live Your Life With Care	Cedar Music	?/27/1960
Lost Without You	OHPM	2/1/1980
My Sweet Little Pretty Brown Eyes	OHPM	12/26/1985
Play Like —	OHPM	5/26/2006
Rainbow Joe	OHPM	5/26/2006
Rock and Roll Atom	OHPM	1980
She's Coming Home Today	OHPM	5/26/2006
Talk to the Lord in Prayer	OHPM	7/10/1987
Tears Mixed with Raindrops	OHPM	10/12/2003
Tomorrow I May be Gone	OHPM	5/26/2006
Tragic Love Affair	OHPM	5/26/2006
Walking By Your Side	OHPM	5/26/2006
What Will Your Heart Say	OHPM	4/29/2006
What's The Use	OHPM	5/26/2006
When God Called Daddy Away	OHPM	5/26/2006
When God Calls You Away	OHPM	7/10/1987
When I Reach My Journey's End	OHPM	7/10/1987
Words	OHPM	7/10/1987
3,000 Miles Lonesome	OHPM	5/26/2006

* OHPM - Old Home Place Music, owner Wayne Busbice

RECORDS PRODUCED BY WEBCO

WLPS 0101	Buzz Busby	Pioneer of Traditional Bluegrass	1981
WLPS 0103	Buzz Busby	Bluegrass Sounds of Buzz Busby Yesterday and Today	1982
WLPS 0104	Bill Rouse & the Uptown Grass Band	Waiting for the Sunshine	1982
WLPS 0105	Jack Fincham & the Dixie Grass	Deep in the Heart of Bluegrass	1982
WLPS 0106	Carl Nelson	On Pine Lake	1982
WLPS 0108	Darrell Sanders	West Virginia Style	1983
WLPS 0109	Grass Reflection	Turn the Green Hills Brown	1983
WLPS 0110	Jim Eanes & the Shenandoah Valley Boys	Shenandoah Grass, Yesterday and Today	1983
WLPS 0111	Overland Express	First Stage Out	1984
WLPS 0112	Bob Purkey & the Blueridge Travellers	Old Dominion Bound	1984
WLPS 0113	Al Jones, Frank Necessary & the Spruce Mountain Boys	Traditional Bluegrass at Its Best	1985
WLPS 0114	Bobby Atkins & the Countrymen	Good Times Can't Last	1985
WLPS 0115	Bill Rouse & the Uptown Grass Band	Old Spinning Wheel	1985
WLPS 0116	Karen Spence & Friends of Bluegrass	With Love to Daddy	1985
WLPS 0117	Busby Brothers	Louisiana Grass	1986
WLPS 0118	Chris Warner	Pickin' and Singin'	1986

WLPS 0119	Paul Adkins	My Old Yellow Car	1986
WLPS 0120	Karen Spence & Ernie Sykes	Sleeping in the Summertime	1986
WLPS 0121	Bill Harrell & the Virginians	Ballads and Bluegrass	1988
WLPS 0122	Gloria Belle	Love of the Mountains	1986
WLPS 0123	Bill Emerson & Pete Goble	Tennessee 1949	1987
WLPS 0124	Chris Warner	All Original	1987
WLPS 0125	Busby Brothers	Stained Glass Bluegrass	1987
WLPS 0126	Larry Stephenson	Every Time I Sing a Love Song	1988
WLPS 0127	Jimmy Gaudreau	Classic J. A. G.	1989
WLPS 0128	Bill Emerson & Pete Goble	Dixie in My Eye	1989
WLPS 0129	Patent Pending	Through the Window	1989
WLPS 0130	South Central Bluegrass	We Can't Return to the Homeplace	1989
WLPS 0131	James King	Sings, It's a Cold, Cold World	1989
WLPS 0132	Chris Warner	Chris Warner and Friends	1989
WLPS 3301-C	Joe Boucher	Dee Jays Don't Make It Easy	1984
WLPS 3302	Hobbs & Partners	Centreville	1984

WLPS 3303-C	D.J. & the C.B. Pickers	Memories of Home	1984
WLPS 3309	D.J. & the C.B. Pickers	Touch of Blue	1987
WLPS No. #	Jack Fincham & the Dixie Grass	Waiting for the Sunrise	1982
WLPS 102	Brooke Johns	Treasures of Broadway	1981
WLPS 5001	Brooke Johns	Return of the Roaring Twenties	1984
Custom	Flora Molton	I Want to Be Ready to Hear God When He Calls	1987
Custom	Judie Pagter and Joe Boucher	Fifty Miles Available Room	1987
Custom	Browningsville Cornet Band	The First Hundred Years	1981
WLPS 3307-C	Spiritual Gospel Singers	He Made a Change in Me	1986
WLPS 107	Blackthorn Stick Ceili Band	Come Dance with Me in Ireland	1982
Custom	Society of Colonial Wars	The Roast Beef of Old England	1982
Custom	Lee Royal and the Sawdusters	Lunchtime at the Sawmill	1986
Custom	Gaithersburg High School Presents	The Music Department	1982

OLD HOME PLACE MUSIC PUBLISHERS
Affiliated with Broadcast Music, Inc.
President: Wayne Busbice   **Vice President: John Busbice**

Song Title	Writer	Date Registered
Adrienne's Reel	Gaudreau, James Arnott	11/16/1988
Amtrak Express	Sanders, Darrell	03/25/1983
At The End	Busby, Buzz	11/07/1980
Back Home in the Ang	Busbice, Wayne	05/26/2006
Ballad of Hobie Young	Presley, Dean O	10/16/1989
Banjo Blues	Warner, Chris R.	08/29/1986
Bar Hoppin Woman	Royal, Lee	08/23/1982
Be Careful of Your Father's Name	Busbice, Wayne	05/26/2006
Bradshaw Mountain Breakdown	Barney, John & Payne, Susan	06/17/1982
Bright Lights and Honky Tonks	Royal, Lee	08/23/1982
California Bound	Pagter, Judith Elaine	09/25/1987
Call Out to Jesus	Eanes, Jim & Lowry, Lora L.	11/04/1983
Culling Me	Busbice, Wayne	07/10/1987
Camptown Breakdown	Nelson, Carl	08/09/1982
Chapel in the Valley	Purkey, Bobby H.	05/08/1984
Chase	Whitehead, Lenny	01/12/1984
Classic J A G	Gaudreau, James Arnott	11/16/1988
Coal Miner's Gold	Presley, Dean O.	03/29/1990
Coal Miner's Gold	Presley, Dean O.	10/16/1989
Come Home Children	Presley, Dean O. & Presley, Jeffrey Dean	10/16/1989
Come Home Daddy	Warner, Chris	09/07/1989
Comin Home to Heaven Above	Spence, Karen F.	06/20/1983
Coming Home	Poindexter, Frank Edward	04/08/1985
Corn Fed	Warner, Chris R.	03/10/1987
Cornbread and Beans in the Pot	Fincham, Jack	02/26/1982
Country Proud	Jones, Lee F.	05/03/1984
Crossing the Summit	Necessary, Frank Marion	12/20/1984
Cuddle Up	Johns, Brooke	08/14/1981
Curly Maple	Emerson, Bill & Goble, Pete	11/20/1986
D J Bounce	Jones, Lee F.	05/03/1984
Darling Do	Busbice, Wayne	05/26/2006
Death's Other Side	McKeon, John W.	06/08/1982
Dee Jays Don't Make It Easy	Sipe, Willis Daniel	05/08/1984
Dieter's Weak	Ryan, Frances Virginia	08/10/1987
Do You Know Who Loves You	Busbice, Wayne	05/26/2006
Don't Be Knockin	Warner, Chris R.	03/10/1987
Don't Leave Me Alone	Busby, Buzz	12/01/1980
Don't Leave Me Here Dear Savior	Fincham, Jack	02/26/1982
Dream	Busby, Buzz	05/13/1982
Earl	Warner, Chris R.	09/07/1989
East West Highway Blues	Rosenberg, Sidney Edward	09/07/1983
Empty Pocket Blues	Bullock, Robin	06/20/1983
Faded Blue Jeans	Warner, Chris	09/07/1989
Fiddler's Potpourri	Nelson, Carl	08/09/1982
Fiddler's Stew	Jones, Lee F.	06/30/1987
Fire Bird	Warner, Chris	09/07/1989
First Battle of Bull Run	Busbice, Wayne	05/26/2006
First Stage Out	Buford, David J.; Jenkins, Mike; Whitehead, Lenny; Wittenberg, Terry A.	03/13/1984

Song Title	Writer	Date Registered
Florentine Waltz	Gaudreau, James A.	11/16/1988
Foldin Out My Hand	Ellis, Robert W. & Malloy, John P.	07/01/1982
Forgotten How to Pray	Necessary, Frank Marion	03/12/1985
Free and Easy	Warner, Chris R.	08/29/1986
Free Free Lovin	Royal, Lee	08/23/1982
Gandy Dancer	Warner, Chris	09/07/1989
Ganja	Wickert, William	08/25/1982
Gathering Storm	Busby, Buzz	05/13/1982
Go Square Yourself Away	Ellis, Robert W. & Malloy, John P.	07/01/1982
God Called Jim Reeves Away	Busbice, Wayne	05/26/2006
Going Back to Dixie	Busbice, Wayne	09/30/1958
Going Back to Stay	Finneyfrock, Buster	01/12/1984
Golden Ring	Hamby, Bill & Schaffer, Chuck	05/26/1981
Good Times Can't Last	Poindexter, Frank Edward	04/08/1985
Good to Go	Gaudreau, James A.	07/23/1996
Grey Ghost	Emerson, Bill	11/20/1986
He'll Be Walking By Your Side	Busbice, Wayne	07/10/1987
Headin Back to Dixie	Busbice, Wayne	12/26/1985
Heart of A Fool	Hale, Robert L; Spence, Karen F; Sykes, Ernie C. Jr.	09/02/1986
Heartbroke and Lonesome	Laird, Charles R.	05/10/1991
Heather's Reel	Warner, Chris R.	03/10/1987
Heaven is a Beautiful Place	Kerns, Catherine Louise	06/17/1985
Heaven is My Home	Busbice, Wayne	12/01/1980
Heaven's Door	Jones, Lee F.	06/30/1987
High and Dry	Warner, Chris R.	03/10/1987
Hoe Kicker	Emerson, Bill	11/20/1986
Home of Greene	Boucher, Joseph E. Jr & Pagter, Judith Elaine	05/29/1987
I Can't Get No Lovin From You	Royal, Lee	08/23/1982
I Carry A Torch	Busbice, Wayne	05/26/2006
I Heard My Savior Calling	Busbice, Wayne	05/26/2006
I Just Couldn't Tell You Goodbye	Busbice, Wayne	05/26/2006
I Just Want to Grow Old Lovin You	King, James E.	06/30/1989
I Want to See Mother Again	Busbice, Wayne	05/26/2006
I'll Be Back After Peach has come to Berlin	Busbice, Wayne	05/26/2006
I'll Be Leaving Bye and Bye	Boucher, Joseph E. Jr & Pagter Judith Elaine	05/29/1987
I'll Have to Make It On My Own	Presley, Dean O.	05/10/1991
I'll Keep You in My Heart	Spence, Karen F.	09/02/1986
I'll Love You Forever	Busbice, Wayne	1957
I'll Pick Pretty Flowers	Pagter, Judith Elaine	09/25/1987
I'll Share It with You	Busbice, Wayne	05/26/2006
I'm On My Way	Fream, Kenneth B.	05/30/1984
I'm Sorry for the Heartaches	Spence, Karen F. & Sykes, Ernie C. Jr.	09/02/1986
I Need A Song	Presley, Dean O.	05/10/1991
I Want to Go Back Home Again	Hale, Robert L. & Sykes, Ernie C. Jr.	09/02/1986
I Will Meet You Bye and Bye	Boucher, Joseph E. Jr. & Pagter, Judith Elaine	06/10/1987
I Wish I Was A Bird	Eanes, Jim & Lowry, Lora L.	11/07/1983
It Must Be Love	King, James E.	06/30/1989
It's a Cold, Cold World	King, James E.	06/30/1989
It's Looking Like Rain	Busby, Buzz	07/01/1981
Jake's Joshin	Jacob, Joe	02/26/1982
Jumpin Gully Louisiana	Busby, Buzz	12/26/1985
Just For Me	Busbice, Wayne	05/26/2006
Just One Look	Martin, Larry	01/12/1984
Kiss Me First	Royal, Lee	08/23/1982

295

Song Title	Writer	Date Registered
Knights of the Golden Horseshoe	Emerson, William Hundley	05/24/1990
Knock On the Door	Purkey, Bobby H.	05/08/1984
Last Call	Finneyfrock, Buster	01/12/1984
Last Drink in the Bottle	Duvall, Dewey	04/01/1982
Lazy Man's Lament	Warner, Chris R.	03/10/1987
Let Jesus Come Into Your Heart	Busbice, Wayne	05/26/2006
Let Me Go Too	Pagter, Judith Elaine	09/25/1987
Let Me See It in Your Eyes	Settle, Mary Glynn	03/28/1989
Let's All Bow Our Heads for Thanksgiving	Rosenberg, Sidney Edward	07/01/1985
Let's Grow Old Together	Busbice, Wayne	05/26/2006
Life Is Hard	Jones, Lee F.	06/30/1987
Like I Used To Do	Spence, Karen F. & Sykes, Ernie C. Jr.	09/02/1986
Live in Heaven Someday	Purkey, Bobby H.	05/08/1984
Live Your Life With Care	Busbice, Wayne	08/27/1980
Living In Suburbia	Busbice, John & Wickert, William	09/10/1982
Lock, Stock and Barrel	Warner, Chris R.	03/10/1987
Log Cabin Memories	Rosenberg, Sidney Edward	09/07/1983
Lonesome Heart	Purkey, Bobby H.	05/08/1984
Long Haul Truckin	Warner, Chris	09/07/1989
Long to See the Mansion	Lawson, Todd Andrew & Lawson, Troy Jeffery	11/24/1985
Lost, Lonesome and Blue	Presley, Jeffrey Dean	10/16/1989
Lost Love	Jones, Lee F.	06/30/1987
Lost Without You	Busbice, Wayne	12/01/1980
Love I cannot Hide	Pagter, Judith Elaine	09/25/1987
Love's Sweet Song	Boucher, Joseph E. Jr. & Pagter, Judith Elaine	06/10/1987
Love That Went Away	Spence, Karen F. & Sykes, Ernie C. Jr.	09/02/1986
Love's Sweet Song	Boucher, Joseph E. Jr. & Pagter, Judith Elaine	05/29/1987
Mansion God is Building	Fincham, Jack	02/26/1982
McDonald's Farm According to Ham and Scram	Busby, Buzz	05/13/1982
Melonie	Poindexter, Frank Edward	04/08/1985
Memories of Home	Jones, Lee F.	05/03/1984
Memories of You	Warner, Chris R.	03/10/1987
Moon Shines Down on Me	King, James E.	06/30/1989
Mr. Bartender	Fincham, Jack	02/26/1982
Mr. Heartache	Jones, Lee F.	06/30/1987
My Darlin's Gone	Finneyfrock, Buster	01/12/1984
My Friend Don Reno	Jones, Albert	03/12/1985
My Little Mountain Home	Pagter, Judith Elaine	09/25/1987
My Lord Keeps A Record	King, James E.	06/30/1989
My Old Paint Mare	Pagter, Judith Elaine	09/25/1987
My Sweet Little Pretty Brown Eyes	Busbice, Wayne	12/26/1985
Natural High	Jones, Lee F.	06/30/1987
Nelson's Hornpipe	Nelson, Carl	05/13/1982
New Sweet Home	Gaudreau, James Arnott	11/16/1988
No One To Blame	Jones, Lee F.	06/30/1987
No Reason To Stay	Ryan, Jenny	08/10/1987
Nothin is for Free	Ellis, Robert W. & Malloy, John P.	07/01/1982
Old Dominion Bound	Purkey, Bobby H.	05/08/1984
Old Union Church	Pagter, Judith Elaine	09/25/1987
On Pine Lake	Nelson, Carl	08/09/1982
On The Farm	Warner, Chris	09/07/1989
One Plus One	Bailey, Raymond Daymond Sr.	06/06/1983
One Tear At A Time	Bailey, Raymond Daymond Sr.	06/06/1983

Song Title	Writer	Date Registered
Our Love Will Never End	Presley, Dean O.	10/16/1989
Out on the Range You and I	McCoy, Justine	07/17/1985
Pages of Time	Warner, Chris	09/07/1989
Pain He's Caused	Pagter, Judith Elaine	09/25/1987
Paint The Town	Warner, Chris R.	03/10/1987
Pennsylvania	Pagter, Judith Elaine	09/25/1987
Pickin On The Run	Fream, Kenneth B. & Snyder, Shawn	05/30/1984
Play Like—	Busbice, Wayne	05/26/2006
Pouring Out Love	Royal, Lee	08/23/1982
Pretty Blue Eyes	Cassada, Calvin & Eanes, Jim	11/07/1983
Pretty Lady	Ellis, Robert W. & Malloy, John P.	07/01/1982
Promises and Lies	Poindexter, Frank Edward	04/08/1985
Psalms 121	Presley, Jeffrey Dean & Presley, Robin L.	05/10/1991
Purk O Lator	Purkey, Delbert G.	05/08/1984
Rabbit On The Run	Jones, Lee F.	06/30/1987
Rainbow Joe	Busbice, Wayne	05/26/2006
Rakin The Coals	Warner, Chris	09/07/1989
Red Lion Rag	Warner, Chris R.	03/10/1987
Reynard In The Cane Breaks	Emerson, William Hundley	05/24/1990
Riding The High Iron	Emerson, William Hundley	05/24/1990
Ring The Bells For The Federals	Rosenberg, Sidney Edward	09/07/1983
River Mighty River	Whitehead, Lenny	01/12/1984
Rock N Roll Atom	Busbice, Wayne	08/27/1980
Rockwell's Last Ride	Warner, Chris R.	03/10/1987
Rolling Hills and Cedar Fences	Pagter, Judith Elaine	09/25/1987
Room in the Master's Mansion	Henderson, Mike	06/20/1983
Running Away	Busby, Buzz	12/01/1980
Rush Hour	Sanders, Darrell	03/25/1983
Rushing World	Royal, Lee	08/23/1982
Same Game	Royal, Lee	08/23/1982
Sandy	Warner, Chris R.	08/29/1986
Save All Your Love	Presley, Dean O. & Presley, Harry	05/10/1991
Scothorn Branch	Busby, Buzz	12/26/1985
She Waits For Me	Poindexter, Frank Edward	04/08/1985
She's Coming Home Today	Busbice, Wayne	05/26/2006
Sleeping In The Summertime	Spence, Karen F.	09/02/1986
Smoky Mountain Fever	Ferguson, Gary G.	04/02/1990
South Central Breakdown	Presley, Jeffrey Dean	10/16/1989
Steppin Out On You	Jones, Albert	03/12/1985
Sweetheart On The Mountain	Spence, Karen F.; Spence, Susan K.; Spence, Steven E.	06/20/1983
Talk To The Lord In Prayer	Busbice, Wayne	07/10/1987
Talking To The Walls	Morgan, Harry	07/01/1981
Taxes, Troubles And Heartaches	Swam, Carroll B.	05/10/1991
Tears Mixed with Raindrops	Busbice, Wayne	10/12/2003
That Old Mountain	Ferguson, Gary G.	04/02/1990
Thinkin Bout You	Ferguson, Gary G.	04/02/1990
Tomorrow I May Be Gone	Busbice, Wayne	05/26/2006
Tragic Love Affair	Busbice, Wayne	05/26/2006
True Blue	Gaudreau, James A.	05/24/1990
Turn The Green Hills Brown	Henderson, Mike	06/20/1983
Uptown Bounce	Rouse, William E.	07/01/1985
Walking by Your Side	Busbice, Wayne	05/26/2006
Waltz of Virginia	Nelson, Carl	05/13/1982

Song Title	Writer	Date Registered
Wasting My Teardrops On You	Duvall, Dewey	04/01/1982
We Can't Return To The Homeplace	Presley, Dean O. & Presley, Jeffrey Dean	10/16/1989
We Don't Make Love	Royal, Lee	08/23/1982
West Virginia Memories	Presley, Dean O.	05/10/1991
What Is A Home Without Love	Fincham, Jack	02/25/1982
What Will Your Heart Say	Busbice, Wayne	04/29/2006
What's The Use	Busbice, Wayne	05/26/2006
When God Called Daddy Away	Busbice, Wayne	05/26/2006
When God Calls You Away	Busbice, Wayne	07/10/1987
When Her Eyes Met Mine	Royal, Lee	08/23/1982
When I Reach My Journey's End	Busbice, Wayne	07/10/1987
When Jesus Comes Down	Warner, Chris	09/07/1989
When They Were Young	Presley, Jeffrey D. & Presley, Robin L.	05/10/1991
Where's The Beef	Jones, Lee F.	05/04/1984
Where The Mountain Laurel Blooms	Pagter, Judie Cox	07/01/1987
White Water Creek	Sipe, Willis Daniel	12/26/1985
Why Did Tom Go Away	Poindexter, Frank Edward	04/08/1985
Winter Storm	Rosenberg, Sidney Edward	09/07/1983
Wish I Was Free Again	Royal, Lee	08/23/1982
Woman Making Believe	Royal, Lee	08/23/1982
Words	Busbice, Wayne	07/10/1987
Yellowstone Gap Kentucky	Necessary, Frank Marion	12/20/1984
You Can Run But You Can't Hide	Emerson, Bill & Meadows, Ralph Joe	11/20/1986
You Can't Live Alone	Poindexter, Frank Edward	04/08/1985
3,000 Miles Lonesome	Busbice, Wayne	05/26/2006

Printed in the United States
94768LV00003B/133-201/A